Lecture Notes in Computer Science 11677

More information about this series at http://www.springer.com/series/7409

Hideyuki Nakanishi · Hironori Egi ·
Irene-Angelica Chounta ·
Hideyuki Takada · Satoshi Ichimura ·
Ulrich Hoppe (Eds.)

Collaboration Technologies and Social Computing

25th International Conference, CRIWG+CollabTech 2019
Kyoto, Japan, September 4–6, 2019
Proceedings

Springer

Editors
Hideyuki Nakanishi
Osaka University
Osaka, Japan

Irene-Angelica Chounta
University of Tartu
Tartu, Estonia

Satoshi Ichimura
Otsuma Women's University
Tokyo, Japan

Hironori Egi
University of Electro-Communications
Tokyo, Japan

Hideyuki Takada
Ritsumeikan University
Shiga, Japan

Ulrich Hoppe
University of Duisburg-Essen
Duisburg, Germany

ISSN 0302-9743   ISSN 1611-3349 (electronic)
Lecture Notes in Computer Science
ISBN 978-3-030-28010-9   ISBN 978-3-030-28011-6 (eBook)
https://doi.org/10.1007/978-3-030-28011-6

LNCS Sublibrary: SL3 – Information Systems and Applications, incl. Internet/Web, and HCI

This Springer imprint is published by the registered company Springer Nature Switzerland AG
The registered company address is: Gewerbestrasse 11, 6330 Cham, Switzerland

Preface

This volume contains the papers presented at the 25th International Conference on Collaboration Technologies and Social Computing. The conference was held during September 4–6, 2019, in Kyoto, Japan. This year two major conferences CRIWG (International Conference on Collaboration and Technology) and CollabTech (International Conference on Collaboration Technologies) were merged after having been jointly held since 2014, with a slight renewal of its name to represent expanding the scope of the field. Supported by the Collaborative Research International Working Group (CRIWG), the CRIWG conferences have been held since 1995, focusing on collaboration technology design, development, and evaluation. The CollabTech conferences have been held since 2005, offering a unique forum for academics and practitioners to present and discuss innovative ideas, methods, or implementations related to collaboration technologies. The merger of these conferences expected papers to propose innovative technical + human + organizational approaches to expand collaboration support, often backed up by theory brought from various disciplines including computer science, management science, design science, cognitive science, and social science.

This year we received 28 submissions, each of which was carefully reviewed by 3 or 4 Program Committee members. As a result, the committee decided to accept 12 full and 8 work-in-progress papers. The accepted papers present relevant and interesting research works related to theory, models, design principles, methodologies, and case studies that contribute to better understand the complex interrelations between collaboration and technology. The program also includes an invited talk.

As editors, we would like to thank the authors of all submissions and the members of the Program Committee for carefully reviewing the submissions. Our thanks also go to our sponsors who allowed us to make the conference attractive to participants by providing a rich opportunity for socializing among them. In addition, we attribute the success of the conference to the efforts of the Special Interest Group (SIG) on Groupware and Network Services of the Information Processing Society of Japan, the SIG on Cyberspace of the Virtual Reality Society in Japan, and the SIG on Communication Enhancement of the Human Interface Society. Last but not least, we would like to acknowledge the effort of the organizers of the conference, as well as thank the Steering Committee for the opportunity to organize the conference and all the help provided during the process.

September 2019

Hideyuki Nakanishi
Hironori Egi
Irene-Angelica Chounta
Hideyuki Takada
Satoshi Ichimura
Ulrich Hoppe

Organization

Conference Co-chairs

Hideyuki Takada   Ritsumeikan University, Japan
Satoshi Ichimura   Otsuma Women's University, Japan
Ulrich Hoppe   University Duisburg-Essen, Germany

Program Co-chairs

Hideyuki Nakanishi   Osaka University, Japan
Hironori Egi   The University of Electro-Communications, Japan
Irene-Angelica Chounta   University of Tartu, Estonia

Financial Co-chairs

Atsuo Hazeyama   Tokyo Gakugei University, Japan
Junko Ichino   Tokyo City University, Japan

Publicity Chair

Takashi Yoshino   Wakayama University, Japan

Local Arrangement Chair

Hiroaki Ogata   Kyoto University, Japan

Local Arrangement Members

Maki Ichimura   Ritsumeikan University, Japan
Juan Zhou   Ritsumeikan University, Japan

Publication Chair

Nelson Baloian   Universidad de Chile, Chile

Registration Chair

Kentaro Takano   Fuji Xerox, Japan

Steering Committee

Hideaki Kuzuoka	University of Tsukuba, Japan
Ken-ichi Okada	Keio University, Japan
Jun Munemori	Wakayama University, Japan
Minoru Kobayashi	Meiji University, Japan
Hiroaki Ogata	Kyoto University, Japan
Tomoo Inoue	University of Tsukuba, Japan

Program Committee

Gwo-Dong Chen	National Central University, Taiwan
Yannis Dimitriadis	University of Valladolid, Spain
Orlando Erazo	Universidad Técnica Estatal de Quevedo, Ecuador
Jesus Favela	CICESE, Mexico
Mikhail Fominykh	Norwegian University of Science and Technology, Norway
Benjamim Fonseca	UTAD/INESC TEC, Portugal
Kinya Fujita	Tokyo University of Agriculture and Technology, Japan
Cédric Grueau	Research Center for Informatics and Information Technologies, Portugal
Pablo Haya	Instituto de Ingeniería del Conocimiento, Spain
Atsuo Hazeyama	Tokyo Gakugei University, Japan
Davinia Hernandez-Leo	Universitat Pompeu Fabra, Spain
Valeria Herskovic	Pontificia Universidad Católica de Chile, Chile
Satoshi Ichimura	Otsuma Women's University, Japan
Claudia-Lavinia Ignat	Inria, France
Indratmo Indratmo	Grant MacEwan University, Canada
Tomoo Inoue	University of Tsukuba, Japan
Yutaka Ishii	Okayama Prefectural University, Japan
Kazuyuki Iso	NTT Corporation, Japan
Jongwon Kim	Gwangju Institute of Science and Technology, South Korea
Ralf Klamma	RWTH Aachen University, Germany
Wim Lamotte	Hasselt University, Belgium
Thomas Largillier	GREYC, France
Liang-Yi Li	National Taiwan Normal University, Taiwan
Tun Lu	Fudan University, China
Stephan Lukosch	Delft University of Technology, The Netherlands
Wolfram Luther	University of Duisburg-Essen, Germany
José Martins	INESC TEC, University of Trás-os-Montes e Alto Douro, Portugal
Sonia Mendoza	CINVESTAV-IPN, Mexico
Roc Meseguer	Universitat Politècnica de Catalunya, Spain
Carmen Morgado	Universidade NOVA de Lisboa, Portugal

Psychological Analysis in Social Media
(Keynote Abstract)

Yoshinori Hijikata

Kwansei Gakuin University

This keynote addresses psychological aspects in social media. It has been 30 years since the idea of the World Wide Web has been proposed as a distributed hypertext system. Some types of web services have evolved into social media. The Web and social media brought two contributions in the academic research field. One is for computer science. Artificial intelligence, whether it is developed by production systems or machine learning algorithms, had never had much knowledge or learning data before the birth of the Web. Because many people write contents on the Web, this gave much knowledge or data to computers. Another is for social science and psychology. Researchers in these areas should rely on the questionnaire survey and the interview to the limited number of people, which cannot fully present the user's behavior or internal mind. However, social media changed the paradigm of the research in these areas. Because many people share their experience on social media, it gave the researchers the user's actual action logs. This helps them to know or infer what is going on in society or what each user thinks in their situation. This keynote focuses on the latter perspective especially on user psychology, and shows some research works related to it. Examples of the research works are the relationship between the user's rating activity and their personality in recommender systems, the relationship between the user's self-expression, especially the type of profile image and the quantity of activities in the social media, the relationship between the user's self-disclosure, especially the name, face photo and affiliation, and their privacy awareness (anonymity consciousness), and the relationship between the user's general activity on social media and their susceptibility of envy. Finally, this keynote shows the future direction on the psychology on IT environment.

Contents

Full Papers

Awareness of Complementary Knowledge in CSCL: Impact on Learners' Knowledge Exchange in Small Groups

Melanie Erkens[✉] [iD], Sven Manske, H. Ulrich Hoppe [iD],
and Daniel Bodemer [iD]

University of Duisburg-Essen, 47057 Duisburg, Germany
{melanie.erkens,bodemer}@uni-due.de,
{manske,hoppe}@collide.info

Abstract. Existing research covers the positive impact of two significant support measures on reciprocal knowledge exchange in small groups: grouping learners with complementary knowledge and enhancing the awareness on co-learners by providing cognitive information on them (cognitive group awareness). Although a combination of both seems obvious, its benefits have not yet been investigated. Thus, we conducted an experimental study in a real classroom setting using a 2 × 2 mixed design to investigate the effects of support in knowledge-complementary groups (with/without cognitive group awareness) and the level of co-learners' knowledge (high/low) on self-assessed communication behavior. Although our results did not confirm interaction effects, the additional objective observation of one third of the learning groups (6 out of 18) yielded a different picture: In supported groups, co-learners exchanged knowledge in a more intended way and chose a better order of talking about topics, both indicating an added value of providing the learners cognitive information.

Keywords: Group formation · Cognitive group awareness · CSCL

1 Theoretical Background

There are many good reasons for learning collaboratively (see Johnson et al. 2000). Especially apparent is the positive effect of performing activities such as asking and explaining on learners' cognitive structure (Ploetzner et al. 1999) that can be easily promoted by group formation. One commonly used schema of group formation is the jigsaw schema ensuring that the knowledge of learners is distributed complementary across learning groups (Dillenbourg and Jermann 2007). Forming groups of learners with complementary knowledge has a positive impact on learning processes as learners acquire knowledge by receiving explanations from others (Webb and Palincsar 1996) and cognitively elaborate existing knowledge due to explaining to others (Ploetzner et al. 1999). These effects can be evoked either by forming groups of learners with 'real' complementary knowledge or by providing co-learners with complementary information to induce the desired knowledge distribution (Dillenbourg and Jermann 2007).

© Springer Nature Switzerland AG 2019
H. Nakanishi et al. (Eds.): CRIWG+CollabTech 2019, LNCS 11677, pp. 3–16, 2019.
https://doi.org/10.1007/978-3-030-28011-6_1

In any case, co-learners commonly need further guidance during their communication ensuring the appearance of the required learning processes (Stegmann et al. 2004). Such guidance needs to take into account that co-learners have to meet several socio-cognitive requirements during their collaboration: linking the content of their conversation with the learning material, establishing a shared knowledge base, and structuring the communication in a goal-oriented way (see Bodemer 2011; Clark and Brennan 1991). To meet these requirements, cognitive group awareness tools (CGATs) provide learners with cognitive information on group members that is usually not directly observable (even in face-to-face settings) and that suggests performing desired behaviors (Janssen and Bodemer 2013). Specifically, these tools (1) highlight or list significant aspects of learning materials to organize co-learners' communication, (2) provide cognitive information on learning partners to facilitate (partner) modeling and grounding processes, and (3) enable co-learners to easily compare said cognitive information to draw their attention to specific constellations such as conflicting opinions or knowledge differences (see Dillenbourg and Bétrancourt 2006; Bodemer and Scholvien 2014). Considering knowledge differences, the visualization of knowledge distributions causes cognitive regulation as co-learners adapt their help seeking based on the visualized levels of knowledge: They prefer to ask questions on topics with own missing knowledge, and also take into account that their learning partner is knowledgeable on the topic, if this information is given (Dehler et al. 2011; Erkens et al. 2016a; 2016b; Erkens and Bodemer 2017). Another function is that visualized knowledge distributions cause cognitive elaboration: Making learners aware of deficits in learning partners' knowledge does not only lead to more or longer explanations (Dehler Zufferey et al. 2011; Erkens and Bodemer 2017), but also more elaborated explanations (Dehler Zufferey et al. 2011; Erkens and Bodemer 2019). Taken together with the findings of complementary group formation, we can conclude that particularly co-learners in groups with complementary knowledge distribution can profit from the additional visualization of this distribution. First, knowledge acquisition might be optimized, since the visualization allows learners to regulate the requests of explanations in terms of asking focused questions on missing knowledge and receiving explanations on it. Second, cognitive elaboration might be better, since learners explain more elaborated, if they are aware of their learning partners' knowledge gaps. Third, they might better prioritize topics to be discussed and thereby better sequence their communication, since knowing about shared and unshared knowledge resources can trigger discussions about topics, with which only one learner in a group is familiar (Schittekatte and Van Hiel 1996).

To exploit the potential of these three benefits, it appears preferable to form groups of learners with real complementary knowledge. To assess the learners' knowledge, methods from learning analytics provide efficient solutions that can be applied to educational data such as essays or homework (Erkens et al. 2016a). One of such methods is text mining, converting semi- or unstructured text into a structured, numerical format (Miner et al. 2012). These structured data can in turn be used for grouping learners based on complementary knowledge. For instance, Erkens et al. (2016a) used Euclidian distances and grouped learners starting from the highest difference downwards to form learning groups. Although they found a relation between distance and knowledge acquisition and a suitability of text mining values to illustrate degrees to which learners wrote on specific topics (Erkens et al. 2016a), the average distance of these groups was not higher than it was in randomly assigned groups. Manske and Hoppe (2017) tackled this problem by creating the semantic group formation algorithm that assigns a diversity score to each grouping and selects the set of groups that satisfies two conditions: total coverage of knowledge items is maximized in the set, and overlap is minimized (Manske and Hoppe 2017). Taken together, text-mining generated distances thus can be used to form groups of real complementary knowledge and to visualize the cognitive information resulting from learners' text (or even from complementary learning material), which might improve cognitive group awareness.

Although the potential of combining complementary group formation with group awareness support seems obvious, especially as it is easily applicable based on text mining generated distance values, it still needs to be tested in the field (see Erkens 2019). For this purpose, we investigate the research question, if group awareness support improves the exchange of knowledge (asking questions, giving explanations, sequencing the discussion) in learning groups with complementary knowledge distribution. We assume that learners with group awareness support communicate in a more intended way than learners without support: Regarding questioning behavior, we expect supported learners to ask more questions in the case of low knowledge and less questions in the case of high knowledge (H1a), and less questions in the case of learning partners' low knowledge and more questions in the case of high learning partners' knowledge (H1b). Regarding explanation behavior, we expect that they give explanations more often in the case of high own knowledge and less explanations in the case of low own knowledge (H2a), and that they give explanations more often in the case of learning partners' low knowledge and less explanations in the case of learning partners' high knowledge (H2b). Further, we qualitatively examine to what extent learners with group awareness support differ from learners without such support regarding their structuring of communication (RQ1) and to what extent we can trace this back to the level of own knowledge and to the knowledge distribution in the learning group (RQ2).

2 Method

Our study was conducted in a real classroom setting with 45 high school students of a German secondary school (26 men; 19 women; age: $M = 16.33$, $SD = 0.67$). We randomly assigned them to the control or experimental group, and further divided them into dyadic or triadic learning groups based on the semantic group formation algorithm that we further describe in the section "Grouping of learners with semantic group formation". To test our hypotheses, we used a 2×2 mixed factorial design with randomly assigned group membership (CGAT vs. No CGAT) as between-subject factor, the level of learners' own knowledge or the learning partners' knowledge (high vs. low) as within-subject factor and learners self-assessed questioning and explanation behavior as a dependent variable. Additionally, we observed three learning groups from each condition regarding their sequencing of discussed topics and other patterns of communication.

2.1   Procedure and Instructions

We conducted the survey in two sessions during regular school hours, each class being supervised by a teacher and three researchers. In the first session, students learned 90 min individually. Each student had a computer with access to a web-based inquiry-learning environment of Go-Lab, an online portal linking personal learning spaces to numerous online labs (de Jong et al. 2014). The specific learning space engaged learners with a project on renewable and blue energies. In this scenario, the learners take the role of a member from the city council of "EnergyCity" and have to decide whether to build an osmotic power plant (see Manske et al. 2015). As a preparation for this decision in a later collaborative session, learners were provided with learning material on several related topics (see topics in Fig. 1).

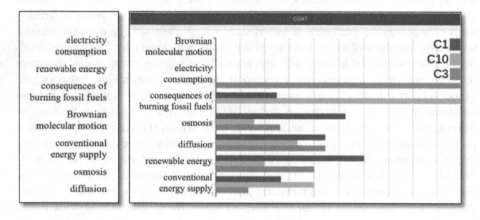

Fig. 1. Example visualizations from learning groups with No CGAT as a topic list (left) and with CGAT as topics including cognitive group awareness information (right).

Further, learners were asked to perform some tasks related to the topical space of the learning material: writing down answers to interview questions of a local news-paper, creating a concept map (see Fig. 2), and writing another text on general assumptions of the possible functioning of osmotic power plants. We used these learner-generated artifacts as a basis to apply the grouping algorithm and (1) formed groups for the collaborations in the second session, and (2) visualized learning part-ners' cognitive information (see "Group formation and provided information"), as needed for the collaboration. In the second session one week later, the students had 90 min to learn collaboratively in their assigned learning groups. Each group had a computer available and the Go-Lab environment posed several collaborative tasks. At the beginning of the collaboration, we informed the students that a shared under-standing of concepts was important to collaborate successfully with each other, and instructed them to exchange their knowledge on relevant topics to create a common knowledge base and to collaboratively write a text on the relevance of salt and fresh water for osmotic power plants. During this phase restricted to 10 min, we supported thcm (or not) with a visualization representing their topic-related knowledge distributions (see Fig. 1). Subsequently to their exchange, we asked the learners to self-assess their collaborative communication behavior (see "Dependent variables").

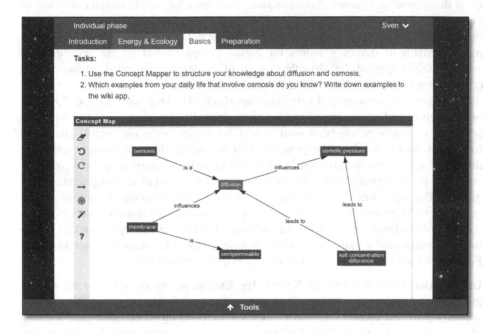

Fig. 2. The learning environment used in this study features different tools for learner-generated content, such as concept mapping.

2.2   Group Formation and Provided Information

Grouping of Learners with Semantic Group Formation. The grouping was based on the algorithm of *semantic group formation* (Manske and Hoppe 2017) that automatically processes text artifacts and extracts knowledge items for each student using semantic technologies for keyword and topic extraction. Based on the extracted knowledge items, a diversity score for each grouping can be assigned. The measure for the diversity of a grouping is the product of the groups' diversity scores. While similarity scores such as the Jaccard index quantify the overlap of two sets, its complement ("Jaccard distance") can be used to characterize the diversity. All pairwise calculated diversities between two students' sets of knowledge items contribute to the group diversity score $D(g)$. The following formula for the diversity of a cohort is constructed based on these premises (with $J(a, b)$ representing the Jaccard similarity of pairs of students in the student group S_g and $1 - J(a, b)$ representing the dissimilarity).

$$D(\text{Grouping}) = \prod_{g \in \text{Grouping}} D(g) = \prod_{g \in \text{Grouping}} \sum_{a,b \in S_g} \frac{1 - J(a, b)}{C_g}$$

C_g is the number of (pairwise) combinations per group, i.e., the binomial coefficient of $|S_g|$ over 2. This normalizes the sum of all diversity scores inside a group respecting that the number of students per group might differ. Otherwise, the scoring leads to major benefits of diversity scores for bigger groups caused by the combinatorial explosion. We applied the algorithm on all of the learner-generated artifacts (texts, concept maps) resulting from the individual learning phase. In a first step, we used a dictionary-based network-text-extraction approach (Hecking and Hoppe 2015) to process given artifacts and to extract keywords related to the aforementioned topics. In addition, an ontology has been used to add synonyms to the dictionary. The group formation algorithm selects the grouping with the highest diversity score in total. The diversity score formula has been constructed in order to maximize the knowledge coverage for each group, and to preserve an even distribution of diversity scores for all groups. The algorithm selects a grouping with a global maximum in diversity. This resulted in 18 learning groups with complementary knowledge distribution: 8 groups in the control condition, of which 4 were assigned to triads and 4 to dyads, and 10 groups in the experimental condition, of which 6 were assigned to triads and four to dyads. Further, we used the results to visualize knowledge distributions.

Information Provided During Knowledge Exchange. As members of the control group should exchange their knowledge without group awareness support (No CGAT), we only provided them with a list of topics corresponding to the individual learning phase (see Fig. 1 on the left). Learning groups in the experimental condition had additionally information on their learning partner(s) available (CGAT). In the latter case, we visualized bars next to each topic, their length determined by the algorithm and representing how much each student of the learning group had written on said topic (see Fig. 1 on the right).

2.3 Dependent Variables

Self-assessment of Questioning and Explaining Behavior (H1 & H2). After exchange of knowledge, learners self-estimated their questioning and explaining behavior on a self-developed questionnaire. Therefore, we presented them 8 utterances related to the previous phase, e.g. "I asked questions, if my knowledge given on a topic was high." or "I gave explanations, if the knowledge of my learning partner was low". Besides differentiating between questions and explanations, we systematically varied the utterances with regard to learners' own level of knowledge (high vs. low) and the learning partners' level of knowledge (high vs. low). For each utterance, learners should specify how much they comply with it on a six-point-Likert-scale ranging from 1 ("not correct at all") to 6 ("fully correct").

Observation of Sequences and Patterns of Communication Processes (RQ1 & RQ2). Beyond learners' self-assessment, we observed six groups to learn more about their structuring of knowledge exchange dependent on knowledge level and knowledge distribution. In each class, we randomly selected one group with CGAT support and one group without support (No CGAT). For the coding, one researcher sat behind the respective group and evaluated each utterance of students with regard to its type (differentiating between question (Q) or explanation (E)), the purpose (differentiating between content-related (C) and organizational (O)), and the topic (differentiating between the topics as they were used in the visualization). We recorded who made the statement and observed the temporal sequence. To give an example: Student A asks a content-related question on osmosis (Os) and student B provides an explanation. In this case, the coding is A: QCOs, B: ECOs. Corresponding to RQ 1 and 2, we used the coded sequences for two purposes: (1) to observe learners' self-regulated determination of sequencing and how much their sequencing of knowledge exchange deviates from a chronological order, and (2) how much this deviation might be caused by other patterns arising from level of knowledge and knowledge distribution. To pursue purpose (1), we created line charts from our results representing the order, in which students talked about topics, and how this order corresponds to the topics' position in the visualization. To pursue purpose (2), we counted the number of content-related and organizational questions and explanations by taking into account the level of visualized knowledge and knowledge distribution. We describe our observations in more detail in the results section.

3   Results

For answering our overall research question on improved communication due to group awareness, we first observed the impact of awareness support on self-assessed questioning and explaining behavior on an individual level. Therefore, we used two-factorial mixed ANOVAs with support (CGAT vs. No CGAT) as between-subject factor and levels of knowledge (high vs. low) as within-subject factors. We reported effects as significant at $p < .05$, and have to note that the distribution of normality was skewed in all cases. In a second step, we qualitatively analyzed the structuring of communication process between learning partners on a group level.

3.1   Self-assessed Questioning Behavior (H1)

Concerning questions, we hypothesized that supported learners behave in a more intended way than learners without support dependent on their level of knowledge (H1a). The results indicate that there was no such significant interaction effect of support (CGAT vs. No CGAT) and learners' level of knowledge (high vs. low) on questioning behavior, $F(1, 43) = 1.48$, $p = .230$, $\eta_p^2 = .03$. Further, we found a significant main effect of learners' level of knowledge, $F(1, 43) = 61.92$, $p < .001$, $\eta_p^2 = .59$, and no significant main effect of support, $F(1, 43) = 0.02$, $p = .899$, $\eta_p^2 < .01$. Moreover, we assumed that learners supported by the CGAT behave also in a more intended way dependent on the level of learning partners' knowledge (H1b). Again, there was no such significant interaction effect of support (CGAT vs. No CGAT) and learning partner's level of knowledge (high vs. low) on questioning behavior, $F(1, 52) = 3.67$, $p = .062$, $\eta_p^2 = .08$. Further, we found a significant main effect of learning partners' level of knowledge, $F(1, 43) = 141.39$, $p < .001$, $\eta_p^2 = .77$, and no significant main effect of support, $F(1, 43) = 0.22$, $p = .641$, $\eta_p^2 = .01$. Table 1 shows relating means and standard deviations. The descriptive statistics illustrate that rather participants in the unsupported than in the supported groups behaved in a desired way.

3.2 Self-assessed Explaining Behavior (H2)

Concerning explanations, we hypothesized that supported learners behave in a more intended way than learners without support dependent on their level of knowledge (H2a). Results indicate that there was no such significant interaction effect of support (CGAT vs. No CGAT) and learners' level of knowledge (high vs. low) on explaining, $F(1, 43) = 0.89$, $p = .351$, $\eta_p^2 = .02$. We found a significant main effect of learners' knowledge level, $F(1, 43) = 311.80$, $p < .001$, $\eta_p^2 = .88$, and no significant main effect of support, $F(1, 43) = 0.05$, $p = .822$, $\eta_p^2 < .01$. Moreover, we assumed that learners supported by the CGAT behave in a more intended way dependent on learning partners' level of knowledge (H2b). Again, there was no such significant interaction effect of support (CGAT vs. No CGAT) and learning partner's level of knowledge (high vs. low) on explaining behavior, $F(1, 52) = 1.41$, $p = .241$, $\eta_p^2 = .03$. Further, we found a significant main effect of learning partners' level of knowledge, $F(1, 43) = 36.07$, $p < .001$, $\eta_p^2 = .46$, and no significant main effect of support, $F(1, 43) = 1.59$, $p = .214$, $\eta_p^2 = .04$. Again, descriptive statistics show that rather the unsupported than the supported students reported to behave in a desired way (see Table 1).

Table 1. Self-assessed extent of asked questions and given explanations during the knowledge exchange

	CGAT - 10 groups ($n = 25$)		No CGAT - 8 groups ($n = 20$)		Total – 18 groups ($N = 45$)	
Questioning behavior	*M*	*SD*	*M*	*SD*	*M*	*SD*
Learner's knowledge high	2.32	1.46	1.90	1.02	2.13	1.29
Learner's knowledge low	4.44	1.33	4.80	1.40	4.60	1.36
Partner's knowledge high	4.44	1.47	4.75	1.02	4.58	1.29
Partner's knowledge low	2.20	1.12	1.65	0.67	1.96	0.98
Explaining behavior	*M*	*SD*	*M*	*SD*	*M*	*SD*
Learner's knowledge high	5.12	0.73	5.35	1.18	5.22	0.95
Learner's knowledge low	1.84	0.85	1.70	0.98	1.78	0.90
Partner's knowledge high	2.96	1.21	2.90	1.41	2.93	1.29
Partner's knowledge low	4.40	1.32	5.05	1.10	4.69	1.26

3.3   Observed Sequences of Communication Processes (RQ1)

To investigate RQ1, we visualized the communication sequences, in which the small groups in the control and experimental condition discussed content-related topics. We created line charts with the x-axis representing the order, in which students talked about topics, and the y-axis representing the position of the topic in the visualized list (see Fig. 3). An exchange about all topics, as determined by the visualized list, is depicted as a dark gray diagonal line that we included in each chart to better illustrate deviations from this chronological order. To take into consideration whether learners talked about a topic several times, we further differentiated between an initial mention of a topic (light gray line) and multiple mentions of topics (middle gray line). From these line charts, we can conclude that learning groups without awareness information (No CGAT) more often proceeded with their exchange of knowledge following the order that is prescribed by the order of listed topics in the visualization. In contrast, groups supported by the CGAT more often deviated from this order.

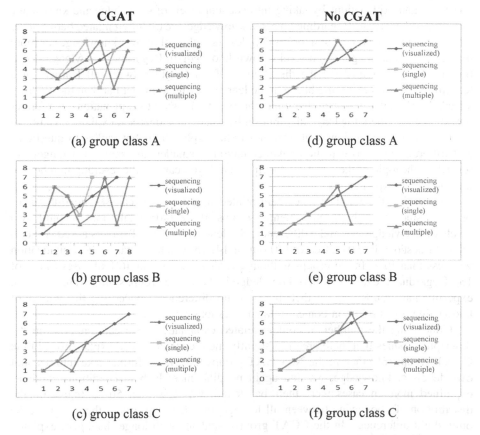

Fig. 3. Sequences of groups with CGAT (a–c) and without CGAT (d–f). X-axes represent the order, in which students talked about topics, y-axes represent the position of topics in the list.

One exception is the CGAT group in class C that shows a similar pattern as the groups without CGAT support. Here, we found that this group is a special case, since the visualization illustrated the learners that they have no knowledge on the first topic ("Brownian molecular motion") and highly heterogeneous knowledge on the second topic ("development of power demand"). Thus, they apparently talked first about the only topic with missing knowledge and then about the topic with most differences before continuing with osmosis, but also in a chronological order. The other groups in the experimental group started immediately talking about osmosis. Another finding is that learners in the CGAT supported groups talked multiple times about topics in comparison to the group without awareness information, e.g. the CGAT group from class A talks two times about osmosis (4 on y-axis), the CGAT group from class B even 3 times (2 on y-axis).

3.4   Observed Patterns of Communication Processes (RQ2)

To investigate RQ2, we counted the number of content-related and organizational questions and explanations by taking into account levels of knowledge and knowledge distributions per topic. Regarding levels of knowledge, we (a) differentiated between the length of a visualized bar for a topic being less (small level of own knowledge) or more than 50% of total length (high level of own knowledge). Regarding knowledge distribution, we investigated (b) the distribution of bar length between all learners of a learning group differentiating between the learner having a smaller bar than the other(s), a bar in the middle or a longer bar than other(s). With regard to explanations, we further investigated (c) the knowledge distribution between questioner and explainer. Here, we only observed explanations that were not initial explanations but replies to questions, and differentiated between the explainer having a smaller, the same or a longer bar regarding the topic of the question. From Table 2, you can see the resulting numbers of questions and explanations.

Concerning the number of content-related questions, we can see no differences between students of both experimental groups. If we further take into account own levels of knowledge, we find a difference: Students in the CGAT groups asked content-related questions in 71% of cases (10 out of 14), in which the bar in the visualization was less than 50%. In the groups without CGAT it was just in 46% of cases (6 out of 13). Regarding the distribution of knowledge in the whole group, similar values in both experimental groups suggest that there are no differences concerning the impact of knowledge distribution on content-related questions.

Concerning the number of content-related explanations, we can gather from the descriptive values that there are only slightly more content-related explanations in the CGAT groups (60) than in the No CGAT groups (53). If we further take into account own levels of knowledge, we find again no difference: In both conditions, students explained more in cases were their bar length was less than 50%. Regarding the distribution of knowledge between all learners of a learning group, there seem to be only slight differences: In the CGAT groups, students with longer bars give explanations in 40% of cases (24 out of 60) and students with shorter bars in 30% of cases (18 out of 60). In No CGAT groups, students with longer bars gave explanations in 36% of cases (19 out of 53) and students with shorter bars in 49% of cases (26 out of 53).

Regarding knowledge distributions between questioner and explainer, we found some differences: Students in the CGAT groups answered in 77% of cases questions with an explanation (13 out of 17), if their bar was the same or higher; and only in 23% of not intended cases. By contrast, students in the No CGAT groups only answered questions with explanations in 50% of cases (5 out of 10) if their bar was the same or higher; and in 50% of not intended cases. Concerning the number of organizational questions and explanations, we found that students without support seem to focus slightly more on organizational issues than supported students: In the CGAT group, 42% of questions (10 out of 24) and 12% of explanations (8 out of 68) are about the organization of communication. In the No CGAT groups, 55% of questions (16 out of 29) and 25% of explanations (18 out of 71) are about the organization of communication.

Table 2. Number of questions and explanations dependent on own knowledge level and knowledge distribution.

Class	CGAT				No CGAT			
# groups	A 3	B 3	C 3	$\sum 9$	A 3	B 2	C 3	$\sum 8$
# content-related questions	3	7	4	14	7	5	1	13
(a) bar length < 50%	1	6	3	10	3	2	1	6
(a) bar length > 50%[a]	2	1	1	4	4	3	0	7
(b) smaller bar than other(s)	1	4	0	5	1	2	1	4
(b) in the middle	1	0	3	4	3	0	0	3
(b) longer bar than other(s)	1	3	1	5	3	3	0	6
# content-related explanations	22	12	26	60	12	8	33	53
(a) bar length < 50%	7	10	19	36	7	5	24	36
(a) bar length > 50%	15	2	7	24	5	3	9	17
(b) smaller bar than other(s)	6	5	7	18	3	5	18	26
(b) in the middle	5	2	11	18	5	0	3	8
(b) longer bar than other(s)	11	6	7	24	4	3	12	19
(c) smaller bar than questioner	0	3	1	4	3	2	0	5
(c) same bar as questioner[c]	2	2	0	4	3	0	1	4
(c) longer bar than questioner[c]	1	6	2	9	0	1	0	1
# organizational questions	3	2	5	10	7	5	4	16
# organizational explanations	2	1	5	8	6	8	4	18

4 Discussion

We conducted the current study to investigate the impact of providing knowledge-complementary groups with text-mining generated group awareness information on knowledge exchange. Contrary to our expectations, learners' self-assessment did not confirm that group awareness support guides co-learners to behave more in an intended way than learners without support. In fact, descriptive results even suggest that primarily learners without group awareness support ask questions in the case of own missing knowledge or knowledgeable learning partners and give explanations in the case of own expertise or missing learning partners' knowledge. However, learners' self-assessment yields another picture than the results of our observation considering knowledge exchange in one third of all learning groups. Here, it was suggested, on the one hand, that the level of own knowledge impacts questioning behavior, as learners in the learning groups with support asked more questions on topics for which their missing knowledge was detected in the individual learning phase. This indicates an improved cognitive regulation in CGAT groups. On the other hand, results indicated that the knowledge distribution impacts explaining behavior as supported learners more often replied to questions on topics on which they wrote more than their learning partner in the individual learning phase. Thus, knowledge distributions were not more important in the CGAT groups regarding initial explanations, but for deciding to answer a content-related question with an explanation.

These results are in accordance with former results that the level of own missing knowledge guides cognitive regulation (e.g., Dehler et al. 2011; Erkens and Bodemer 2019) and that knowledge distribution guides explaining behavior (e.g., Dehler Zufferey et al. 2011; Erkens and Bodemer 2019). As we only observed a third of groups, we cannot generalize our findings, but the disagreement of subjectively and objectively generated results seems to be systematic. One possible interpretation of this might be that unsupported learners self-assessed their behavior in accordance with an optimal (but obviously not factual) procedure, whilst learners with group awareness support were aware of their actual strategies and behaviors during the collaboration and/or considered also other influencing factors in their self-assessment. This interpretation is supported by the one-sided distributions of normality for the self-assessment and by different orders of discussing topics that learners followed dependent on their experimental group. Learners without group awareness information available mainly followed a chronological order suggesting that said order rather than levels of knowledge guided them, whilst learners with group awareness support deviated from this order. However, the question remains what other factors influence the sequencing of co-learners in the groups with group awareness support. One possible explanation might be derived from the visualizations of the communication sequences: Learners with group awareness support talked more often multiple times about topics, especially on osmosis. Osmosis was an important topic for the first collaborative task of writing a short text on the relevance of salt and fresh water for osmotic power plants. This implies that learners with group awareness support had this task more in mind, related osmosis to other topics and thus integrated contents of learning material better in their exchange of knowledge.

Further research should examine to what extent content-related information might be an influential factor here, and what value it adds on learning when combined (or not) with group awareness information. Moreover, we did not investigate differences between groups of two and three learners that might also be relevant and should be considered in future studies. Finally, it stays unclear how accurately the semantic group formation algorithm gathered and visualized co-learners' levels of knowledge. We should further investigate this to ensure that group formations are optimal and visualizations do not misdirect learners due to making them aware of levels of knowledge that deviate from actual values. However, overall we found indications that knowledge-complementary groups can benefit from additionally provided cognitive information, since it seems to guide behavior in a target-oriented way and to support a metacognitive awareness. Beyond that, text mining provides an efficient way to support the group formation but also the creation of visualizations that trigger these processes.

Moreover, it could even be implied to complementary learning material, if no student-generated texts are given to analyze real complementarities.

Acknowledgments. We thank the Otto-Hahn-Gymnasium in Dinslaken for the great cooperation. Furthermore, we thank Jessica Gärtner for helping us collect the data and coding the questions and explanations, and Patrick Schlottbom for analyzing the communication sequences and visualizing the results. Special thanks go to our deceased colleague and friend Sören Werneburg, who, as a former teacher at the school where the study was conducted, not only established the contact with the teachers and made the cooperation possible, but also accompanied the study with the greatest enthusiasm.

References

Bodemer, D.: Tacit guidance for collaborative multimedia learning. Comput. Hum. Behav. **27**(3), 1079–1086 (2011)

Bodemer, D., Scholvien, A.: Providing knowledge-related partner information in collaborative multimedia learning: isolating the core of cognitive group awareness tools. In: Liu, C.-C., Ogata, H., Kong, S.C., Kashihara, A. (eds.) Proceedings of the 22nd International Conference on Computers in Education, ICCE 2014, pp. 171–179 (2014)

Clark, H.H., Brennan, S.E.: Grounding in communication. In: Resnick, L.B., Levine, J.M., Teasley, S.D. (eds.) Perspectives on Socially Shared Cognition, pp. 127–149. American Psychological Association, Washington (1991)

Dehler, J., Bodemer, D., Buder, J., Hesse, F.W.: Guiding knowledge communication in CSCL via group knowledge awareness. Comput. Hum. Behav. **27**(3), 1068–1078 (2011)

Dehler Zufferey, J., Bodemer, D., Buder, J., Hesse, F.W.: Partner knowledge awareness in knowledge communication: learning by adapting to the partner. J. Exp. Educ. **79**(1), 102–125 (2011)

de Jong, T., Sotiriou, S., Gillet, D.: Innovations in STEM education: the Go-Lab federation of online labs. Smart Learn. Environ. **1**(3), 1–16 (2014)

Dillenbourg, P., Bétrancourt, M.: Collaboration load. In: Elen, J., Clark, R.E. (eds.) Handling Complexity in Learning Environments: Research and Theory, pp. 142–163. Elsevier, Amsterdam (2006)

Dillenbourg, P., Jermann, P.: Designing integrative scripts. In: Fischer, F., Kollar, I., Mandl, H., Haake, J.M. (eds.) Scripting Computer-Supported Collaborative Learning, pp. 275–301. Springer, New York (2007). https://doi.org/10.1007/978-0-387-36949-5_16

Erkens, M.: Guiding knowledge exchange in collaborative learning: mechanisms and potential of text-mining support. University of Duisburg-Essen, Duisburg (2019)

Erkens, M., Bodemer, D.: Which visualization guides learners best? Impact of available partner- and content-related information on collaborative learning. In: Smith, B.K., Borge, M., Mercier, E., Lim, K.Y. (eds.) Making a Difference: Prioritizing Equity and Access in CSCL, 12th International Conference on Computer Supported Collaborative Learning, CSCL 2017, pp. 127–134 (2017)

Erkens, M., Bodemer, D.: Improving collaborative learning: guiding knowledge exchange through the provision of information about learning partners and learning contents. Comput. Educ. **128**, 452–472 (2019). https://doi.org/10.1016/j.compedu.2018.10.009

Erkens, M., Bodemer, D., Hoppe, H.U.: Improving collaborative learning in the classroom: text mining based grouping and representing. Int. J. Comput. Support. Collab. Learn. **11**(4), 387–415 (2016a)

Erkens, M., Schlottbom, P., Bodemer, D.: Qualitative and quantitative information in cognitive group awareness tools: Impact on collaborative learning. In: Cress, U. (ed.) Transforming Learning, Empowering Learners: The International Conference of the Learning Sciences (ICLS) (2016b)

Hecking, T., Hoppe, H.U.: A network based approach for the visualization and analysis of collaboratively edited texts. In: Proceedings of the First International Workshop on Visual Aspects of Learning Analytics co-located with 5th International Learning Analytics and Knowledge Conference, LAK 2015, pp. 19–23 (2015)

Janssen, J., Bodemer, D.: Coordinated computer-supported collaborative learning: awareness and awareness tools. Educ. Psychol. **48**(1), 40–55 (2013)

Johnson, D.W., Johnson, T., Stanne, M.B.: Cooperative Learning Methods: A Meta-Analysis. University of Minnesota, Minneapolis (2000)

Manske, S., Hecking, T., Chounta, A., Werneburg, S., Hoppe, H.U.: Using differences to make a difference: a study on heterogeneity of learning groups. In: Lindwall, O., Häkkinen, P., Koschmann, T., Tchounikine, P., Ludvigsen, S. (eds.) Exploring the Material Conditions of Learning: The Computer Supported Collaborative Learning (CSCL) Conference 2015, pp. 182–189 (2015)

Manske, S., Hoppe, H.U.: Managing knowledge diversity: towards automatic semantic group formation. In: 2017 IEEE 17th International Conference on Advanced Learning Technologies (ICALT), pp. 330–332 (2017)

Miner, G., Delen, D., Elder, J., Fast, A., Hill, T., Nisbet, R.: The seven practice areas of text analytics. In: Fast, A., Delen, D., Miner, G., Elder, J., Nisbet, R., Hill, T. (eds.) Practical Text Mining and Statistical Analysis for Non-Structured Text Data Applications, pp. 29–41. Elsevier, Amsterdam (2012)

Ploetzner, R., Dillenbourg, P., Preier, M., Traum, D.: Learning by explaining to oneself and to others. In: Dillenbourg, P. (ed.) Collaborative Learning: Cognitive and Computational Approaches, pp. 103–121. Elsevier, Oxford (1999)

Schittekatte, M., Van Hiel, A.: Effects of partially shared information and awareness of unshared information on information sampling. Small Group Res. **27**, 431–449 (1996)

Stegmann, K., Weinberger, A., Fischer, F., Mandl, H.: Scripting argumentative knowledge construction in computer-supported learning environments. Presented at the First Joint Meeting of the EARLI SIGs Instructional Design and Learning and Instruction with Computers, pp. 320–330 (2004)

Webb, J.M., Palincsar, A.S.: Group processes in the classroom. In: Berliner, D., Calfee, R. (eds.) Handbook of Educational Psychology, pp. 841–873. Macmillan, New York (1996)

Identifying Socio-Technical Means to Support Small Loosely Coupled Groups of Volunteers

Alexander Nolte[1,2(✉)] and Rosta Farzan[3]

[1] University of Tartu, Tartu, Estonia
alexander.nolte@ut.ee
[2] Carnegie Mellon University, Pittsburgh, PA, USA
[3] University of Pittsburgh, Pittsburgh, PA, USA
rfarzan@pitt.edu

Abstract. Volunteers provide a large variety of valuable services to society spanning from local community efforts to global non-profit organizations and online communities. While larger volunteer groups and online communities in particular have been studied extensively, there is a lack of research on small loosely coupled volunteer groups especially with respect to the way they collaborate to organize activities. Our work attempts to shed light onto such groups. In this paper, we present results from an exploratory study of five student organizations. Based on a literature analysis we developed an interview protocol and corresponding coding scheme that allowed us to analyse how such groups cooperate and how they use technology to communicate and organize activities. Our findings indicate areas of improvement around higher levels of transparency, well defined procedures, effective knowledge management and exchange between similar groups. We discuss these potentials and propose an initial socio-technical conceptualization to overcome current issues and support collaboration in such groups.

Keywords: Volunteer collaboration · Exploration · Loosely coupled groups

1 Introduction

Technology that fosters group collaboration has been of continuous interest to researchers and practitioners alike [47]. The early years of research in this field, was mainly dominated by work on the needs of groups within large organizations. In more recent years however, the context has considerably diversified and researchers and practitioners have also started to investigate solutions to support unpaid volunteers in small locally oriented projects [52], large non-profit organizations [49] and online production communities [54]. Supporting volunteer collaboration poses a unique challenge compared to collaboration in large organizations as coordination is often loosely structured. Contributors within such groups oftentimes come from diverse backgrounds, have adopted a variety of team work styles, use a diverse set of tools, and may drop out at any point in time.

Most work investigating volunteer collaboration focuses on non-profit organizations and online communities [3, 10, 50] while small loosely coupled groups have not

H. Nakanishi et al. (Eds.): CRIWG+CollabTech 2019, LNCS 11677, pp. 17–35, 2019.
https://doi.org/10.1007/978-3-030-28011-6_2

been a strong focus so far. Small loosely coupled volunteer groups often focus on organizing series of dedicated activities such as discussion meetings, food giveaways or social events. Student organizations are one example of such small volunteer groups that organize series of activities – often for their fellow students. However despite studies showing that student organizations positively affect their members as well as the university community [2] they are rarely studied. Moreover, student organizations often do not focus on the university alone. Some organizations specifically aim to support local communities by using knowledge and skills that they gained during their studies for a good cause [53]. It thus appears reasonable to study and propose support for such groups as one important example of loosely coupled volunteer groups.

To cope with their loosely structured nature, members of such organizations have to develop practices and adopt technology well-suited to their fluid nature. At the same time, members of these groups often strongly identify with the cause of an organization and are often formed by individuals that are enthusiastic about similar values [6, 8]. At the same time however, they might not spend much effort on planning the way they collaborate since they are focused on the goals they set for themselves as a group.

Designing approaches to support collaboration within student organizations requires understanding their ad-hoc nature and their lack of a common organizational or technological infrastructure. Despite them all being students of the same university they typically have to establish common technologies and practices themselves since their activities take place outside of their studies and are thus not directly connected to the university infrastructure. We thus aim to first gain an understanding of the way these groups currently operate and the challenges they face in order to achieve their goals. Specifically, our work aims to the question of how volunteers in such organizations collaborate currently (**RQ1**) and what role technology plays in their current practices (**RQ2**). Based on our findings we propose means to improve collaboration within and between such groups.

To answer the two main research questions, we conducted an interview study with five student organizations from two large North-American universities. The interview protocol and the corresponding coding scheme are grounded in literature from the field of computer supported collaboration and volunteer group work to ensure that we cover relevant aspects that have been discussed as important in prior work on volunteer collaboration. Results from our analysis supported our initial assumptions about the unique challenges these groups face and provided insights into how they collaborate (Sect. 4). Based on our findings we propose a socio-technical concept to support them (Sect. 5). The contribution of this paper is thus threefold: (1) Developing and applying a coding scheme based on a comprehensive literature review, (2) conducting a qualitative study of collaboration practices in an under-studied context of small loosely coupled volunteer groups and (3) developing guidelines to foster collaboration in these groups.

2 Background

Our work lies at the intersection between volunteer engagement and computer supported cooperative work. Throughout this section, we will situate our research within these fields and highlight where we intend to go beyond the state of the art.

2.1 Volunteer Groups in Computer Supported Cooperative Work

Collaboration in small loosely coupled groups of volunteers shares commonalities with other similar groups in organizational contexts in which people are also *"mobile, widely dispersed, and autonomous, and team members communicate with each other only intermittently"* [42]. Such groups rely on suitable means of communication that allows them to coordinate and share information. The groups we study, however differ from those studied by Pinelle and Gutwin in that they do not operate within the confines of an organization which binds group members to certain explicit (contract) or implicit (norms) rules including common practices and technologies used. Such common practices and technologies that can facilitate collaboration within a group are not present for the groups we study due to episodic participation of members. Coordination can rather change based on individuals leaving and others joining a group which in the case we study is common due to members graduating and potentially even moving out of the are they studied. The episodic nature of participation also complicates designing technologies for such groups. There is a number of different approaches that focus on analyzing, structuring and supporting collaboration through technology [7, 18, 22, 25, 36, 38, 43]. Such approaches however are only marginally applicable in this context since they require upfront planning, do not take the episodic nature of membership of the groups we study into account or take place around a common technology that every member needs to use to participate. There are also approaches that propose light-weight means to analyze group collaboration using heuristics [38] or incremental process reflection and improvement [37]. These approaches are however also only marginally applicable since they require expert support which might not always be available for the groups we study.

More recently work has emerged around flash groups [45] or flash organizations [48] which are comprised of people that are not familiar with each other and come together to conduct a time bounded project. They are thus similar to the groups we study in that they consist of people that come together for a common purpose but have no common practices or technologies to build on. They are however different in the way that flash groups or organizations have a project leader ultimately deciding on the direction of the project. The groups we are studying instead are democratically organized. Moreover, flash groups typically disband after a project has been completed while the groups we study are more permanent and often continue even when no founding member is part of the group anymore.

2.2 Volunteering and Volunteer Collaboration

There is a large body of work around volunteering and volunteer collaboration. Scholars have studied volunteers supporting elections [3], sports events [10] or natural disasters [8]. There are also studies covering individuals that volunteer their time for longer term activities such as political activism [46] or contributing to online production communities [50]. The groups we study, operate in the latter space in that they follow a specific goal over a longer period of time.

Literature on volunteer engagement commonly distinguishes between different phases of volunteering: Before, during and after being a volunteer [24, 39]. Most work in this field has focused on understanding motivations for individuals to volunteer in order to attract more volunteers [6, 8, 27] and on volunteer retention to ensure that individuals continue to volunteer after they initially took the decision to do so [17, 20, 26]. In our work, we mainly focus on individuals that have already taken the decision to volunteer. We do however consider initial motivations as well as antecedents of retention behavior since both have been found to influence volunteer behavior.

Our main focus lies in the way volunteer groups collaborate (RQ1) and in the way they use technology for this (RQ2). Most studies that cover this aspect focus on (non-profit) organizations that employ coordinators which split larger projects into manageable tasks and distribute them to volunteers [12, 17, 23]. There is also work on groups in which a stable core of volunteers takes over coordination tasks while the remaining volunteers can decide on which tasks they would like to carry out [4, 10, 32]. Our study is related to this work in that the groups we study are organized around an elected leadership group who coordinates activities. Our study however differs from this work because the aforementioned groups usually have the potential to develop members and prepare them for a leadership role over time. This is not always possible for the groups that we study due to the way that they are organized. Our study thus adds to our understanding how leadership tasks are passed on between different generations of volunteer members.

3 Empirical Method

To answer our research questions, we conducted an exploratory interview study. We developed an interview protocol and a corresponding coding scheme based on a systematic literature review [28]. We will provide a description of this process the following (Sect. 3.1) before outlining the context of the study (Sect. 3.2), the interview protocol (Sect. 3.3) and corresponding coding scheme (Sect. 3.4) and the data collection and analysis procedure (Sect. 3.5).

3.1 Literature Review

We started the systematic literature review with the identification of relevant search terms[1] that are related to how such groups collaborate (RQ1) and how they use technology (RQ2). We used them to search for articles in GoogleScholar that were published after 2006. During an initial screening we focused the first ten pages of the

---

[1] Volunteer + {collaboration, team, work, organization, participation, sustainability, retention, turnover}, loosely coupled collaboration, ad-hoc teams, flash teams.

result list for each search term. In addition, we also analyzed papers from high ranking journals and conferences in both the fields of computer supported cooperative work and information systems using the same strategy (c.f. Table 1 for a complete list of the conferences and journals we considered). For those conferences and journals, we limited our analysis on work that was published after 2006. This combined strategy led to a total of 130 papers that were examined more closely.

In a first pass we scanned the titles, abstracts and methodology sections of the identified articles in order to assess their fit to our context. We only included peer-reviews papers written in English that contained empirical studies of volunteer groups and reported findings related to the way they organize and use technology. We included both quantitative and qualitative studies. Moreover, we added referenced papers to our list of relevant papers if they met the aforementioned criteria. This procedure resulted in a reduced set of papers 60 which served as a basis for the interview protocol and coding scheme. We will discuss both in detail below.

Table 1. Conferences and journals considered in the literature review

Name	Type
ACM Conference on Human Factors in Computing Systems (CHI)	Conference
ACM Conference on Computer-Supported Cooperative Work and Social Computing (CSCW)	Conference
European Conference on Computer-Supported Cooperative Work (ECSCW)	Conference
ACM International Conference on Supporting Group Work (Group)	Conference
International Conference on the Design of Cooperative Systems (COOP)	Conference
Computer Supported Cooperative Work (CSCW)	Journal
International Conference on Information Systems (ICIS)	Conference
European Conference on Information Systems (ECIS)	Conference
Management Information Systems Quarterly (MISQ)	Journal
European Journal of Information Systems (EJIS)	Journal
Information Systems Journal (ISJ)	Journal
Information Systems Research (ISR)	Journal
Journal of the Association for Information Systems (JAIS)	Journal
Journal of Information Technology (JIT)	Journal

3.2 Context

The student organizations we studied are volunteer groups that are created and run by students for students. Each organization defines its own mission (c.f. Table 1 for an overview of the groups we studied) and they are established upon students' request. They have to follow certain rules dictated by the university, such as alignment to a specific school, the ability to attract a certain number of members (usually ten), and electing and maintaining a leadership team. The leadership team is usually (re-)elected annually and is comprised of a president, a vice-president and a business manager. There are also examples of student organizations with a larger leadership board. Neither leadership nor members receive any monetary compensation for their service.

Minor funding that can be granted from the university has to be spent for activities related to the purpose of the organization.

3.3 Interview Protocol

Our interview study is designed to investigate how volunteers in student organizations collaborate (RQ1) and the role of technology in such collaboration (RQ2). Interview questions included (1) motivations to join (e.g. *"What were the reasons for you to join this student organization?"*); (2) individual's commitments to the organization after joining (e.g. *"What were the commitments you made when you first entered this organization?"*); (3) the organization of specific activities (e.g. *"Please provide a short description of an activity [you recently (co-)organized]."*); and (4) the role of technology in their organizational activities (e.g. *"Which technology did you use to communicate/coordinate while organizing this particular activity?"*)[2].

3.4 Coding Scheme

Our coding scheme was developed through an iterative process starting based on relevant dimensions from our literature review. The initial coding scheme covered different motivations (code 1, [6, 8, 27]), commitments and intentions (code 2, [16, 19, 40]) and coordination and decision-making activities (code 3, [11, 24, 29, 34, 35]) as well as aspects of awareness (code 5, [14, 21, 32]) and satisfaction (code 9, [5, 17, 19, 40]) which are partly based on different means of feedback (code 8, [5, 40, 41]). It was refined through multiple rounds of coding of a sample of interview responses following an open-coding process. Following this procedure was necessary since student groups engage in specific activities (code 3) related to themselves as well as individuals outside of their organization (code 4). They also have a specific organizational structure with unique roles (code 2) and they use different technologies (code 6) for specific purposes (code 7) that could not be identified from prior work on volunteer collaboration. Moreover, this procedure also allowed us to specify sources of feedback (code 8) and technologies that organizations we studied used (codes 6 and 7).

Our final coding scheme (Table 2) included codes on (1) individual characteristics of the organization and its leaders and members (code 1), their tenure and role within the organization, their commitment to the organization (code 2) and their satisfaction with their participation (code 9) which can be influenced by feedback (code 8); (2) organization and coordination of activities, communication, decision making, recruitment, turnover and transition (code 3) including the target of such activities (code 4); and (3) the role of technology (code 6) and its purpose (code 7). An important dimension orthogonal to most of the aforementioned processes is related to level of awareness about members and processes within the organization. Awareness can be related to individuals, technology and the group as such (code 5).

---

[2] The full interview protocol can be retrieved from the authors upon request.

Table 2. Coding scheme

Code	Category	Coded aspects
1	Motivation	Socialize (1a), Having fun (1b), Interest in topic (1c), Identification with values (1d), Networking (1e), Career opportunities (1f), Gain new skills (1 g), Prior commitments (1 h), Bonds with members outside of the organization (1i)
2	Official role	Current role (2a), Commitments and responsibilities (2b), Tenure within current role (2c), Previous role (2d), Intention to continue (2e), Intention to quit (2f)
3	Activities	Organize events (3a), Coordination (3b), Decision making (3c), Face-to-face gathering (3d), Manage money (3e), Marketing (3f), Recruitment (3 g), Transition (3 h)
4	Target of activities	Group internal (4a), Parent organization (4b), Externals (4c)
5	Awareness	Group as whole (5a), Individuals in the group (5b), Task awareness (5c)
6	Technology	Social media (6a), Email (6b), Instant Messenger (6c), Content management (6d), Wiki or Blog (6e), Phone (6f)
7	Purpose of technology	Coordination (7a), Marketing (7b), Reporting (7c), Communication (7d)
8	Feedback	From fellow officers (8a), From members and event participants (8b)
9	Satisfaction	Expectations met (9a), Support received (9b), Perceived effort (9c)

3.5 Interview Study and Analysis

We interviewed a total of ten officers of five student organizations from two different North American universities. Organizations were chosen based on their level of activity, diversity of their mission and diversity of students (c.f. Table 3 for more information). Since the focus of our study was on organization and collaboration processes, we exclusively interviewed officers who are responsible for all operational activities of the organizations. Our interview participants served in different leadership roles within the student organizations we studied including president, vice-president, business manager and board member. Some of the student organizations we studied require leadership to change every year (e.g. SO4) while others do not have such a requirement (e.g. SO2). The interviewees had varying tenures within the respective student organization ranging from seven months to seven years.

The interviews lasted from 40 to 57 min each. After transcribing the interviews, we conducted three rounds of pre-coding in which two researchers independently applied the coding scheme (c.f. Table 2) to the same parts of the first interview. After each round, we calculated the inter-coder agreement based on Cohens-Kappa [9] for individual answers. We discussed codes with low agreement scores in order to refine the coding scheme and in order to reach a common understanding about how to apply the codes. After three rounds of pre-coding both researchers coded the remainder of the

Table 3. Student organizations analyzed

ID	Goal/mission	Interview participants
S01	Support women in Information Sciences	President (I0, I2) and Business manager (I6)
S02	Support doctoral students in Information Sciences	President (I3)
S03	Support students in Library Sciences	President (I5) and Business manager (I4)
S04	Support international students in Information Sciences	President (I7) and Vice-president (I1)
S05	Support local community organizations by providing data-driven services	Board members (I8, I9)

interviews. Following the guidelines by Landis and Koch [30] we found moderate (0.41–0.60) to substantial (0.61–0.80) scores for Cohens-Kappa for all but the codes related to socializing, prior commitments, and reporting which we subsequently removed from analysis. We then analyzed the coded content to discover emergent themes regarding our two main research questions. In total, our data set consisted of 660 answers and we analyzed a total of 2,045 codes.

4   Findings

The results of the interview analysis have been organized into three aspects (1) Individual disposition to volunteering in student organizations; (2) Current practices of collaboration in student organizations; and (3) The role of technology in current practices.

4.1   Individual Disposition to Volunteering in Student Organizations

Before analyzing current practices and the role of technology we first have to understand individual motivations and the fulfilment of expectations since those are important for volunteer engagement.

Individual Motivations.
As expected, most students joined an organization because they identified with its values. This is not only evident by the fact that 22% of all mentions of any motivation were related to this but also by every interviewee stating this as one of their motivations to join. Examples for such statements are: *"I definitely think that it is important that there is a space that is carved out for women and their specific issues"* (I2), *"our values [...] are very important to me."* (I5), *"I got very interested in this organization because I am a minority in the US"* (I7) and *"it seemed like a community of like-minded people"* (I9). Identification with the values of a student organization were followed by other motivations such as career opportunities (16%), interest in topic (15%), bonds with members outside of the organization (12%) and networking (11%). Having fun (7%) and gaining new skills (6%) were also mentioned but only in a few

cases. It should also be noted that every interviewee mentioned between three and seven different motivations to join a particular student organization.

Moreover, we observed that there was a connection between specific motivations mentioned by the interviewees and the nature of the organizations. For example, for SO3 which serves as a student chapter of a professionally oriented library organization, interviewees highlighted career-oriented motivations. They mentioned that participation in this group allowed them to interact with other professionals working in the field of their desired future career (*"this organization provided an opportunity for networking"*, I4). Similarly, for SO5 which has the main mission to support local communities using their technical skills, interviewees expressed related interests highlighted by the following quote: *"[the organization] really allows me to apply the data skills that I am learning in a real-world setting"* (I8). At the same time, student organizations with broader scope attract students with broader motivations as well. For example, interviewees of S01 expressed diverse sets of motivations as the organization tried to address a very set of interests related to women in technology. Examples for such diverse motivations are e.g. *"I think one of the core values is to provide a space where women [...] can come and share their experience"* (I2) and *"briefly summarizing what are the values of S01 I would say networking"* (I6).

Fulfilment of Expectations.
Volunteer organizations rely on free participation of individuals who join a group with various motivations. Satisfying their expectations in response to their individual motivations, is essential for their continued participation. Our interviewees mainly expressed satisfaction with respect to their expectations about the goals of an organization being fulfilled. However, our interviewees were not always satisfied with their involvement in the organization. Most interviewees expressed both positive and negative attitudes when speaking about their expectations of their participation in the organization. Especially the oftentimes low attendance of activities they organized was mentioned as being disappointing (*"sometimes you feel frustrated that there is not enough members"*, I0, *"we just had 3 or 4 students in the talk"*, I3, *"we didn't get that many people"*, I5). Low attendance, however was not the only negative aspect that was mentioned. Some interviewees also expressed their frustration with the coordination or the lack of such (*"I think that we could have been more on top"*, I2, *"I think as an organization [...] we could be doing better"*, I4). Others also expressed dissatisfaction with the kinds of events organized by the group: *"I would definitely like to see more talks"* (I6).

In some cases, dissatisfaction was related to other students within the same organization. Some interviewees expressed their frustration that students did not fulfil tasks they agreed to fulfil: *"People had agreed to send out emails and those emails still have not gone out"* (I4); *"There are some people that commit to something and don't make it"* (I9). This happens despite the generally responsible attitude: *"I would say my fellow officers have exceeded my expectations"* (I5); *"everyone was helping in all the process"* (I6); *"I cannot remember that I asked some of them to do something and then they just forfeited"* (I3). This contradictory observation might hint at challenges with respect to coordinating and organizing events. Individuals might have misinterpreted or misunderstood what was expected of them or might not had the right means to communicate challenges that arose from the tasks they agreed to carry out.

4.2 Current Practices

In this section, we focus on the way students within student organizations collaborate (RQ1). Starting by analyzing their activities we then outline the process of their practices followed by an analysis of how they manage the inevitable turnover of individuals.

What Do These Organizations Do? Due to the nature of the student organizations we considered in this study, their main focus is on organizing events that cover a broad range of themes such as speaker series, brainstorming sessions, socializing, welcoming new students, or raising funds. This is evident not only by the fact that 54% of all mentions of any activity during the interviews were related to organizing events but also by responses of interviewees such as: *"My role [...] is to organize events"* (I0); *"My responsibilities are primarily to organize and oversee [...] events"* (I5); *"My particular responsibility would be to coordinate and initiate events"* (I7). The different student organizations we studied organize between four and more than 20 events per year. As a result, a major part of current practices involves coordination around organizing events (67% of all mentions of coordination were reported in the context of event organization). Other practices involved coordination around activities such as managing money, marketing and transition.

Student organizations are involved in activities that require collaboration with other groups outside of the university. A collaboration with members of the local community is an example of a non-event related activity (*"the Boys and Girls Club [...] wanted to make sure that their clubs are in the places where they are most needed"*, I8). Student organizations also engage in the recruitment activities (12% of all mentioned activities). Recruiting new members and officers is particularly important, given the high-turnover nature of these groups. New officers are mainly recruited from within the organization as evident by the frequent co-occurrence of the code "recruitment" and the code "group internal". Some interviewees also mentioned that they recruit new officers among other students in the university (29%). However, despite all interviewees mentioning recruitment as an important activity, there is no evidence that recruitment is organized. It rather takes place as an individual activity without much of coordination or organization which is evident by statements such as: *"I am still encouraging other people to go"* (I5) or *"she invited me to join"* (I0). Also focusing on recruitment within the same group only seems feasible when students actually stay within the same group for a considerable amount of time. This is not always the case as some student organizations such as S03 are run by students that are on a one-year program which in turn results in the necessity of recruiting new members and officers every year.

What is the Process of Their Practices? We observed their current practices to involve the following five steps:

Initiation: The organization of an activity starts either as (1) an officer proposes an activity (e.g. *"I was the one who proposed that we make one of these"*, I2); or (2) based on an activity that is regularly organized by the organization (e.g. *"we host a couple of annual events during the year"*, I7).

In-person planning meeting: The initiation is then followed up by an officer meeting to discuss about the upcoming activity: *"We need an officer meeting to decide all of the logistic things"* (I0). These in-person meetings usually involve planning activities and identifying tasks that need to be conducted for the activity to take place (*"that took some brainstorming and also some realistic talk about what we could get done"*, I1). Commonly, an activity is planned by a senior officer based on previous experiences (*"it is kind of a routine"*, I3). This officer then sometimes serves as a coordinator for that particular event (*"I was in charge of organizing everything"*, I3).

Distribution of tasks: Tasks are usually distributed among the officers by *"sort of self-picking"* (I0). Potential leftover tasks are then picked up by the coordinator who is in charge of the event (*"at the end whatever is left I pick them up"*, I3). The distribution of tasks rarely leads to conflicts as officers within an organization generally know each other well. Oftentimes they are able to even guide each other on which tasks fit their expertise (*"s/he is not good at business stuff"*, I2), the schedule of specific members (*"getting busy with school"*, I4), or their specific skills (*"some people are better with responding to emails than others"*, I4).

Following up: After tasks are distributed during the meeting, coordination mainly takes place on a needs basis. Sometimes individuals check on the progress: *"I would go to their office and ask them"* (I2). However, mostly individuals are expected to fulfil their responsibilities without any further input (*"tasks are divided once and considered done afterwards"*, I6). Communication and follow-up are thus quite infrequent.

Assessing success of an event: After an event, attendees or fellow officers oftentimes provide feedback which usually focuses on the event itself (*"some students came to me and said that this was a very helpful experience to them"*, I7, *"people said that they thought it was successful"*, I9). Feedback from attendees as well as fellow officers was reported on about equally often (attendees 46%, officers 54%) and there was no clear difference in the content or the quality of the feedback. Feedback is generally positive and focused on the event but sometimes participants were not happy with an event and would express that to the organizers: *"People might not be happy with a talk and say it is not useful for them"* (I3). This feedback however is never systematically evaluated. It rather stays with the person that received it and it is not used to reflect and discuss what went right and what can be improved in the future.

What Happens Next? Student organizations face high turn-over and quick transition. Seven out of ten interviewees mentioned that they intended to stop serving in their current role after their term ends or cut down their engagement due to their studies (*"I knew I was going to have a lot of milestones for my PhD"*, I6, *"that is something that you can manage when you are in the first or second year of your PhD program"*, I7). It is thus not surprising that 13% of all mentioned activities are transition related.

Student organizations indeed dedicate some effort to the transition process (unlike recruitment which is mainly uncoordinated as discussed before). However, each organization has their own strategy. Some attempt to support the transition through documentation (*"we are trying [...] to create documents describing what we did"*, I4) while others try to manage it as part of their recruitment process by forming a leadership team consisting of tenured and new members (*"I was vice president last year and [...] this year I became the president"*, I0). One of the organizations even ran an event dedicated to passing on knowledge from one leadership group to the next (*"during the leadership retreat was a [...] we wanted to connect the incoming board members [...] with the outgoing ones"*, I9).

In all cases, however, we observed that the main focus of transition-related activities is on handling the interaction between the student organization and the university. Those interactions cover questions of how to *"start the organization"* (I4) or *"where we get our money"* (I5). There was no indication of passing on knowledge about the inner workings of the respective organizations. The transition of this knowledge however is particularly important for such loosely coupled groups since there is often no chance to repeat the same event within the same semester or year and mistakes or difficulties can easily be forgotten and repeated. Moreover, while the same person can serve as an officer for a few years, they eventually will have to leave as they finish their studies. Therefore, in cases that the same leadership group is in place for a long time, lack of transition of knowledge can become even more of an impediment as evident by the following statement: *"If I were the president for four/five years when I leave it will be kind of a bummer for the next president to realize how to do that"* (I3).

4.3 The Role of Technology in Current Practices

In addition to the way student organizations operate, we are also interested in how they use technology (RQ2). We will report on our findings related to technology in this section starting with which technology is being used followed by how it is used.

Which Technologies Do Student Organizations Use? Our anticipation that student organizations use a wide range of technologies was confirmed by the interview results. Starting with email as the technology that was mentioned the most (56% of all mentions of technology), most interviewees also mentioned using different instant messengers (15%) such as WhatsApp (I1, I3, I8, I9), Slack (I2, I6), iMessage (I5) and SMS (I5). We also observed an almost equal number of mentions of different content or document management systems (12%) such as GoogleDrive (I0, I2, I4, I6, I9), Dropbox (I7) or Box (I8). There were also mentions of the usage of voice chat (7%), social media (5%) and wikis or blogs (4%) as well as other technologies such as the school website (I0, I4), doodle polls (I0, I1) and GoogleForms (I4). We also found individuals that use up to six different technologies for different purposes. This can lead to uncoordinated technology use among the members of an organization (e.g. I8 and I9, both part of SO5, use different document management systems, I8 uses GoogleDocs while I9 uses Box) which in turn can complicate coordination.

What is most cumbersome, however, is that none of the tools are being significantly utilized and most interviewees resort to emails for most activities. This becomes obvious when analyzing the way technology is being used.

Usage Strategies Overall, we observed that technology is mainly utilized for coordination purposes. Both email ($r = 0.60$, $p < .001$) and instant messengers ($r = 0.39$, $p < .001$) were significantly mentioned in relation to coordination activities. In fact, we observed that with relation to coordination, there is significantly more mention of technology (60%) than face-to-face meetings (40%). This does not imply though that coordination indeed mainly takes place using technology since most coordination happens during the first in-person planning meetings as discussed in Sect. 4.2. However, most coordination that takes place after a meeting is done using technology (*"we send an email to ask what happened"*, I0). The organizing officers particularly utilize email threads (*"usually we just talk through our email threads"*, I4) which makes it hard for individuals that are not part of this thread to be informed about the planning of an activity. They have to either actively ask for information or wait for the involved officers to decide to inform them.

Coordination around the organization of activities as reported by the study participants mainly happens via email and instant messenger as evident by the significant correlation between the respective codes ($r = 0.60$, $p < .001$ for coordination and email and $r = 0.39$, $p < .001$ for coordination and instant messenger). However, considering the way that communication happens it is surprising that individuals do not perceive a general lack of task awareness. In fact, multiple interviewees stated that awareness is not a problem because *"I have the list in my booklet"* (I3) or they would *"go to office and ask"* (I2) if there was a problem. However, when looking deeper into the interview content it becomes clear that individuals are not really aware of tasks that are currently conducted and that this indeed leads to issues. Individuals assume that *"tasks are divided once and considered done afterwards"* (I6) which is not always the case (*"a day before I was notified that the meeting would happen tomorrow"*, I6). There is thus a clear need to improve task awareness.

For activities other than coordination, technology only plays a minor role. Feedback is never delivered via technology but rather face-to-face. This significantly limits the potential for documenting and reflecting on feedback in order to improve the organization of activities. Technology is also only marginally considered as a means to support the transition from one generation to the next or to recruit new members. In fact, only one interviewee stated that s/he currently working on creating a GoogleDocs document that focuses on the interaction between the student organization and the university (*"describing what we did to start the organization"*, I4). This document however does not cover information about how the student organization operates internally. Similarly, recruitment is only marginally conducted using email as a technology (*"I sent out the email to the new PhD students that I knew that came to the school"*, I0).

5   Discussion and Limitations

Our findings provide an insight into how volunteers within student organizations currently collaborate (RQ1) and how they utilize technology for their collaboration (RQ2), indicating a number of areas where technology combined with well-designed practices can improve collaboration within such small loosely coupled volunteer groups. Specifically, we identified three main areas of improvement: (1) **higher level of transparency**, (2) **well defined task procedures**, (3) **more effective knowledge transfer within and between groups**.

Awareness is an essential ingredient of effective collaboration. Our results indicate a **lack of transparency and awareness**, especially with regards to planning of activities. This can become a significant roadblock in effectively managing organizations as previously discussed in the context of collaborative work [14, 21]. Similarly, **well-defined procedures** play a significant role to support the organization of activities, especially if those activities are recurring. Common means to achieve this are approaches related to business process management [15]. The student organizations we studied have a clear need for such processes since activities are currently organized on a needs basis and guided by individual experiences. There are also no practices in place that support organizations in dealing with feedback and reflecting on past activities to improve their practices. This lack of well-defined procedures does not only harm the organization of activities. It also harms the process of recruiting new members and new officers. Such procedures are commonly designed managed by employed coordinators [12, 17, 23] or a stable core of volunteers [4, 10, 32] both of which are not available in the context we studied. Lack of transparency and well-defined procedures can further lead to challenges in **knowledge transfer**. Within current practices, we observed only non-structured arbitrary knowledge exchange between current members and officers as well as between current and future members and officers. As a result, existing knowledge often gets lots and does not transfer from one generation of members and officers to another. This finding is similar to work discussing corporate knowledge management [1] and it is particularly hard to overcome for small loosely coupled volunteer groups as they face high turnover and loose commitment levels. Membership in such organizations has by definition an expiration date as it depends on a terminal education period. Therefore, designing and practicing highly transparent, well-defined procedures to document and transfer knowledge is critical to their longer-term success. Also, despite the fact that the student groups we studied undoubtedly have commonalities and similar problems, there is almost no exchange between the leadership of different groups about their practices. There is work suggesting structured process reflection [38] but such approaches can be difficult to implement in the context we studied.

We also observed that technology currently is significantly under-utilized even though many different tools are used by different members. There is no standard procedure for how technology can support their collaboration effectively without adding additional barriers in the process. Currently, there is high reliance on email as a main means of communication which can introduce additional challenges, especially with regards to transparency, awareness and transfer of knowledge as mentioned before. Common technology can serve as a means to overcome such challenges as evident e.g. in the context of online communities [44]. We will discuss this aspect in the following.

5.1 A Proposal Towards a Solution

An important goal of our research was to discover how technology can support collaboration within small loosely coupled volunteer groups. We aim to complement existing practices since these groups have been around for some time and thus exemplify an interesting success story. While we provide a first step towards a solution in this direction, we believe that a longer term solution needs an iterative participatory design process [7, 18, 22, 36]. The future direction of our research aims at introducing our proposed technology to a number of student organizations for a trial period. We will then analyze their practices in presence of the new technology in order to refine the technology and practices over time as best fits the needs of each individual organization.

In particular we propose an approach that is based on complementing current practices, orchestrating existing technologies and providing support for the missing opportunities. In particular, we propose to use the group messenger Slack [51] as a core means of communication since it is light weight and it can easily be adapted to suit the needs of a student organization. Slack is easy to set up, easy to use and maintain, works on almost any device and has been successfully applied in similar collaborative contexts such as small software teams [33]. Slack also provides a lot of flexibility in that it allows users to connect it with other technologies of their choice such as Facebook, GoogleDrive, Dropbox and others.

Slack promotes **transparency** in that all individuals that are part of a channel can follow the stream of messages and have the opportunity to become part of the conversation at any point of time. This allows individuals that were not part of the initial planning meetings to become part of the conversation and offer ideas and support. It provides a basis for assessing the membership of an organization in that it allows members of a channel to see who is a part of it, assess the level of engagement based on interaction in the channel and get in contact with them. It also supports **knowledge transfer** within and between organizations in that previous messages can be retrieved and used for future purposes which makes it a light weight and simple knowledge management mechanism [13]. Furthermore, it provides a communication channel for the leadership of different volunteer groups to discuss about common ideas and challenges. Finally, it provides the opportunity for former members to stay in touch and potentially offer support if required. Slack by itself does not solve the previously mentioned lack of **procedures**. It does however provide a basis for procedures to evolve because it provides a platform for sharing documents, discussing feedback and organizing reflection even beyond the boundaries of a single organization. The evolving of those practices can also be supported by bots [31] which can monitor the activity in specific channels and e.g. suggest towards reflecting on a previous activity based on the date of that activity or suggest for engaging new and old members in transfer activities based on the typical transition period of an organization. Bots can enable or promote practices, but they cannot guarantee for them to form. It still remains in the responsibility of the members and officers to build them and pass them on to future generations. We also acknowledge the fact that following these suggestions requires student organizations to commit to this particular technology and that it might steer resentment by individuals since it is another tool to use and to maintain. We are however confident that its ability to blend in with other technologies, its aforementioned potential to support the operation of student organizations and its ease of use will serve as a means for them to try and potentially adopt it. Moreover, some interviewees even mentioned that they use it in their professional life and suggested using it for their student organization as well.

5.2 Limitations

The exploratory nature our research poses limitations. First, we focused our work on one particular type of small loosely coupled volunteer groups by studying student organizations. While it can be argued that these organizations are generally comparable to other similar organizations it has to be noted that these organizations operate within a specific context that has an impact on the way they collaborate. We aimed at mitigating this effect by including organizations of different sizes from different universities that have different goals. Second, our work was driven by an interview guide and a corresponding coding scheme that were developed based on existing literature. While we conducted and exhaustive literature analysis, it is possible that we did not cover all aspects that can be found in real life volunteer organizations. We tried to mitigate this effect by conducting an analysis that allowed for adding codes based on our interview data. Third, our conclusions are based on a relatively small sample of ten interviewees and five student organizations from two North-American universities. This poses a threat to the generalizability of our results. However, our work is meant to shed light onto an area that has not been extensively studied by focusing on small volunteer groups. It thus seems reasonable to conduct a study that provides initial insights which are rather informative than generalizable. Finally, we calculated percentages and correlations between codes and included them into our analysis which can lead to misinterpretations since just the fact that certain aspects are mentioned more often together does not constitute causality between them. To mitigate this threat, we abstained from drawing causal conclusions based on the calculations but rather utilized them as a complement to our qualitative analysis. We also backed them up with interview quotes to set them into context.

Acknowledgements. Dr. Nolte's contributions to this research were partially funded by Deutsche Forschungsgemeinschaft (DFG) under grant no. NO 1302/1-1.

References

1. Alavi, M., Leidner, D.E.: Knowledge management and knowledge management systems: conceptual foundations and research issues. MIS Q. **25**, 107–136 (2001)
2. Baker, C.N.: Under-represented college students and extracurricular involvement: the effects of various student organizations on academic performance. Soc. Psychol. Educ. **11**(3), 273–298 (2008)
3. Boulus-Rødje, N., Bjorn, P.: Design challenges in supporting distributed knowledge: an examination of organizing elections. In: Proceedings of the 33rd Annual ACM Conference on Human Factors in Computing Systems, pp. 3137–3146. ACM (2015)
4. Cataldo, M., Herbsleb, J.D.: Communication networks in geographically distributed software development. In: Proceedings of the 2008 ACM Conference on Computer Supported Cooperative Work, pp. 579–588. ACM (2008)
5. Chevrier, F., et al.: Factors affecting satisfaction among community-based hospice volunteer visitors. Am. J. Hosp. Palliat. Med. **11**(4), 30–37 (1994)
6. Clary, E.G., et al.: Volunteers' motivations: a functional strategy for the recruitment, placement, and retention of volunteers. Nonprofit Manag. Leadersh. **2**(4), 333–350 (1992)

7. Clegg, C.W.: Sociotechnical principles for system design. Appl. Ergon. **31**(5), 463–477 (2000)
8. Cobb, C., et al.: Designing for the deluge: understanding & supporting the distributed, collaborative work of crisis volunteers. In: Proceedings of the 17th ACM Conference on Computer Supported Cooperative Work & Social Computing, pp. 888–899. ACM (2014)
9. Cohen, J.: Weighted kappa: nominal scale agreement provision for scaled disagreement or partial credit. Psychol. Bull. **70**(4), 213 (1968)
10. Crowston, K., et al.: Self-organization of teams for free/libre open source software development. Inf. Softw. Technol. **49**(6), 564–575 (2007)
11. Crowston, K., Howison, J.: A ten-year retrospective. Hum.-Comput. Interact. Manag. Inf. Syst. Found. **120** (2006)
12. Cuskelly, G., et al.: Volunteer management practices and volunteer retention: a human resource management approach. Sport Manag. Rev. **9**(2), 141–163 (2006)
13. Dennerlein, S., et al.: Web 2.0 messaging tools for knowledge management? Exploring the potentials of slack. In: European Conference on Knowledge Management, p. 225. Academic Conferences International Limited (2016)
14. Dourish, P., Bellotti, V.: Awareness and coordination in shared workspaces. In: Proceedings of the 1992 ACM Conference on Computer-Supported Cooperative Work, pp. 107–114. ACM (1992)
15. Dumas, M., et al.: Fundamentals of Business Process Management. Springer, Heidelberg (2013). https://doi.org/10.1007/978-3-642-33143-5
16. Farmer, S.M., Fedor, D.B.: Volunteer participation and withdrawal. Nonprofit Manag. Leadersh. **9**(4), 349–368 (1999)
17. Farrell, J.M., et al.: Volunteer motivation, satisfaction, and management at an elite sporting competition. J. Sport Manag. **12**(4), 288–300 (1998)
18. Fischer, G., Herrmann, T.: Socio-technical systems: a meta-design perspective. Int. J. Sociotechnology Knowl. Dev. IJSKD. **3**(1), 1–33 (2011)
19. Galindo-Kuhn, R., Guzley, R.M.: The volunteer satisfaction index. J. Soc. Serv. Res. **28**(1), 45–68 (2002)
20. Garner, J.T., Garner, L.T.: Volunteering an opinion: organizational voice and volunteer retention in nonprofit organizations. Nonprofit Volunt. Sect. Q. **40**(5), 813–828 (2011)
21. Gross, T., et al.: User-centred awareness in computer-supported cooperative work-systems: structured embedding of findings from social sciences. J. Hum.-Comput. Interact. **18**(3), 323–360 (2005)
22. Grudin, J.: Why CSCW applications fail: problems in the design and evaluation of organizational interfaces. In: Proceedings of the 1988 ACM Conference on Computer-Supported Cooperative Work, pp. 85–93. ACM (1988)
23. Harrison, D.A.: Volunteer motivation and attendance decisions: competitive theory testing in multiple samples from a homeless shelter. J. Appl. Psychol. **80**(3), 371 (1995)
24. Haski-Leventhal, D., Bargal, D.: The volunteer stages and transitions model: organizational socialization of volunteers. Hum. Relat. **61**(1), 67–102 (2008)
25. Herrmann, T., et al.: Evaluating socio-technical systems with heuristics - a feasible approach? In: Proceedings of the 2nd International Workshop on Socio-Technical Perspective in IS Development (STPIS 2016), pp. 91–97. CEUR-WS (2016)
26. Hibbert, S., et al.: Understanding volunteer motivation for participation in a community-based food cooperative. Int. J. Nonprofit Volunt. Sect. Mark. **8**(1), 30–42 (2003)
27. Karr, L.B., Meijs, L.C.P.M.: Sustaining the motivation to volunteer in organizations. In: Fetchenhauer, D., Flache, A., Buunk, B., Lindenberg, S. (eds.) Solidarity and Prosocial Behavior. Critical Issues in Social Justice, pp. 157–172. Springer, Boston (2006). https://doi.org/10.1007/0-387-28032-4_10

28. Kitchenham, B.: Procedures for performing systematic reviews (2004)
29. Kraut, R., et al.: Dealing with newcomers. Evid. Soc. Des. Min. Soc. Sci. Build Online Communities **1**, 42 (2010)
30. Landis, J.R., Koch, G.G.: The measurement of observer agreement for categorical data. Biometrics, 159–174 (1977)
31. Lee, M., et al.: Bots mind the social-technical gap. In: Proceedings of 15th European Conference on Computer-Supported Cooperative Work-Exploratory Papers. European Society for Socially Embedded Technologies (EUSSET) (2017)
32. Liao, Q.V., et al.: Improvising harmony: opportunities for technologies to support crowd orchestration. Urbana **51**, 61801 (2016)
33. Lin, B., et al.: Why developers are slacking off: understanding how software teams use slack. In: Proceedings of the 19th ACM Conference on Computer Supported Cooperative Work and Social Computing Companion, pp. 333–336. ACM (2016)
34. Malone, T.W., Crowston, K.: The interdisciplinary study of coordination. ACM Comput. Surv. CSUR. **26**(1), 87–119 (1994)
35. Malone, T.W., Crowston, K.: What is coordination theory and how can it help design cooperative work systems? In: Proceedings of the 1990 ACM Conference on Computer-Supported Cooperative Work, pp. 357–370. ACM (1990)
36. Mumford, E.: Effective Systems Design and Requirements and Analysis - the ETHICS aproach. Macmillan Press LTD, Houndsmill, Basingstoke, Hampshire and London (1995)
37. Nolte, A.: Exploring potentials of process reflection to support communities of small volunteer groups. In: Workshops and Work-in-Progress Contributions at S-BPM ONE 2018. CEUR-WS (2018)
38. Nolte, A., et al.: Supporting collaboration in small volunteer groups with socio-technical guidelines. In: Proceedings of 16th European Conference on Computer-Supported Cooperative Work - Exploratory Papers, Reports of the European Society for Socially Embedded Technologies (2018)
39. Omoto, A.M., Snyder, M.: Considerations of community: the context and process of volunteerism. Am. Behav. Sci. **45**(5), 846–867 (2002)
40. Pearce, J.L.: Volunteers: The Organizational Behavior of Unpaid Workers. Routledge, Abingdon (1993)
41. Peterson, D.K.: Recruitment strategies for encouraging participation in corporate volunteer programs. J. Bus. Ethics. **49**(4), 371–386 (2004)
42. Pinelle, D., Gutwin, C.: Designing for loose coupling in mobile groups. In: Proceedings of the 2003 International ACM SIGGROUP Conference on Supporting Group Work, pp. 75–84. ACM (2003)
43. Qiu, H.S., et al.: Going farther together: the impact of social capital on sustained participation in open source. In: International Conference on Software Engineering. IEEE (2019)
44. Ransbotham, S., Kane, G.C.: Membership turnover and collaboration success in online communities: explaining rises and falls from grace in Wikipedia. Mis Q., 613–627 (2011)
45. Retelny, D., et al.: Expert crowdsourcing with flash teams. In: Proceedings of the 27th Annual ACM Symposium on User Interface Software and Technology, pp. 75–85. ACM (2014)
46. Saeed, S., et al.: Analyzing political activists' organization practices: findings from a long term case study of the european social forum. Comput. Support. Coop. Work CSCW **20**(4–5), 265–304 (2011)

47. Schmidt, K.: Riding a tiger, or computer supported cooperative work. In: Bannon, L., Robinson, M., Schmidt, K. (eds.) Proceedings of the Second European Conference on Computer-Supported Cooperative Work ECSCW '91., pp. 1–16. Springer, Dordrecht (1991). https://doi.org/10.1007/978-94-011-3506-1_1
48. Valentine, M.A., et al.: Flash organizations: crowdsourcing complex work by structuring crowds as organizations. In: Proceedings of the 2017 CHI Conference on Human Factors in Computing Systems, pp. 3523–3537. ACM (2017)
49. Voida, A., et al.: Homebrew databases: complexities of everyday information management in nonprofit organizations. In: Proceedings of the SIGCHI Conference on Human Factors in Computing Systems, pp. 915–924. ACM (2011)
50. Wang, L.S., et al.: Searching for the goldilocks zone: trade-offs in managing online volunteer groups. In: Proceedings of the ACM 2012 Conference on Computer Supported Cooperative Work, pp. 989–998. ACM (2012)
51. Slack. https://slack.com/
52. Social Kitchen - the Other Person. http://www.aljazeera.com/indepth/inpictures/2015/09/greece-social-kitchen-person-150921110028671.html
53. SUDS. http://suds-cmu.org/
54. Wikipedia. https://www.wikipedia.org/

The Analysis of Collaborative Science Learning with Simulations Through Dual Eye-Tracking Techniques

I-Chen Hsieh[1(✉)], Chen-Chung Liu[1(✉)], Meng-Jung Tsai[2],
Cai Ting Wen[1], Ming Hua Chang[1], Shih-Hsun Fan Chiang[1],
and Chia Jung Chang[3]

[1] Graduate Institute of Network Learning Technology,
National Central University, Taoyuan City, Taiwan
hsiehichen@g.ncu.edu.tw, ccliu@cl.ncu.edu.tw
[2] Program of Learning Sciences, National Taiwan Normal University,
Taipei City, Taiwan
[3] Department of Information Technology, Takming University of Science
and Technology, Taipei City, Taiwan

Abstract. Collaborative problem solving is a core ability that has been highly valued in recent years. Collaborative problem solving activities allow learners develop collaboration skills. In science education, collaborative learning with simulations enables learners to manipulate a science problem to explore scientific concepts. However, the collaboration during such a learning context is a complicated process and researchers face difficulties in understanding learners' mental effort in using the simulations. The use of dual eye-tracking techniques is helpful to uncover learners' visual attention, and thus to better analyze student collaboration in activities. In this paper, the research focus on learners' difficulties when they learn together with the simulation in different places. The results show that the techniques are helpful to identify the subtle interaction problem including the problem of lacking coordination, the process misunderstanding problem, and misunderstanding in partners' attention. Educators may need to address these problems when simulations are applied to support remote collaborative science learning.

Keywords: Eye-tracking · Collaboration · Science learning

1 Introduction

In recent years, collaborative problem solving (CPS) is one of the core competencies [1]. Therefore, collaborative problem solving activities are frequently applied to help students develop such a competency as they learn to coordinate with the partners to solve problems together. In the past, researchers applied questionnaires or survey to understand collaboration quality during collaborative learning. However, it is suggested that such subjective approach often can not reflect the actual collaboration and mental efforts during collaborative learning [2].

© Springer Nature Switzerland AG 2019
H. Nakanishi et al. (Eds.): CRIWG+CollabTech 2019, LNCS 11677, pp. 36–44, 2019.
https://doi.org/10.1007/978-3-030-28011-6_3

To better capture learners' mental effort, many experts applied eye-tracking analysis technique to analyze students' visual attentions to understand the students' problem solving process [3, 4]. These studies mostly focused on the individual problems solving process, not on the collaboration process. How two individuals' attentions coordinate to solve a problem is not clearly depicted. To conquer such a limitation, dual eye-tracking techniques which collect and analyze two individuals' gaze movements were applied to uncover how two students learn together [5]. The literature has demonstrated the usage of such techniques for the research of collaborative learning.

The present study thus attempts to understand the collaboration process through dual eye-tracking techniques when students at different places learn science together with computer simulations. Collaborative learning with simulations enables learners to manipulate a science problem to explore scientific concepts. It is hoped that the dual eye-tracking techniques can uncover the limitations of the computer simulation in supporting collaborative problem solving. Although eye-tracking techniques are not a completely novel research method [6–8], this study contributed to understand the application of dual eye-tracking techniques in understanding the use and design of computer simulation in supporting science learning.

2 Methods

This study recruited students from a national university in Taiwan. Only students who had normal vision or normal vision after correction and who never participated in similar experiments are included in this study. This study selected two pairs of students as the focus group for detail case study. The two participants of each pair did not know each other before the experiment and they sit in different rooms and talk with the mobile phone system. Such an arrangement simulates the learning situation when students do not co-present in a classroom but learn in different places.

The simulation used in this study is "how much rain" (Fig. 1) that simulates how much rain will fall on to a character who run in different speed. The simulation displays both of the animation and the amount of the rain falling onto the character in three charts.

With the simulation, the student pairs needed to understand whether the character needs to run to avoid getting wetter. This simulation allows students to manipulate the running speed and rainfall density. The students could check the top, side and the total rain falling on the character.

In this study, we defined seven area of interest (AOI) for the analysis of gaze movement (Fig. 1), including the problem description area (AOI1), the simulation control area (AOI2), the simulation animation area (AOI3), the top rain chart displaying the rain falling to the head (AOI4), the side rain chart displaying the rain falling to the character from the side (AOI5), the overall rainfall chart (AOI6) and learning material area (AOI7).

The participants operate the simulation on an individual basis. In other words, the simulations operated by the two students of the student pairs were not synchronized. One pair member's operations on his/her simulation did not interfere with each other. In this scientific learning activity, the two partners must coordinate closely to solve the

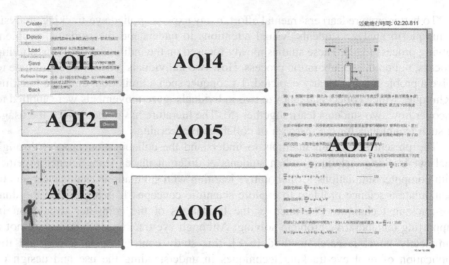

Fig. 1. The "how much rain" simulation.

scientific problems. This experiment was 20 min. After the activity, the participants answer a teamwork quality (TWQ) questionnaire [9] to understand their perception about the collaboration.

This study applied the Tobii Eye Tracker 4C at 90 Hz to collect students gaze movement. The Real-time Fixation Identification and Analysis Module (RFIAM) [10] was used to collect the gaze movement. Several AOIs (Area of Interest) regions were defined according to the different components of the simulation (Fig. 1). When student gaze at an AOI, the eye-tracking system will detect such a fixation and recorded the start time and end time of the fixation and the AOI area. This study applied the cross-recurrence plot (CRP) function in MATLAB [11, 12] to analyze the students' joint attention. The CRP analysis, students' discourse and their feedback to the TWQ questionnaire was analyzed together to better understand the collaboration process.

3   Results and Discussion

Figure 2 displays the CRP of a pair of this study. The x-axis and y-axis of the matrix represent the activity time of different students. If student A gazed an AOI at time x and student B also gazed the same AOI at time y, then the cell (x, y) at the CRP will be marked. Therefore, the diagonal line represents that the two students observed the same AOI at the same time. This study firstly integrated students' fixation records with their screen videos to better present students' visual attention and their screen behaviors. The videos were then analyzed with students' discourse data. As shown in Fig. 2, Block B shows the two students demonstrated noticeable joint attention. From the discourse B1–B7 (Table 1) we observed that the two are coordinating on the manipulation of the simulation, and thus they both closely watched the AOI2. Therefore, they demonstrated high level of visual joint attention from the intensive marked area around Block B.

However, triangulating the CRP with discourse data (as shown in Table 1) also found that the two experimenters were not aware of the other party's operation. More specifically, while one person was waiting for the other person to operate the simulation, the other person had thought he already completed the simulation (see the discourse A1–A6). We observed that STUDENT A is still watching AOI2, while STUDENT B has visually moved to AOI6 in the chart area. Such results suggest that student will encounter the process misunderstanding problem when they use simulations individually to collaborate to learn. From the difference between Block A and Block B, we found that the CRP can reflect how two individuals pay attention to the simulation and work together.

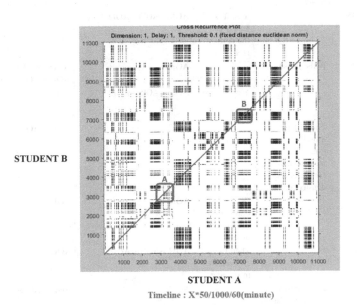

Fig. 2. Introduction to the Cross-Recurrence Plot cooperation status of the pair A.

In another case, as shown in Fig. 3 and Table 2, it is observed that there is a problem in the communication between the two people at the beginning (C1–C3). More specifically, STUDENT A suggested to directly discuss the answer of the question and terminate the activity (C2). This is because STUDENT A has already completed the simulation while STUDENT B was still waiting for STUDENT A to discuss how to manipulate the simulation. From discourse C3, we could find that STUDENT B doesn't observe any chart area (AOI4, AOI5, AOI6), while STUDENT A has moved to the chart in AOI5. Such an instance reflects that students encounter the problem of lacking coordination. Such a problem occurred again from D1 to D4. More specifically, when STUDENT A has already completed simulation and was watching the chart of AOI6, STUDENT B was still waiting for STUDENT A to discuss about the variable in the AOI2.

Table 1. Partial dialogue during the experiment and AOI conversion of the pair A.

Number	Timeline (min)	STUDENT A	STUDENT B	AOI_ STUDENT A	AOI_ STUDENT B
A1	02:27		If he run faster and he speed is 3, he gets wet	AOI2→AOI3→AOI2→AOI3	AOI2→AOI6→AOI3→AOI6
A2	02:32		When he arrived at place, he wet value is 202	AOI3→AOI6→AOI2→AOI6	AOI6
A3	02:42	Are you setting 3 now?		AOI6	AOI2
A4	02:45		Yes, it is V = 3 and the density is 4	AOI6→AOI3→AOI2	AOI2
A5	02:48	Is the density 4?		AOI2	AOI5→AOI4→ AOI5→AOI3→AOI4
A6	02:50		Yes˙	AOI2→AOI5→AOI2	AOI2
⋮					
B1	05:46	Then I have tested it a few times, I measured…Is setting of rain density high?		AOI2	AOI5→AOI1→AOI2
B2	05:55		Ok, I set the rain density setting to high	AOI2	AOI2
B3	06:02		Then I set the slowest one in running	AOI2→AOI1→AOI2	AOI2
B4	06:08	High density. Which the fastest or the slowest in your setting		AOI2	AOI2→AOI3→AOI2
B5	06:10		I set the slowest one	AOI2→AOI5→AOI2	AOI2→AOI5→AOI3
B6	06:11	Then I set the fastest one		AOI2	AOI3

Furthermore, the discourse E1–E6 display another problem, that is attention misunderstanding. However, from E1–E6, it can be found that STUDENT A is talking about the cumulative rainfall of AOI6 while STUDENT B was not sure which AOI to observe and transited among different AOIs. Thus, it reveals that the two students encounter misunderstanding in their visual attention and thus cause ineffective collaboration.

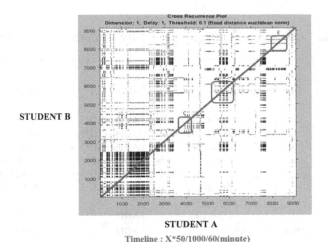

STUDENT A

Timeline : X*50/1000/60(minute)

Fig. 3. Introduction to the Cross-Recurrence Plot cooperation status of the pair B.

This study found that the two pairs demonstrated different patterns of collaboration. It can be inferred by the CRP that pair A demonstrated more marked blocks in the activity than pair B did. The dialogue data also demonstrate that pair A members will inform each other of the operation status and thus demonstrated better joint attention. On the contrary, pair B lacked coordination and cause misunderstanding in both of the process and attention. Such a difference can be also shown in their feedback to the TWQ (See Table 3) indicating that pair A perceived a higher level of collaboration quality than pair B did.

Table 2. Partial dialogue during the experiment and AOI conversion of the pair B.

Number	Timeline (min)	STUDENT A	STUDENT B	AOI_ STUDENT A	AOI_ STUDENT B
C1	03:13		Well, so are we going to make this problem now?	AOI4→AOI5→AOI7	AOI1→AOI7→AOI2
C2	03:19	Well, should we discuss it? Then press End		AOI7→AOI5→AOI7	AOI2
C3	03:25		Do we run this simulation? Or do we have to answer the question on the right side?	AOI5→AOI2→ AOI5→AOI7→ AOI5→AOI2→AOI7	AOI2→AOI1→ AOI7→AOI1→ AOI7→AOI2→AOI3

(*continued*)

Table 2. (*continued*)

Number	Timeline (min)	STUDENT A	STUDENT B	AOI_ STUDENT A	AOI_ STUDENT B
⋮					
D1	04:20	Then we are end?		AOI6	AOI2
D2	04:22		Do you want to run the simulation? From speed 2, the rainfall density is fixed, and adjust to the speed is 4, I press run	AOI6→AOI5→ AOI4→AOI5→ AOI6→AOI2→ AOI3→AOI7→ AOI2→AOI5→ AOI6→AOI2→AOI4	AOI2→AOI1→ AOI2→AOI4→ AOI2→AOI5→ AOI6→AOI3→ AOI2→AOI4→ AOI5→AOI3→AOI2
D3	04:58		I do reset	AOI2	AOI2→AOI5→AOI2
D4	05:00	Well... in fact, your numbers will not affect my data		AOI4	AOI2→AOI5→ AOI6→AOI2
⋮					
E-1	06:50	So, the shorter your time, the faster your speed, and the more rainfall there will be		AOI6	AOI3→AOI2→ AOI6→AOI3
E-2	06:59		The less rainfall there will be	AOI6	AOI3
E-3	07:02	The more rainfall there will be		AOI6	AOI3
E-4	07:05	It will be...		AOI6	AOI3
E-5	07:07		Wait, so who is the rainfall?	AOI6	AOI3
E-6	07:11	It is the relatively large amount of rainfall		AOI6	AOI3→AOI2→AOI5

Table 3. Two pairs of cooperation quality.

	Pair A	Pair B
Communication	4.125	2.875
Coordination	3.875	2.875
Balance of member contributions	4.75	3.5
Support	4.167	2.75
Effort	4.375	3.125

4   Conclusion

In the case study above, the marked blocks on the diagonal of the CRP display the degree to which two individually jointly pay attention to the same AOI together. In the two pairs of this study, pair A demonstrated higher quality of collaboration than the pair B did. Through the dual eye-tracking technique, we also identified three main problems when the computer simulations are used to support online synchronous collaborative learning, that is, the problem of lacking coordination, the process misunderstanding problem, and misunderstanding in partners' attention. It is worthwhile to investigate what mechanism is helpful to amend these problems. For instance, collaborative simulations which enforce the synchronization of all operations to the simulation of all participants may be helpful to guide students to jointly attend to the shared focus. Furthermore, this study triangulated students discourse records with visual attention through eye-tracking techniques. It is found that such approach help the researcher gain more insight on the detail process of the collaboration. Researchers may find such an approach helpful to look into the constraints and affordances of other new collaborative learning systems.

References

1. Griffin, P., McGaw, B., Care, E.: Assessment and Teaching of 21st Century Skills: Methods and Approach. Springer, New York (2012). https://doi.org/10.1007/978-94-017-9395-7
2. De Koning, B., Tabbers, H., Rikers, R., Paas, F.: Attention guidance in learning from a complex animation: seeing is understanding? Learn. Instr. 20(2), 111–122 (2010)
3. Tsai, M.J., Hou, H.T., Lai, M.L., Liu, W.Y., Yang, F.Y.: Visual attention for solving multiple-choice science problem: an eye-tracking analysis. Comput. Educ. 58, 375–385 (2012)
4. Tai, R.H., Loehr, J.F., Brigham, F.J.: An exploration of the use of eye-gaze tracking to study problem-solving on standardized science assessment. Int. J. Res. Method Educ. 29(2), 185–208 (2006)
5. Nüssli, M.-A.: Dual eye-tracking methods for the study of remote collaborative problem solving. Doctoral dissertation (2011). https://doi.org/10.5075/epfl-thesis-5232
6. Schneider, B., Sharma, K., Cuendet, S., Zufferey, G., Dillenbourg, P., Pea, R.: Using mobile eye-trackers to unpack the perceptual benefits of a tangible user interface for collaborative learning. ACM Trans. Comput. Hum. Interact. 23(6), Article 39 (2016)
7. Othlinghaus-Wulhorst, J., Jedich, A., Ulrich Hoppe, H., Harrer, A.: Using eye-tracking to analyze collaboration in a virtual role play environment. In: Rodrigues, A., Fonseca, B., Preguiça, N. (eds.) CRIWG 2018. LNCS, vol. 11001, pp. 185–197. Springer, Cham (2018). https://doi.org/10.1007/978-3-319-99504-5_15
8. Sharma, K., Caballero, D., Verma, H., Jermann, P., Dillenbourg, P.: Looking AT versus looking THROUGH: a dual eye-tracking study in MOOC context. In: Proceedings of 11th International Conference of Computer Supported Collaborative Learning, pp. 260–267 (2015)
9. Hoegl, M., Gemuenden, H.G.: Teamwork quality and the success of innovative projects: a theoretical concept and empirical evidence. Organ. Sci. 12(4), 435–449 (2001)

10. Hsu, C.-Y., Chiou, G.-L., Tsai, M.-J.: A pilot study on developing and validating a fixation-based scaffolding learning system. Poster presented at 2016 International Conference of East-Asian Association for Science Education, Tokyo, Japan (2016)
11. Marwan, N., Kurths, J.: Nonlinear analysis of bivariate data with cross recurrence plots. Phys. Lett. A **302**(5–6), 299–307 (2002)
12. Marwan, N., Romano, M.C., Thiel, M., Kurths, J.: Recurrence plots for the analysis of complex systems. Phys. Rep. **438**(5–6), 237–329 (2007)

Hybrid Meetings in the Modern Workplace: Stories of Success and Failure

Banu Saatçi[1]([✉])(iD), Roman Rädle[2](iD), Sean Rintel[3](iD), Kenton O'Hara[3](iD), and Clemens Nylandsted Klokmose[1](iD)

[1] Digital Design and Information Studies, Aarhus University, Aarhus, Denmark
`banu.saatci@cc.au.dk, clemens@cavi.au.dk`
[2] Computer Science, Aarhus University, Aarhus, Denmark
`roman.raedle@cs.au.dk`
[3] Microsoft Research, Cambridge, UK
`{serintel,keohar}@microsoft.com`

Abstract. Hybrid meetings, in which co-located and remote participants connect via video or/audio, have become ubiquitous in the globalized modern workplace. Despite, or perhaps because of this ubiquity, conducting hybrid meetings is not straightforward. In this paper, we investigate the opportunities and challenges of hybrid meetings. We conducted a multi-site study of hybrid meetings in two global software companies in Europe, using participant observation, semi-structured interviews and video-analysis. Our findings show that there is a significant diversity in formats and requirements for hybrid meetings in different working environments. Further, hybrid meeting participants perceive and handle a range of both expected and emergent problems. While some problems can be attributed to difficulties or failures of technical infrastructure, others arise out of asymmetries of interaction and social and cultural context across the co-located and remote settings. We argue that managing these asymmetries is key to a successful hybrid meeting.

Keywords: Hybrid meetings · Video conferencing · Remote collaboration

1   Introduction

Hybrid meetings are video- and audio-based meetings that include both co-located and remote participants. With the advancements of video-conferencing software and technologies, business meetings in the increasingly globalized world go beyond the physical meeting room. The hybrid meeting has become ubiquitous in modern international and multi-site workplaces, and their success (or failure) has significant economic and societal impact. Yet, most of our understanding of video- and audio-based communication is from studies conducted in laboratory or controlled settings.

© Springer Nature Switzerland AG 2019
H. Nakanishi et al. (Eds.): CRIWG+CollabTech 2019, LNCS 11677, pp. 45–61, 2019.
https://doi.org/10.1007/978-3-030-28011-6_4

In this paper, we will take a holistic approach to better understand how hybrid meetings take place in the workplace today, and identify when they succeed and when they fail. We present a multi-site and multi-method study where we observed hybrid meetings at two global software companies in Denmark and in the United Kingdom. We raise and seek answers for the following questions: What are the main problems of people in hybrid meetings taking place in the business setting? How are hybrid meetings diversified across different working environments, departments or companies? How do certain instances emerge as problems in hybrid meetings and how are these problems constructed by different users? Our findings show that hybrid meeting experiences are diverse, and what makes a hybrid meeting a success or a failure is a complex socio-technical phenomenon shaped by the technical infrastructure and social and cultural context.

2   Related Work

Within the fields of HCI and CSCW, there has been a long history and large amount of research on video-mediated communication and video-based meetings. Researchers focused on how to improve people's experiences with hybrid/virtual meetings and virtual collaboration by studying diverse physical and social factors including but not limited to gaze awareness [15,26], audio [22,28], camera angle [12], seating position [27], social presence [3], culture [5,6,21], gesture [8,18], trust [1,24], as well as telepresence [14,16,17].

There are a number of user and case studies, which inspired us for conducting our research. Based on their naturalistic analysis of individuals collaborating on different tasks in the workplace, Heath and Luff claim that video-mediated communication causes asymmetries in interaction, which refer to changing reciprocity and manners in communication with the existence of a "technological medium" [9,10]. According to the authors, the asymmetries of interaction do not necessarily limit or prevent the video-mediated communication, but also pave the path for new forms of interaction and collaboration at work [9].

In their study, Isaacs and Tang compare video-based, audio-based and face-to-face interactions by analyzing a small teams' collaboration using a desktop video conferencing prototype [13]. They find that while using video improves both verbal and nonverbal communication compared to audio-based meetings, video-based interactions are still inefficient in terms of securing peripheral cues, floor control and side conversations, and need to be supported with other shared tools making the collaboration experience as natural as possible [13].

Based on the long-term experiences of developers, researchers and users, Dourish et al. call for departing from the presumption of comparing the experiences of video-mediated communication with face-to-face interaction and underline how complex conducts in media spaces occur in individual, interactional, communal and societal levels in the long run. [7]. Authors claim that media spaces are also part of the "real world" and interactions within media spaces are larger than person-to-person interaction [7].

Another interesting example is a combination of the internal company and external costumer study through surveys and interviews focusing on understanding user's problems with hybrid meetings in order to prototype a more effective remote collaboration tool [30]. The authors categorize problems with hybrid meetings at conference rooms as "audio problems", "remote attendee problems" and "conference room problems" and find that remote participants feel disadvantaged as they are mostly disengaged, forgotten and ignored by the co-located participants and even moderators of those meetings [29]. The same study also underlines that co-located participants accuse remote participants for not paying attention to them, which causes them to ignore the remote participants even more and remote participants remain isolated from the meeting, which continues like a vicious circle [29].

In another study, Tan and Kondoz focus on understanding obstacles to a seamless virtual collaboration through a longitudinal and multi-method ethnographic research based on the use of a virtual collaboration desk [23]. By examining the virtual meetings of a software project group for around ten months and collecting both quantitative and qualitative data, researchers find that the success or failure of virtual collaboration is based on diverse factors ranging from the "team participation and cultural differences" to "management and policy issues" and "technology barriers" in an organization [23].

3   Methodology

We conducted a multi-site study combining three qualitative methods: participant observation, semi-structured interviews, and video-analysis.

3.1   Collection of the Empirical Materials

We conducted fieldwork in two global software companies located in Denmark and United Kingdom (Table 1). In Denmark we conducted participant observation at the Global Business Services section of a large software company (*Company A*) and observed four daily scrum meetings and one retrospective meeting. Scrum is an "iterative and incremental project management" approach especially applied in global software development projects [11]. Scrum meetings take place mostly early in the morning for fifteen minutes standing up, and once every five weeks a longer so-called retrospective meeting is held, during which they assess the implementation process of the project and teamwork. The team we observed at *Company A* consists of 27 members, 20 of which are based in Denmark and seven of which are based in India. Therefore, they have daily scrum and retrospective meetings in a hybrid meeting format. In all meetings there were scrum masters, who are also team members and intervene when there is a problem during the meetings regardless of whether the issue is technical or social.

In the United Kingdom we observed another large software company (*Company B*). At *Company B* we conducted fieldwork at diverse departments including but not limited to Sales, Marketing, Finance, Cloud Solutions and Research.

Table 1. Overview of the observed meetings at Company A and B. Each meeting is represented with the company letter (A, B) and the number of the meeting (1–5). (Example: A3 - Third meeting at Company A)

	A1	A2	A3	A4	A5	B1	B2	B3	B4
Format[a]	VH	VH	VH	VH	VH	VH	VH	VH	AV
Duration (min)	15	15	15	5	90	90	60[b]	45	30[c]
Number of Participants[d]	4C 1R	14C 5C	6C 3C	2C 2C	17C 6C	11C 3R	8C N/A	8C 2R	104R
Type	Scrum	Scrum	Scrum	Scrum	Retrospective	Status Update, Brainstorming Update	Monthly Business Update	Acquaintance Meeting	Status Update
Department	Global Business Services	Global Business Services	Global Business Services	Global Business Services	Global Business Services	Sales, Finance, Marketing	Sales, Finance, Sales	Sales, Finance, Marketing	Cloud Solutions
Software	Zoom Meetings	Zoom Meetings	Zoom Meetings	Zoom Meetings	Zoom Meetings, Mural	Microsoft Teams	Microsoft Teams	Microsoft Teams	Skype for Business
Visuals	Large Screen	Large Screen	Large Screen	Large Screen	Large Screen	Large Screen, Microsoft RoundTable	Microsoft Surface Hub	Large Screen	Personal Computer
Audio[e]	Portable Mic, LS	Portable Mic, LS	Portable Mic, LS	Portable Mic, LS	Portable Mic, LS	Microsoft RoundTable, LS	Microsoft Surface Hub, LS	Microsoft RoundTable, LS	Headset
Video Analysis						x		x	

[a]VH: video-based hybrid meeting, AV: audio-based virtual meeting, [b]17 min connection issue, [c]Only observed time, [d] **Bold**: at the observed venue, C: co-located, R: remote, [e]LS: loudspeaker

Overall we observed three video-based hybrid meetings, two of which were also recorded with a steadicam and a portable camera, and one audio-based virtual meeting. Virtual meetings are different from hybrid meetings in the sense that there are no physical rooms in those meetings, meaning that all remote participants are connected through their personal devices.

Apart from the participant observation and video recordings of meetings in both companies, we conducted semi-structured interviews with two employees from *Company A*, one from Denmark and one from the Indian team but currently employed in Denmark for one year, and with 21 employees at *Company B* from diverse departments. All of the interviews were audio-recorded except the one with a software engineer, who refused to be recorded due to being shy, but still accepted to be interviewed. Due to the time constraint of the employees, the average length of the interviews is nine minutes. Interviewees were briefly asked to tell about their department/work/position details, their experiences with hybrid meetings such as how often they have those meetings, what kind of issues/needs they have and whether any further improvements they expect from hybrid meeting tools.

3.2 Analysis

All audio-recorded interviews were transcribed in verbatim format, but in order to avoid difficulties in reading as well as to save space, intonations, interjections as well as missing text are shown as three dots closed with square brackets ([...]). All recorded videos were watched thoroughly a number of times until the saturation point in insight was reached. Relevant parts of the meetings were written down in notes. Interview transcriptions, participant observation and video recording notes were merged in the qualitative data analysis software *NVivo* and analyzed through the stages of open coding, line-by-line coding and focused coding [4].

4 Findings

We categorized our findings into two themes: technical infrastructure and social and cultural context.

4.1 Technical Infrastructure

Size and Functionality of Meeting Rooms. One of the issues *Company A* is facing is that their team is very crowded and the size of the rooms, that are specifically used for daily scrum meetings, are quite small. In these meetings also nobody takes notes on computer or notebook and it is difficult for them to locate the computer in the best position so that the other end of the meeting in India can see everyone in the room. Both employees from *Company A* we interviewed underlined the need for larger and technologically more advanced video-conferencing rooms at both ends.

As we conducted fieldwork in two global software companies in Europe, we observed that they maximized and to a considerable extent standardized their technological resources, meaning that their employees use the same laptops, tablets or other digital devices, at the individual level. However, one of the significant problems, which is harder to normalize, is the unequal meeting infrastructure in both ends of the meeting. Both companies have hybrid or virtual meetings with partners or people located all around the world. They also have better meeting infrastructure such as faster bandwidth connection and more enhanced room functionalities compared to partners located abroad. For instance, the team working at the branch of *Company A* in India, does not have a large screen and the members use their laptop for the meetings, which makes them look down during the meetings since they are standing up all the time and makes the eye contact and social cueing harder for them. Moreover, they do not have the same connection bandwidth compared to the team in Denmark. The situation is also similar in *Company B* as one of our interviewees underlined:

The main issue is that is the quality [...] of the equipment. And [...] quality of line... Quite often [...] at least when we have a real hybrid meeting, when there is a team locally and another team on the other side of the of the network. [...] If we here at [Company's name] have [...] quite good equipment like RoundTables and Surface Hubs, on the other side of the network, the equipment is usually not that good and then it becomes a problem because people in the other [...] side do not hear it clearly what I was saying and it is much more difficult for them to [...] to contribute something to the discussion. Because they feel somewhat out of context of the meeting. (P19)

Even meeting rooms in the same company varies to a considerable extent. Especially in *Company B*, where there are many meeting rooms available, employees cannot be sure about which functionalities each room has and can experience some problems in setting up the meeting and therefore lose time:

Yeah so problems connecting to meetings happen quite often, in my experience it stems through I think just the sheer number of the different types of [...] machines available to connect to different connection points, different ways of joining that we have here on campus, so this is a Surface Hub, there is only a couple of these on campus so we are not used to joining them regularly, we have connectivity issues in some of the meeting rooms because they all contain different technology. So when you walk into a meeting room, you are not quite sure what technology you are gonna have in there, so you may not be prepared or with the right adapters or connectors to be able to join straightaway. (P9)

The diversity of the meeting infrastructure even in the same company causes trouble mostly during the setup process. *Meeting B2* was delayed around seventeen minutes due to problems with setting up the *Surface Hub*. Also in the *Meeting B3*, showing slides on *Surface Hub* took twenty minutes.

According to a participant of *Meeting B2*, setting up a virtual meeting, in which everyone is connected through his/her own personal device, is easier than setting up a physical room connection to a hybrid meeting:

[...] The problems that we have with these technologies at the moment are more of an infrastructure problem, so for us today the network let us down or the technology in the room let us down rather than [...] actually just joining, I tend to have an easier experience when it is just myself joining from my machine [...] rather than connecting in a larger room for hybrid meeting is when we normally experience these delays. (P9)

Another participant from *Company B* addressed as well that joining the meeting through personal devices is a must in order to create a shared, equal space for everyone in the meeting regardless of one's role or task in that particular meeting:

I think we need to start the default to behavior of everyone joining the meeting from a device. Irrespective of whether you are [...] the presenter or organizer of the meeting. Cause quite often [...] you are the organizer of the meeting here and you are the one that presents and joins the conference call. [...] and you have got the knowledge of and, and remembering who is on, who is also in the meeting joining remotely whereas if everyone joins from their device, then there is kind of like this common space, you got the common space, the physical space. And then also the digital life if everyone joins the same space [...] and keep people in the room [...], [be] aware of who is, who is also in the meeting. And to, to pull them in more often. (P13)

Our observations showed us also that virtual meetings can be favored more than hybrid meetings as it is easier to setup and lead the meeting and to form a more equal platform for interaction in the workplace. In this regard *Meeting B4* was interesting in the sense that it was an audio-based virtual meeting that took place among 104 participants and the conversation among participants was very smooth and understandable. It was striking to see that even co-located team members, were all connected to the meeting with their personal devices from their desks. The turn taking among the participants was fluid and participants did not interrupt each other.

Hardware and Software. We observed that for audio-based virtual meetings, especially with participants working in an open office environment, using high quality headsets is a must for having an efficient meeting. This also applies for remote participants, who work in an open office environment. Audio quality is similarly important in hybrid meetings, which can be observed especially when there are breakdowns during those meetings. Different workplaces or teams have diverse coping strategies with audio problems or breakdowns. During the meetings we observed at *Company B*, co-located participants suggest the remote participant to turn off his/her video when there is a breakdown in connection. However, in *Company A*, instead of turning off the video in the call, they mute the call, keep the video on and switch to landline phone call:

> By the time I came in 2015 [to Denmark] again, [...] I saw that we were actually more and more towards the video calls and where we stick only to Skype call as well. [...] which sometimes have this network glitch issues when you are having different countries and there was a gap and stuff like those. And then we decided to actually make a balance of this. [...] What we decided is to maintain the video-call [...] without the audio and keeping the phone call quality by this AT&T calls or DIRECT phone calls, which actually helped us understanding and looking at the people as well, and we can understand what they are working on, have the fluidity of the team if somebody is having an opinion, even during the short period of meeting, so if [...] during the fifteen minutes someone actually raised a hand and they want to share an opinion. It, it actually allowed us to, to take an opinion rather than just one person talking all the time. So it allowed more in interacting manner definitely when we have this. (P1)

Sometimes screens are not proportionate with the size of the room, and in *Meeting B1*, a couple of times co-located participants were not able to see the screen clearly and had to stand up and get close to the screen. This happened very often especially when a document similar to a *Microsoft Excel* sheet was shown on the screen. It was not easy for participants to read them from their seats. Also there have been cases where the screens were too bright to see or especially in roundtables, people turning their backs to the screen had difficulties in seeing the remote participants, which minimized their interaction as well.

While *Company A* was relying on the laptop camera in their hybrid meetings, *Company B* was using *Microsoft RoundTable*. We observed that as the camera of a laptop makes co-located participants face the laptop most of the time, panoramic 360° cameras give the co-located participants the opportunity to sit round the table and talk without being forced to look at the screen and at the same time allow remote participants to follow the meeting smoothly. However, this also decreases their interaction with the co-located participants and isolates them from the physical room as co-located participants there can forget to interact with them.

In terms of software, *Company A* and *B* differ from each other in the sense that while *Company A* has been using a special software only for remote meetings, which is called *Zoom Meetings*, *Company B* was in a transition stage from *Skype for Business* to *Microsoft Teams*, which is more of a digital workplace platform, at which all meetings, notes, work-related chat and documents are held and stored. One of the employees we interviewed at *Company A* mentioned that they are using different tools during hybrid meetings and it would be better to rely on one single tool, which could potentially minimize the network glitches.

4.2   Social and Cultural Context of the Meeting

Meeting Task. In *Company A*, we observed that there are more clear and defined meeting tasks, which have been repeated and implemented very often since the team has a very long history and experiences of working together from different countries. In *Company B*, even though there is a better and well established technical infrastructure, these resources are not always used efficiently. This partially stems from the fact that while the section we observed in *Company A* focuses on software development, in *Company B* we examined diverse departments, which do not always have hybrid meetings with the same people, for the same purposes and in the same meeting rooms. One of the participants of the *Meeting B2* claimed that using *Surface Hub*, which caused them around seventeen minutes delay in joining the meeting, was not necessary as it was not an interactive meeting, they were only following it:

> *Yeah so this wasn't a great use of the Hub to be honest because we in this area were more of a listening participants only. In Hub meetings are really much better in these spaces much better used when we are interacting in the Hub, which we weren't doing today. So we could have just done this in front of a normal TV and have [...] the same [...] listening experience, [...] We didn't have any input into that meeting today from this room. So [it] is more of an audience view with the people doing the hard work were [...] signed in the other room. So [...] I think in general it is better to use the Hub in this kind of environment to do interactive meetings where you are on video and you can share your desktop and use the whiteboard on the Hub so, they, they are much better use of this space.* (P9)

Language and Accent. Both team members we interviewed in *Company A* underlined the challenges of understanding the English accents of each other during meetings. Getting used to different accents takes time and requires practice, and participants can ask for help from other local person, who is in the room:

> *In the beginning I used to pretend. [laughs] [...] It takes, it takes some time. [...] Like for instance when I was [...] in another project [with] some Indian resources [...], I have difficulties understanding what they were actually saying. And sometimes we would look at each other here in the room when everybody who was present here and then we always have a landed resource and for instance at the moment we have a guy from India here and he, he gets it. So [...] we would look to him and he would sort of say it again so we would all understand it. But now as time has passed, I understand what they say.* (P2)

Cultural Behaviors. In the scrum meetings of *Company A*, participants from both sides interacted standing up and gave status updates one by one. However, while co-located people on the Danish side were talking to each other and often interrupting each other, participants connected from India were not interacting with each other at all, they were focusing on the conversations in the Danish side and answering only when they were directly asked any questions. We were curious about whether Indian participants were afraid or shy of interrupting the boss and asked about it to the Danish interviewee. She called this a matter of cultural behavior and differentiated Danes and Indians in social interaction:

> I think that is very much a matter of cultural behavior. [...] The Danish people are very used to talking among each other and talking all the time and there is not, I don't know if I should say, it's the respect thing but it's just I feel that the Indian culture is more like, they wait until they are asked to speak whereas Danish people they just speak. They don't wait. If I have something I wanna say, I'll just say it. I am not waiting for my turn or waiting for somebody to ask me to speak, I'll just speak out. Whereas in India the, the culture is very different, so they will wait. [...] In our case, so this is the safe place, everybody could speak, everybody can say, you can say whatever you want. [...] That takes a lot of time for everybody to get used to that culture and be comfortable in it. (P2)

Team Dynamics and Proximity. Most of the team members in both *Company A* and *B* know their remote participants better and meet and work with them often physically too. Therefore, during the hybrid meetings with these team members, they can recognize their voices well and do not necessarily need to see them on the screen when they are talking. However, two of the researchers we interviewed in the *Company B* mentioned that they do not meet with their remote collaborators physically and feel the need to be aware of who are in the other end of the hybrid meeting when they are talking. Thus, when there is a breakdown in connection, turning off the video is not an option for them. Awareness of others in the meeting is vital if the participants do not know each other well. Secondly, hierarchical relations among the participants shape the physical setting of the co-located participants as well as the direction of the conversation in hybrid meetings. In both companies' meetings, the bosses were sitting or standing up close to both the co-located people and the screen, where the remote participants or the other physical room can be seen. Due to their managerial role in the team, they prefer to be in the center of the conversation, since they lead and/or respond to the discussions during those meetings.

Personal Habits. During the meetings in *Company A*, we observed that the distance to the microphone and how much to increase the voice is an issue. Especially during the *Meeting A5*, participants, who were sitting far to the microphone and the screen, did not seem to care about how much the Indian team can hear them. They seemed to ignore their distance to the microphone and preferred to talk at the same voice level. In our interview, the scrum master from *Company A* mentioned the difficulty of changing people's behavior especially with the microphone:

[...] And then there is a habit part as well. People have a tendency not to go close to the microphone. [...] For instance if I join from home, I can very clearly hear people who are also joining in from a phone, but people who are here in the room, I cannot hear them very well because they don't come close to the phone. We try [...], we have an extension microphone and everything, but still it is a matter of habit. [...] "Okay, make sure you do it! Make sure you do it! Make sure you do it!" And a lot of times [...] we would say to people "Okay, could you please get closer? Could you please remember, please remember?" (P2)

A habitual success in virtual meetings could be the *Meeting B4*, at which we observed that the turn-taking and conversation during the meeting was very smooth as participants were very literate in observing through the software who is talking and since their work is always based on remote audio meetings, they were very familiar with the manners of establishing digital dialogues such as waiting 1–2 s after the person finishes his/her talk or speaking clearly and distinctly. One of the participants of *Meeting B4* underlined the importance of following the etiquettes for every meeting case:

One thing, this term "etiquettes", that need to be the kind of the manners [...] having [...] within those kind of hybrid meetings, is well also annoying in different places, you may be in a, in a quite meeting room and maybe in an open plan area. It is to make your sound mute when you are not talking, things like that. So it is important to make sure people know what those etiquettes are and what they should do because they don't always do. (P10)

Digital Literacy. While both companies we observed are specialized in software, still the employees in different departments have diverse levels of knowledge in terms of setting up the meeting and fixing the technical problems. The case of *Company B* was interesting in the sense that for their all remote meetings, they use their own software and technical equipment, which makes them more literate and skilled of the digital tools they are using. Interestingly, when we were conducting fieldwork there, *Company B* was doing in-house testing of a new hybrid meeting software for businesses, which was not released to the market at that time but was allowing the guest users to enter the remote meeting, meaning that they could use this software not only among their team members, but also with their customers. However, the adaptation and shift of a particular department or group to the new, rapidly evolving software was diverse and it was challenging for some participants to adapt to more than ten major updates a day. One of the employees told us that he feels embarrassed when he is using the software with his customers as it is still not a mature product and can have some errors, which he cannot fix. He mentioned that during these in-house testing processes he considers himself like a guinea pig, due to having hybrid meetings with the new software based on the trial and error. Not having sufficient knowledge regarding the technology used is definitely an inconvenient situation for the employees.

Stress. In relation to meeting task, hierarchical relations among the team members as well as the outsiders may affect the stress level of the participants, causing them not to make rational decisions when they need to fix an issue. *Meeting B3* had such a moment. A Marketing company wanted to give a presentation to the Sales team at the *Company B* in order to convince the team to work together in the future. Since the team leader and another team member were not at the office, the presentation had to be done in a hybrid meeting format. 360° panoramic camera and the new software were used. The meeting started with a 20 min delay because the presenters from the Marketing company could not manage to connect to the Wi-Fi of the company in order to share the slides through the new software. In the end, instead of uploading the presentation to another computer and sharing the slides with the remote participants through that computer, the employee from the *Company B*, who was also the facilitator of the meeting, decided to broadcast the presentation slides, which were shown on the large screen of the meeting room, through her mobile phone, causing one of the employees of the Marketing company hold her phone for around half an hour. She could not think about any other solution as the head of the team, who was connected remotely, complained that there is not enough time left and they should hurry with their presentation.

Inclusiveness of Remote Participants. According to one of our interviewees, having limited awareness of other participants in the physical room makes the interaction unequal and even unfair for remote participants:

> *[Remote participants] they have a little bit of a disadvantage of not being there. [...] Information access might not be easy or for them, to take a turn in the conversation isn't quite as easy. It's more of an active process to invite them in and then clearly stating to whom they are talking, who they are addressing, [...] through the verbalization what they would like to achieve. [...] Especially when [...] you have got many people that are remote and in different locations as well, for them figuring out who is taking turn [...] especially if there is a camera feed and [...] you have a lack of verbal and non-verbal cues as well, figuring out what's the dynamics in the group is just a little bit harder, you have to be really explicit in just saying specific people and it's harder if you wanna say something to know when it is the right time to chip in.* (P15)

In *Meeting B1*, we noticed that remote participants' interaction and participation were quite limited. During the whole meeting, they muted their microphones except while they were talking and especially when the brainstorming session started, they did not provide any input or share any idea even though that was expected from all participants in the meeting. They continued working on their own computer and did not focus on the meeting as the brainstorming was taking place on the physical whiteboard in the actual meeting room, which they cannot see properly as well. However, interestingly, in the *Meeting*

A5, the input by the participants during the brainstorming process was provided equally on the *Mural* platform, which is an online brainstorming software. We observed that during this meeting, remote participants were more engaged and productive compared to the *Meeting B1*. Furthermore, again in *Meeting B1*, when there were breakdowns during remote participants' turn, co-located participants made fun of the situation among each other and laughed. One of the co-located participants even took the photo of the screen when the image of the remote participants was hanging to share it with the group. However, since they cannot hear the conversation in the time of a connection problem, remote participants miss even the fun part of their own "remote" participation, mostly being annoyed by the issue and trying to fix it or repeating the same sentences.

In the hybrid meetings of *Company B*, in which mostly 360° panoramic cameras used, co-located participants do not face the screen where they can see the remote participants, which cause the co-located participants to ignore them unless they make a noise. This was also mentioned by one of our interviewees:

> *[...] Why is this [...] a problem? Because quite often conversation focuses [...] in the local table. And then the other party, it is quite difficult to get into this context. It is difficult to switch the context [...] to the other side of the network. [...] [Remote participants] [...] they are just watching it's and because the, the quality of the audio is not very good, [...] and all the [...] people sitting on the table, they turn mostly back to them and the ones that turn that are faced to them are on the other side of the table so they are very small on the screen. You see [...] visually there is no [...] feeling of being part of this meeting [...] It's like you are sitting quite [...] in another room basically and you need to shout to [...] this crowd in order to get attention to yourself. (P19)*

5 Discussion

According to Oulasvirta, today's IT infrastructure, "the real ubicomp" is different from how Weiser foresaw in his famous vision of ubiquitous computing [25]: *"is a massive noncentralized agglomeration of the devices, connectivity and electricity means, applications, services, and interfaces, as well as material objects such as cables and meeting rooms and support surfaces that have emerged almost anarchistically, without a recognized set of guiding principles."* [19]. Bell and Dourish also underlined that ubicomp of today depends on the ways in which users "improvise" and "appropriate" technologies [2]. Our study shows that while a reliable technical infrastructure is a must for a successful hybrid meeting, it is still the user, who has to be knowledgeable and experienced enough to cope with the technical issues and breakdowns of hybrid and virtual meetings. In their study on individuals' handling of different devices during the face-to-face and remote collaboration in the business setting, Oulavirta and Sumari found that employees rely on their prior experiences and knowledge regarding the technologies and physical tools they are using [20]. However, the uncertainties of especially the mobile work and the unpredictability of resources in every situation require changes of plans and strategies, which require additional mental and/or physical efforts of the employees [20]. In our fieldwork we also observed that the unpredictability and uncertainties of remote work and collaboration still require endless mental work by the users, evolving their experiences and coping strategies over and over again. While prior planning is needed for a better meeting experience, still being flexible for last minute changes and efficient solution-making is required.

As we underline the importance of the social and cultural context, we argue that hybrid meetings create asymmetries that extend beyond the reciprocity of perspectives explored by Heath and Luff [9]. In other words, while video-mediated communication itself transforms the look, gestures and manners of bodily conduct, it also broadens the already given asymmetries stemming from the diversity of the social and cultural background of participants. With the proliferation of hybrid meeting technologies and experiences around the world, the asymmetrical inequality in opportunities of communication due to a combination of diverse technical, social and cultural factors becomes crucial to overcome.

One of the major asymmetries in hybrid meetings we observed is the diverse experiences between co-located vs. remote participants. Remote participants feel isolated from the meetings and co-located participants dominate the interaction. Differences in language and accent, cultural behaviors, personal habits, digital literacy and stress as well as technical infrastructure in different geographical locations contribute to the asymmetries of interaction and making meetings more inclusive for everyone is one of the main challenges of hybrid meetings.

It was clear from our fieldwork that all the hybrid meetings we observed were impacted by the effect of socio-technical asymmetries. The only seemingly successful meeting we observed was *Meeting B4*, which was the audio-based meeting with 104 participants. It almost seems counterintuitive that a meeting at that scale would be far better than a small meeting with a handful of co-located and remote participants, but we believe that the lack of asymmetry in the meeting was crucial to its success. Not all meetings can be fully virtual, and we believe the hybrid meeting is here to stay in the modern workplace. How can the experience and effectiveness of hybrid meetings improve? The problems we saw were socio-technical in nature, and we do not believe that the solution only lies in technological innovation. Hybrid meetings open up opportunities for companies to communicate and organize themselves in ways that was previously impossible. However, we observed that they are conducted haphazardly, and a simple recommendation would be to train modern knowledge workers in conducting meetings. Nevertheless, this also requires a more holistic articulation of the challenges that may arise, that we believe we have contributed with in this paper.

From a technological perspective, the video-conferencing software could be equipped with better tools to overcome technical and social asymmetries. We can only speculate in how such tools could be manifested, but one could imagine tools that could better indicate technical issues, for instance when the connection of a remote participant drops, or tools to visualize the activity of participants, which could help an organizer make sure all participants got equal time to speak. However, there is also a danger that such tools could be used for surveillance.

While through this study we do not point out specific implications for design, our findings suggest the following: Apart from improving and equalizing the technical infrastructure for all sides of the meetings, taking the meeting requirements (i.e. the meeting task and content, the number of co-located and remote participants as well as their level of experience) and socio-cultural differences of the participants into account even before setting up the meeting environment play an important role in contributing to the success of the hybrid meetings.

6 Conclusion

Through a holistic study of hybrid meetings in two global software companies in Europe, this paper shows that hybrid meetings are diversified across different working environments and both the technical infrastructure and social and cultural context of the meeting play an important role in shaping the effectiveness of the meeting. While size and functionality of meeting rooms and hardware and software used in meetings form the technical infrastructure of the meeting, meeting task, language and accent, cultural behaviors, team dynamics and proximity, personal habits, digital literacy, stress and the inclusiveness of remote participants are critical social and cultural dynamics that are part of the workplace culture and social relations around it, affecting the experiences of participants with hybrid meetings. Our research brings into light that asymmetries of interaction and social and cultural context in both co-located and remote settings can be considered as decisive factors in making hybrid meetings succeed or fail.

Acknowledgements. Banu Saatçi's work has been supported by Microsoft Research through its PhD Scholarship Programme in EMEA. We thank both companies and their employees for taking part in our research and anonymous reviewers for their valuable feedback along with Christian Remy, Gökçe Elif Baykal, Midas Nouwens, Bjarke Vognstrup Fog, Cristian Roner and Kaya Akyüz for their comments and suggestions on earlier drafts.

References

1. Bekkering, E., Shim, J.P.: Trust in videoconferencing. Commun. ACM **49**(7), 103–107 (2006)
2. Bell, G., Dourish, P.: Yesterday's tomorrows: notes on ubiquitous computing's dominant vision. Pers. Ubiquitous Comput. **11**(2), 133–143 (2007)
3. Bradner, E., Mark, G.: Social presence with video and application sharing. In: Proceedings of the 2001 International ACM SIGGROUP Conference on Supporting Group Work, pp. 154–161. ACM (2001)
4. Charmaz, K.: Constructing Grounded Theory: A Practical Guide Through Qualitative Analysis. Sage, London (2006)

5. Diamant, E.I., Fussell, S.R., Lo, F.l.: Where did we turn wrong?: unpacking the effect of culture and technology on attributions of team performance. In: Proceedings of the 2008 ACM Conference on Computer Supported Cooperative Work, pp. 383–392. ACM (2008)

6. Diamant, E.I., Fussell, S.R., Lo, F.L.: Collaborating across cultural and technological boundaries: team culture and information use in a map navigation task. In: Proceedings of the 2009 International Workshop on Intercultural Collaboration, pp. 175–184. ACM (2009)

7. Dourish, P., Adler, A., Bellotti, V., Henderson, A.: Your place or mine? Learning from long-term use of audio-video communication. Comput. Support. Coop. Work (CSCW) **5**(1), 33–62 (1996)

8. Fussell, S.R., Setlock, L.D., Yang, J., Ou, J., Mauer, E., Kramer, A.D.: Gestures over video streams to support remote collaboration on physical tasks. Hum. Comput. Interact. **19**(3), 273–309 (2004)

9. Heath, C., Luff, P.: Disembodied conduct: communication through video in a multimedia office environment. In: Proceedings of the SIGCHI Conference on Human Factors in Computing Systems, pp. 99–103. ACM (1991)

10. Heath, C., Luff, P.: Media space and communicative asymmetries: preliminary observations of video-mediated interaction. Hum. Comput. Interact. **7**(3), 315–346 (1992)

11. Hossain, E., Babar, M.A., Paik, H.: Using scrum in global software development: a systematic literature review. In: 2009 Fourth IEEE International Conference on Global Software Engineering, pp. 175–184, July 2009. https://doi.org/10.1109/ICGSE.2009.25

12. Huang, W., Olson, J.S., Olson, G.M.: Camera angle affects dominance in video-mediated communication. In: CHI 2002 Extended Abstracts on Human Factors in Computing Systems, pp. 716–717. ACM (2002)

13. Isaacs, E.A., Tang, J.C.: What video can and cannot do for collaboration: a case study. Multimedia Syst. **2**(2), 63–73 (1994)

14. Kristoffersson, A., Coradeschi, S., Loutfi, A.: A review of mobile robotic telepresence. Adv. Hum. Comput. Interact. **2013**, 3 (2013)

15. Mukawa, N., Oka, T., Arai, K., Yuasa, M.: What is connected by mutual gaze?: user's behavior in video-mediated communication. In: CHI 2005 Extended Abstracts on Human Factors in Computing Systems, pp. 1677–1680. ACM (2005)

16. Nakanishi, H., Tanaka, K., Wada, Y.: Remote handshaking: touch enhances video-mediated social telepresence. In: Proceedings of the SIGCHI Conference on Human Factors in Computing Systems, pp. 2143–2152. ACM (2014)

17. Neustaedter, C., Venolia, G., Procyk, J., Hawkins, D.: To beam or not to beam: a study of remote telepresence attendance at an academic conference. In: Proceedings of the 19th ACM Conference on Computer-Supported Cooperative Work and Social Computing, pp. 418–431. ACM (2016)

18. Ou, J., Fussell, S.R., Chen, X., Setlock, L.D., Yang, J.: Gestural communication over video stream: supporting multimodal interaction for remote collaborative physical tasks. In: Proceedings of the 5th International Conference on Multimodal Interfaces, pp. 242–249. ACM (2003)

19. Oulasvirta, A.: FEATURE: when users do the Ubicomp. Interactions **15**(2), 6–9 (2008)

20. Oulasvirta, A., Sumari, L.: Mobile kits and laptop trays: managing multiple devices in mobile information work. In: Proceedings of the SIGCHI Conference on Human Factors in Computing Systems, pp. 1127–1136. ACM (2007)

21. Setlock, L.D., Fussell, S.R., Neuwirth, C.: Taking it out of context: collaborating within and across cultures in face-to-face settings and via instant messaging. In: Proceedings of the 2004 ACM Conference on Computer Supported Cooperative Work, pp. 604–613. ACM (2004)
22. Smith, D., et al.: Overhear: augmenting attention in remote social gatherings through computer-mediated hearing. In: CHI 2005 Extended Abstracts on Human Factors in Computing Systems, pp. 1801–1804. ACM (2005)
23. Tan, A., Kondoz, A.M.: Barriers to virtual collaboration. In: CHI 2008 Extended Abstracts on Human Factors in Computing Systems, pp. 2045–2052. ACM (2008)
24. Teoh, C., Regenbrecht, H., O'Hare, D.: Investigating factors influencing trust in video-mediated communication. In: Proceedings of the 22nd Conference of the Computer-Human Interaction Special Interest Group of Australia on Computer-Human Interaction, pp. 312–319. ACM (2010)
25. Weiser, M.: The computer for the 21st century. Sci. Am. **265**(3), 94–105 (1991)
26. Xu, B., Ellis, J., Erickson, T.: Attention from afar: simulating the gazes of remote participants in hybrid meetings. In: Proceedings of the 2017 Conference on Designing Interactive Systems, pp. 101–113. ACM (2017)
27. Yamashita, N., Hirata, K., Aoyagi, S., Kuzuoka, H., Harada, Y.: Impact of seating positions on group video communication. In: Proceedings of the 2008 ACM Conference on Computer Supported Cooperative Work, pp. 177–186. ACM (2008)
28. Yankelovich, N., Kaplan, J., Provino, J., Wessler, M., DiMicco, J.M.: Improving audio conferencing: are two ears better than one? In: Proceedings of the 2006 20th Anniversary Conference on Computer Supported Cooperative Work, pp. 333–342. ACM (2006)
29. Yankelovich, N., Simpson, N., Kaplan, J., Provino, J.: Porta-person: telepresence for the connected conference room. In: CHI 2007 Extended Abstracts on Human Factors in Computing Systems, pp. 2789–2794. ACM (2007)
30. Yankelovich, N., Walker, W., Roberts, P., Wessler, M., Kaplan, J., Provino, J.: Meeting central: making distributed meetings more effective. In: Proceedings of the 2004 ACM conference on Computer Supported Cooperative Work, pp. 419–428. ACM (2004)

A CSCL Script for Supporting Moral Reasoning in the Ethics Classroom

Claudio Alvarez[1,2(✉)], Gustavo Zurita[3], Nelson Baloian[4],
Oscar Jerez[5], and Sergio Peñafiel[4]

[1] Facultad de Ingeniería y Ciencias Aplicadas, Universidad de Los Andes,
Santiago, Chile
calvarez@uandes.cl
[2] Centro de Investigación En Educación, Universidad de Los Andes,
Santiago, Chile
[3] Facultad de Economía y Negocios, Universidad de Chile,
Santiago, Chile
gzurita@fen.uchile.cl
[4] Facultad de Ciencias Físicas y Matemáticas, Universidad de Chile,
Santiago, Chile
[5] Centro de Investigación Avanzada En Educación (CIAE), Universidad de
Chile, Santiago, Chile

Abstract. In many engineering schools around the world, ethics is a compulsory subject. However, teaching ethics in engineering is not a simple duty, as engineering students usually attribute less value to learning ethics than to other subjects. Hereby, we report on our initial efforts towards developing a CSCL script for fostering meaningful ethical discussions among engineering students in the classroom. The script comprises successive phases in which the students conduct ethical judgments individually, in a small group and in a teacher-mediated class group discussion. The process seeks that students cast their judgments without inhibitions, so it maintains students' anonymity in all phases. A trial with 35 engineering students confirmed that the tool offers a good usability, averaging a 79.9 score in the System Usability Scale (SUS). Furthermore, the trial cohort highlighted the convenience of anonymity when discussing ethical cases. Analysis of student behavior revealed that ethical judgments tend to be stable across the activity. However, judgments changed mostly in groups where more discussion was generated. In the future, we will study whether group composition that maximizes the heterogeneity of the students in the groups according to their individual ethical appraisals increases the likelihood of students varying their ethical judgments, as a result of argumentative and reflexive processes in discussions.

Keywords: CSCL script · Mobile CSCL · Moral reasoning ·
Engineering education

© Springer Nature Switzerland AG 2019
H. Nakanishi et al. (Eds.): CRIWG+CollabTech 2019, LNCS 11677, pp. 62–79, 2019.
https://doi.org/10.1007/978-3-030-28011-6_5

1 Introduction

In many engineering schools around the world, ethics is a compulsory subject in the engineering curriculum at the undergraduate level. Interest in ethics education in engineering has grown in the past decades, mainly because of requirements posed to institutions by accreditation systems such as ABET [1]. In addition, in recent years a number of situations with public and worldwide notoriety have arisen with regard to unethical behavior involving engineers in the workplace [2], as well as engineering students in classrooms [3], which have raised awareness about the necessity to teach students competencies regarding ethical reasoning. Other current concerns such as environmental awareness and advances in areas such as machine learning, cybersecurity and big data have brought about new ethical dilemmas and situations that engineers must be capable to reason about and cope with effectively [4]. Although ethics is present in engineering curricula and is part of the competencies in many graduate profiles of engineering programs around the world, teaching ethics in engineering is not a simple duty, as there are epistemological differences insofar as how teachers and students perceive ethics as an engineering subject [5, 6]. Engineering students usually give less value to learning ethics than to other scientific or technological subjects [7]. On the other hand, there has been a lack of scholarly research as well as teacher awareness regarding pedagogies that can yield the best results in the teaching of engineering ethics [8].

Traditional forms of teaching dominate in engineering classrooms, affording limited possibilities for students to actively participate, and to take an agentic role in learning. Ethical education activities prompting for socialization of points of view, participation in discussions, reflection and student agency are not akin to traditional pedagogy in engineering classrooms, thus for many engineering students it can be challenging to participate in classroom debates about ethical issues, by verbalizing their emotions, reasoning and beliefs. Ethical debates around cases assume that students must not only demonstrate ability to apply moral reasoning and develop ethical judgments, but also to proficiently and meaningfully communicate these processes, expecting to be listened, understood and respected by their peers and the teacher [7, 9].

In this paper we present a Computer-Supported Collaborative Learning (CSCL) script [10] focused on fostering students' reflection around ethical cases in the classroom. Students face the ethical case in several phases comprising individual and collaborative work. The process seeks that students express their judgments without inhibitions, so it maintains the anonymity of the students among themselves, even while working collaboratively. On the other hand, the teacher monitors the activity and he/she can easily notice the groups of students presenting the greatest differences in the ethical evaluation of the case discussed. Lastly, the teacher can engage the entire class group in a discussion, commenting on divergent ethical judgments found, and encourage students to further reason, argue and debate considering different points of view and judgments.

In the following sections, we present a discussion on the current state of ethics teaching in engineering, the design of the proposed CSCL script, a pilot conducted with computer science students and its results, and finally, conclusions and future research avenues.

2 Ethics Education in Engineering

According to Holsapple et al. [5], faculty and administrators in engineering schools often describe ethics education as comprising a balance between knowledge of ethical codes of conduct and understandings of ethical rights and wrongs with a more nuanced, complex understanding of ethical dilemmas that fall into a "gray area". Engineering graduates, however, often report that their ethics education was almost completely based on the application of codes, allowing for a lesser depth and complexity in the analysis of ethical cases. While ethics is meant to be a central component of today's engineering curriculum, it is often perceived as a marginal requirement that must be fulfilled [6].

According to Genova & Gonzalez [7], the pedagogy of ethics for engineers must consider the characteristics of thought inherent in students' scientific training and their future professional focus. The authors characterize the mentality of engineers with the following description: *the real world is what can be touched and measured, the prototype of rational thinking is mathematical-deductive reasoning, and the best results are obtained by following standard procedures.* Therefore, it is a priority to acknowledge the difficulties of engineering students in recognizing the value of philosophical thinking and moral theory. Engineering students may be able to learn ethics based on standards, however, overreliance in this approach may have dangerous consequences, as it may result in reducing ethical reasoning to the application of rules in mechanical or quasi-algorithmic ways, without necessarily developing a deep understanding of the cases or the implications of decisions for the various actors. In addition, under this approach it is clear that students may find themselves in difficulties trying to understand why one ethical standard may be preferable to another or the implications that adopting an ethical standard may have for the student.

In a systematic literature review on interventions for teaching ethics in engineering in the United States, Hess and Fore [8] report that the most common methods involved exposing students to codes or standards, using case studies, and discussion. In half of the analyzed samples, they observed that the interventions integrated ethical units in pre-existing engineering courses. They consider that this is desirable, as teaching ethics in a contextualized manner is achieved by means of adopting more realistic problems and scenarios in engineering practice. The authors emphasize the need to develop learning experiences where students reflect not only on their own emotions, but also on emotions of others and can develop greater empathy with the actors and situations.

May and Luth [11] argue about the importance of students developing moral efficacy, that is, confidence in their ability to actively and positively deal with ethical issues that arise in the workplace, and to overcome obstacles in developing and implementing ethical solutions to ethical dilemmas. Considering Bandura's theorization on self-efficacy [12], as well as Kohlberg's on moral development [8], ethical learning experiences should foster ethical agency, and should not limit students to a role of mere spectators who only seek to apply the most appropriate ethical standard to each situation. In addition, it is desirable that the activities allow all students to participate and express themselves, and facilitate them to conduct their ethical evaluations and argumentation in an honest and authentic way, without feeling inhibited by their peers.

Numerous experiences in Computer-Supported Collaborative Learning (CSCL) settings show that face-to-face discussions supported by computer-mediated communication can provide students with equal opportunities to contribute to the construction of shared knowledge and meanings in the classroom [13]. Furthermore, CSCL scripts provide structure and scaffolding for communication and cognitive processes towards these aims, and can facilitate building on the reasoning of others [14]. Many examples can be found in the literature about CSCL script schemata and patterns, and how these can be instanced (tailored) to suit a specific pedagogical rationale [15]. In particular, in ethics education, AGORA-net [16] is a CSCL script aimed at ethical case analysis. It confronts small groups with the task of identifying and reconstructing different stakeholder positions on controversial ill-structured cases, where students defend their positions in a graphically represented argument by means of interactive software. However, in addition to the tool itself, the authors propose a comprehensive pedagogical framework to apply it in an ethics course effectively. Their approach demands several hours to conduct a single activity, encompassing a variety of individual and collaborative phases, as well as adopting an enabling instructional design that divides the course into parallel tracks; one addressing content issues, and the other ethical skills. Thus, the adoption of this approach demands educators to undergo course transformation that will likely require institutional support and adequate incentives.

Another well-documented technology-enhanced environment supporting the discussions in the class is Peer Instruction (PI), based on either traditional Classroom Response Systems (CRS), or mobile applications, such as Socrative [17, 18]. In these settings, short episodes of lecturing are followed by questions to which students respond to individually and in small groups. The instructor can examine students' responses and provide feedback to the class, based on the observed statistics, commonly depicted as a histogram. However, under the traditional implementation of this activity, it can be difficult for the instructor to present complex ethical cases to the students, prompting them to answer multiple interrelated questions, and track the progress of the groups through these. In addition, students' work in small groups is not anonymous, thus hindering their willingness to propose and defend ethical views and judgments that could appear conflictive with others'.

3 Our Proposal

3.1 Design Principles

Reflecting on the literature discussed above, and taking into consideration the needs of ethics teachers in the educational context of the present study, we adopted the following design principles to create the CSCL script here presented, aimed at supporting teaching of ethical judgment in the classroom:

- **Embeddable in a traditional ethics course:** Ethics educators must be able to embed the script within the time of their face-to-face classes, avoiding other significant curricular or methodological changes in their courses. The script is designed for ethics educators who use to conduct analysis of ethical cases in their classes, thus it should be possible for them to adopt the script with no need to prepare additional materials.

- **Multidimensional judgments:** The script allows students to perform complex ethical judgments considering several relevant dimensions in an ethical case.
- **Anonymity of judgments and interactions:** In order for students to make authentic ethical judgments while lessening their conflict anxiety with their peers, the tool allows anonymous participation. While the teacher can see the identity of the students, it is the teacher's responsibility to keep student identity confidential.
- **Domain independence:** The script makes no assumptions about the professional or scholarly domain in which the ethical cases are situated, so it can be applied to the teaching ethics in different disciplines and at various educational levels.
- **Device independence:** The script can be used on any mobile device or desktop computer. The interface is responsive and can adapt to different form factors, input methods and screen resolutions.
- **Ease of use:** In the best interest of facilitating user adoption of the tool, the design of the tool focuses on achieving ease of use through user interface minimalism and intuitive design. It is relevant to minimize teacher training efforts, as well as facilitating students' intuitive and quick adoption of the script.

3.2   Script Description

The script comprises successive phases in which the students conduct ethical judgment on a given case, while the teacher configures, controls and monitors the activity of individual students and groups. The phases of the script are Prerequisites and Setup, Reading & Individual Appraisal, Appraisal Sharing, Group Discussion, and a teacher-mediated Whole Class Discussion phase. The script draws some inspiration from the pyramid CSCL script pattern [15]. However, rather than co-constructing shared artifacts, learners always work on their own ethical judgements. Their ethical judgements are ought to evolve independently, as a result of sharing them and commenting on them anonymously in small group interactions. Script phases are as follows:

Prerequisites and Setup. To create and configure an activity, the teacher must indicate its title, a brief description, and provide a PDF file containing the description of the case involved. In addition, the teacher defines the ethical judgment rubric for the case, which will be used by the students during the activity. The components of the rubric are a set of statements (or questions) addressing the relevant aspects of the case, and for each of these statements there is a semantic differential scale that allows the student to conduct a quantitative assessment, on a scale from 1 to 7. The intent of the rubric is to make the ethical judgments of students and groups comparable. In addition, it fulfills a role of scaffolding, helping the student to focus on the relevant ethical aspects of the case, and to submit an ethical judgment in the limited time available during a face-to-face session. The teacher can generate an access code for students to easily join the classroom session. Once the students enter the session in the classroom, the teacher triggers the random formation of groups of two to five students. The teacher can see the composition of the groups, but this information remains hidden to the students, so students do not know which are their groupmates at this stage. After the groups are formed, the teacher starts the activity and the students' transition to the Reading & Individual Appraisal phase.

Reading & Individual Appraisal. During this phase, each student reads the case presented and issues his/her first ethical assessment individually, without interacting with others. To carry out the ethical judgment, the student has the rubric defined by the teacher to his avail (see Fig. 1a), which includes statements relevant to the case accompanied with their respective semantic differential scales. The software presents the statements in tabbed interface, i.e., each statement appears in a different tab, and completed tabs (ethical judgments) are marked with a green line. Each ethical judgment entered by the student through a semantic differential scale score must be justified with a brief message. The teacher can monitor the progress of the groups through his/her interface (see Fig. 2, 'Individual Appraisal' phase). The interface displays the score that each student has given to each statement/semantic differential scale in the evaluation of the case. The teacher can also inspect the comments written by the students to justify their individual judgments (see Fig. 3a).

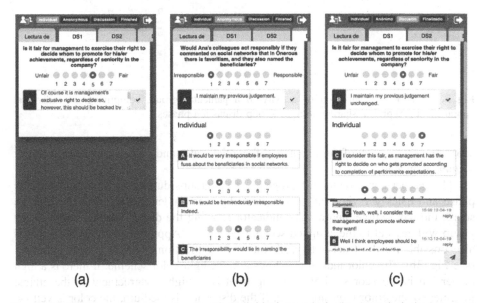

Fig. 1. Students' user interface in the (a) Individual appraisal, (b) Appraisal sharing, and (c) Group discussion phases

Appraisal Sharing. Once the students submit their individual ethical judgment for the case, the teacher triggers the transition to the Appraisal Sharing phase, in which each student sees his/her ethical judgment of the previous phase, along with the evaluations of their classmates (see Fig. 1b). The identity of all groupmates remains hidden. After reviewing the ethical judgments of his/her peers, the student may keep his/her original ethical judgment unchanged, or modify it. In either case, the student must provide a

Group	Phase	Statement 1			Statement 2			Statement 3		
1	Individual Appraisal	5	7	1	4	7	2	2	1	4
1	Appraisal Sharing	7	5	1	7	5	4	1	1	2
		4.3		6.0	5.3		3.0	1.3		1.0
1	Group Discussion	Chat: 23			Chat: 14			Chat: 3		
		1	5	3	7	7	3	1	2	2
		3.0		4.0	5.7		4.0	1.7		1.0

Fig. 2. Teacher's monitoring grid displaying the progress of a group. 'DS' columns show the points given by the students to each scale of the differential semantics. (Color figure online)

Fig. 3. Teacher's visualization of activity in a particular group, comprising (a) Individual appraisal, (b) Appraisal sharing, and (c) Group discussion phases

score to each for each of the semantic differential scales and issue a comment to justify his/her judgments.

The teacher can monitor the progress of the groups during the Appraisal Sharing phase and quickly review the scores given by each student, along with the average score, the score range, and a color indicator showing the dispersion that exists in the group with respect to the assigned scores (see Fig. 2, 'Appraisal Sharing' phase). It is also possible for the teacher to read students' justification for each ethical judgment (see Fig. 3b). The color indicator follows a traffic light color scheme; if there is a high dispersion in the scores within a group (that is, a high disagreement in the ethical judgments), the color indicator is red. If the dispersion is medium, the color is yellow, and the green color indicates there is low dispersion. In addition, the teacher can review in detail all the ethical judgments that students made in each group.

Group Discussion. Once the groups have finished the appraisal sharing phase (i.e., each student has submitted his/her revised ethical judgments), the teacher triggers the transition to the Group Discussion phase of the activity. In this phase, group composition remains as before, and each student can see his/her ethical judgments performed so far, along with the judgments of his/her peers since the individual appraisal. Students can chat through instant messaging (i.e., by means of an interface resembling instant messengers such as WhatsApp Messenger or Telegram), and discuss their judgments about the ethical case (see Fig. 1c). In this phase, the students have one last opportunity to modify their ethical judgment, as a result of interacting with their peers and revising the judgments conducted in the group. The teacher sees the deliverables of the Group Discussion phase in his/her interface (see Fig. 3c). S/he can inspect the conversation chat log in each group to further understand the scores each student has assigned to each semantic differential scale. The teacher might be more interested in reviewing group discussions where there is a higher level of disagreement; therefore, the same traffic light color scheme is used to facilitate identifying groups with higher disagreement among peers. Finally, the teacher sees for each group an indicator with the number of chat messages that have been exchanged among its members (see Fig. 2), which helps finding the groups where there has been greater discussion.

Whole Class Discussion. Once the groups finish the Group Discussion phase, the teacher can advance to a Whole Class Discussion phase where s/he can present the class with conflicting ethical judgments from different groups, and prompt students to express their opinions and judgments. The teacher must be careful to select conflicting or divergent judgments judiciously in order to stimulate a debate leading to an ethically grounded case resolution. The goal is that students recognize the virtues of the resolution reached in this final discussion, which can help them build ethical schemata, as well as ethical meaning they can transfer to different cases in their future as students, or professionals in the workplace.

3.3   Script Implementation

The CSCL script is implemented as a web application based on a stack composed of Node.js [19] as the runtime environment, Express.js [20] as the web application framework, a custom-built data access layer based on JavaScript and SQL, optimized for speed and concurrency. PostgreSQL [21] is used as the underlying database engine, and Embedded JavaScript (EJS) [22] is used in view templates. In addition, the Bootstrap [23] library version 3 is used consistently across the user interface. The technologies used to implement the script support utilizing it with devices with different form factors (i.e., in a device-independent manner), and allow simple migration of the web application to a distributed cloud environment, including dedicated/separate nodes for database and the web application itself, in case scalability to large numbers of concurrent users becomes a necessity.

4   Trial Activity

A trial activity was carried out with the intent to conduct a usability evaluation of the script and its supporting software, together with an exploratory study on the potential of the activity to generate ethical discussion in small groups. The exploratory study is an early attempt to examine the extent to which students modify their ethical judgments when facing the judgments of their peers, as well as analyzing student behavioral patterns in discussions, depending on the homogeneity or diversity of ethical judgments.

4.1   Educational Context

We conducted a pilot activity in a Web Technologies course during the first semester of 2019 in a Latin American university. The course lasts one semester, it is compulsory for students pursuing a computer science major in engineering, and optional for students of other engineering majors. In the course the students learn about the design and functioning of the world wide web, including protocols and application architectures, as well as web application development using well-known tools and frameworks. Although the course does not focus on the ethical aspects of web engineering and technologies, we considered the course cohort was apt for a trial of the CSCL script, as the students had already studied an introductory course in engineering ethics, and thus had experience learning ethics based on case discussions and essay writing.

4.2   Sample Description

The trial cohort was composed of 35 students from the Web Technologies course. Six students were female and 29 male. Ages ranged between 21 and 23 years. As for student enrollment in engineering majors, eleven students were enrolled in computer science, seventeen students in industrial engineering, five students in electrical engineering, and two in civil engineering. The students voluntarily participated in the trial.

4.3   Method

The course performed a complete activity based on an ethical case dealing with employee favoritism in a software development firm. The case was inspired by the 'Onerous Favorites' case available at the Markkula Center for Applied Ethics at Santa Clara University [24] (see Fig. 4). The statements and Semantic Differential Scales

---

Ana is a software engineer working at Onerous, a software development firm with a reputation in banking and finance sectors. Ana has witnessed various incidents of managerial favoritism towards particular employees in the company during her long professional career. Recently, she found a particularly unfavorable scenario because it involved some of his closest collaborators.

Two employees who had recently been hired at Onerous received visible roles in a prominent project. Once the project was completed successfully, management gave the new employees generous promotions. On the other hand, management asked Ana's co-workers to play supporting roles in the project and they were not given any special recognition (ie, promotions) for their work and contribution to the success of the project.

Ana's co-workers were very upset because they perceived that there was favoritism in the company, so they asked Ana for advice, as they knew that she had extensive professional experience in the company. They said that they would leave the company if the management insisted on benefiting the new employees in a clear sign of favoritism.

When Ana listened to her colleagues, she was inclined to take this matter to her manager. However, he felt that would be useless because he considers his manager to be stubborn and inflexible.

Questions:

Is it fair for management to exercise their right to decide whom to promote for his/er achievements, regardless of seniority in the company?

Would it be prudent for Ana to meet with her boss to tell him about discomfort feelings among employees caused by favoritism issues in the company?

Would Ana's colleagues act responsibly if they commented on social networks that in Onerous there is favoritism, and they also named the beneficiaries?

Fig. 4. The ethical case used in the trial activity.

Table 1. Ethical judgment statements and their corresponding Semantic Differential Scales (SDS), as presented in the trial activity.

SDS	Statement/Question	Poles
1	Is it fair for management to exercise their right to decide whom to promote for his/her achievements, regardless of seniority in the company?	Unfair – Fair 1–7 range
2	Would it be prudent for Ana to meet with her boss to tell him about discomfort feelings among employees caused by favoritism issues in the company?	Imprudent – Prudent 1–7 range
3	Would Ana's colleagues act responsibly if they commented on social networks that in Onerous there is favoritism, and they also named the beneficiaries?	Irresponsible – Responsible 1–7 range

(SDSs) utilized in the trial activity are shown in Table 1. The activity lasted for 75 min in total. The first fifteen minutes were used to give instructions to the students, and to wait for the students to connect to the wireless network and join the work session. Then, the activity required 50 min to complete its four phases. Finally, in the final ten minutes an adapted version of the System Usability Scale (SUS) [25] was administered through an online form. Two open-ended items were added to the scale questionnaire, in order to capture students' comments regarding aspects of the tool that were positively valued, and those that should be improved. In addition, a Likert item was added in scale 1–5 asking the student if he would feel satisfied using the tool in a course of the engineering curriculum.

5 Results

5.1 Usability Evaluation

The results of the SUS questionnaire reveal that the script and supporting software were found to be highly usable by the cohort of engineering students. The mean score of the SUS scale, which awards a maximum of 100 points, was 79.9, with a standard deviation of 14.3. For the calculation of the SUS score, only the first 10 items of the questionnaire were used, which correspond to those of the original SUS scale. The distribution of SUS scores is depicted in Fig. 5. According to [25], a score of 72.75 is considered to be ranked as good usability, and a score of 85.58 or above is considered to be excellent. Fifteen students (42.9%) of the sample presented a score equal or above this figure, thus evaluating usability as excellent. Ten students (28.6%) presented a score in the interval [72.75, 85.58), which regards the tool as having a good usability. Of the remaining students, nine (25.7%) considered usability to be 'OK', i.e., SUS score is in the interval [52.01, 72.75), and only 2.8% of the cohort considered usability to be poor.

Table 2 shows the adapted items of the SUS scale that were utilized, together with the descriptive statistics that resulted from administering them to the trial cohort. From the results, it can be observed that students evaluated the tool as easy to learn and use.

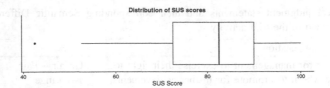

Fig. 5. Distribution of SUS scores as reported in the trial activity.

Table 2. SUS questionnaire item characterization and descriptive statistics.

N	Item stem	Type	M	SD
1	I think that this application could be used frequently in courses that teach ethics	Likert 1–5	4.45	0.66
2	I think this application is unnecessarily complex	Likert 1–5	1.91	0.78
3	I think this application is easy to use	Likert 1–5	3.88	0.93
4	I would need help if I had to use this application again	Likert 1–5	1.46	0.98
5	I think the functions of this application are easy to understand	Likert 1–5	3.94	1.19
6	I think there are many inconsistencies in this application	Likert 1–5	1.66	0.94
7	I imagine that other students could quickly learn to use this application	Likert 1–5	4.54	0.78
8	I found that using this application is uncomfortable and complicated	Likert 1–5	2.26	1.12
9	I feel very confident when using this application	Likert 1–5	4.14	0.94
10	I have to learn many details before using this application well	Likert 1–5	1.71	1.05
11	Do you think something could improve in this application?	Open-ended	-	-
12	What is the best thing you would highlight in this application?	Open-ended	-	-
13	Would you feel comfortable using this application in a course of your career?	Likert 1–5	4.14	0.91

Item 5, i.e., "I think the functions of this application are easy to understand", had the greatest variability of them all. This may be explained by the fact that the students used the tool for the first time in the trial without any previous training, and they received instructions as the activity progressed. However, the average of this item was close to 4, which is satisfactory. Arguably, the result of item 9 reveals that the students perceived that the software functioned stably, as this can likely explain their sense of confidence using it. Finally, item 13, which does not belong to the original SUS scale, indicates that the majority of students would agree with the use of the tool in engineering courses.

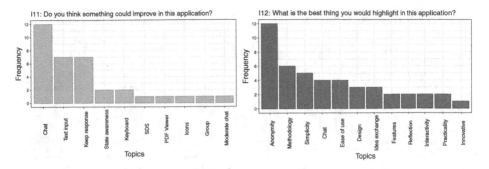

Fig. 6. Responses to open-ended items 11 and 12.

Figure 6 shows the categories of student responses to the open-ended items 11 and 12 of the questionnaire. With respect to the aspects that should be improved, the students emphasized that the chat interface used in the Group Discussion phase should be enhanced. The problems reported relate to the space available on the screen when using the chat interface, since the appearance of the onscreen keyboard pushes the interface upwards, so it becomes difficult to see the chat window and at the same see/read ethical evaluations on the same screen. On the other hand, the text input for SDS comments was uncomfortable for some students, as they claimed it only supported a limited amount of text, and the interface made difficult to scroll along a lengthy line and edit it. Finally, several students stated that it would be convenient for the interface to allow the student to submit the same response generated in the previous phase without changes. We consider that the incorporation of this feature could cause students to misuse it as a shortcut, without consciously making the effort to reconsider their ethical evaluation.

According to the results of item 12, the students valued the anonymity that is afforded by the tool when making ethical judgments, and interact with peers through the chat interface. Several students recognized value in the methodology, which first requires the students to carry out an individual ethical evaluation and then confront it with that of the classmates, to finally participate in a discussion moderated by the teacher. Finally, the students valued the simplicity of the tool and its ease of use, which is consistent with what was reported through the SUS questionnaire.

5.2 Evolution of Ethical Judgments Across the Activity Phases

Figure 7 (a) shows distributions of scores awarded by the students to the three Semantic Differential Scales (SDS) comprised in the trial case. Henceforth, we use colors blue, green and red to identify SDS1, SDS2 and SDS3, respectively. It can be seen that there is little variation in the distribution of scores awarded by students between the phases. Figure 7 (b) complements this information, showing the distributions of the absolute differences of scores of the SDSs between the phases of Individual Appraisal (IA), Appraisal Sharing (AS) and Group Discussion (GD). It can be seen that the most frequent scoring variations are of a single point in each case. In the SDS1, there was only one case of a peer who changed his/her evaluation in three

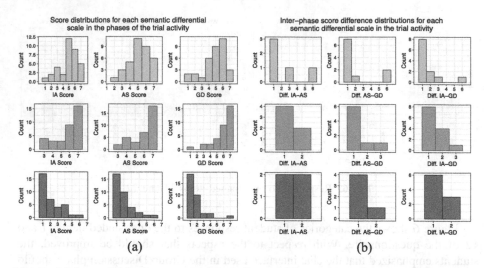

Fig. 7. (a) Score distributions per SDS scale in Individual appraisal (IA), Appraisal sharing (AS) and Group discussion (GD) phases. (b) Distribution of inter-phase SDS score differences (as absolute values). Colors: SDS1 (blue), SDS2 (green), SDS3 (red). (Color figure online)

points between the first and third phase, and another more extreme case of a peer who changed his/her evaluation in 6 points, that is, changed his/her evaluation to the opposite pole of the semantic differential scale. In SDS2, there was only one person who changed his/her evaluation in three points between the first and third phases. In the case of SDS3, there were three subjects who modified their evaluation in two points.

5.3   Chat Comments Versus Variation in Ethical Judgments

Although it is apparent that students modify their ethical judgments scarcely between the successive phases of the activity, we explored whether greater interactions through the chat interface were linked to an increased change in the ethical judgments (i.e., scores of the SDSs). To analyze this, we relied on an environment based on R 3.4.1 and the Quanteda package [26]. We built correlation matrices for each SDS (see Table 3), including sum (i.e., SUM_DELTA) and mean (i.e., MEAN_DELTA) of absolute differences (deltas) in group SDS scores between phases of Appraisal Sharing and Group Discussion, together with the sum (i.e., SUM_NTOKENS), mean (i.e., MEAN_NTOKENS) and standard deviation (i.e., SD_NTOKENS) of the number of tokens generated per group in chatroom conversation.

It can be seen that in the case of SDS1, there is a correlation of 0.72, and highly significant ($p < 0.01$), between the amount of tokens generated by the groups in the chat, and the average score delta, in relation to scores assigned by the members of each group to the SDS. As for SDS2, we did not find relevant correlations between chat activity and changes in ethical judgments. However, in the case of SDS3, we found a correlation of 0.87 ($p < 0.01$), between the average number of tokens written in the chat room by the peers in each group, and the sum of the SDS score deltas of the group

Table 3. Exploring correlations among group chat message statistics per SDS, and SDS absolute score differences per group between Appraisal Sharing and Group Discussion phases.

Statement/SDS 1	SUM_DELTA	MEAN_DELTA	SUM_NTOKENS	MEAN_NTOKENS	SD_NTOKENS
SUM_DELTA	1	0.77**	0.45	0.37	0.29
AVG_DELTA		1	0.72**	0.73**	0.65*
SUM_NTOKENS			1	0.91**	0.87**
AVG_NTOKENS				1	0.97
SD_NTOKENS					1

Statement/SDS 2	SUM_DELTA	MEAN_DELTA	SUM_NTOKENS	MEAN_NTOKENS	SD_NTOKENS
SUM_DELTA	1	0.22	-0.19	-0.12	-0.19
AVG_DELTA		1	-0.05	0.29	0.23
SUM_NTOKENS			1	0.15	0.32
AVG_NTOKENS				1	0.51
SD_NTOKENS					1

Statement/SDS 3	SUM_DELTA	MEAN_DELTA	SUM_NTOKENS	MEAN_NTOKENS	SD_NTOKENS
SUM_DELTA	1	0.96**	-0.06	0.87**	0.75**
AVG_DELTA		1	-0.11	0.79**	0.63*
SUM_NTOKENS			1	0.35	0.54
AVG_NTOKENS				1	0.9
SD_NTOKENS					1

*p < 005, **p < 0.01

peers. Both cases indicate that the more discussion in the chatroom, the greater the likelihood that students will modify their ethical judgments.

To verify the above qualitatively, we reviewed group chatlogs where there was little or no variation of scores between the phases, and on the opposite, groups where there was the highest variation of scores between the phases, in each SDS. Coincidentally, by examining chat interactions related to the three SDSs there was an evident trend that in groups where there were no differences in ethical judgments at the beginning of the GD phase, conversation was trivial and very brief, whereas in the groups in which there was greater change in the ethical evaluation there were significant discussions. To illustrate this, in Table 4 we show discussion transcripts A and B associated with SDS1. Note that both transcripts A and B have been translated to English from original Spanish. In transcript A the group has an extensive discussion where different opinions and points of view are posed. In total there were six points of variation in the ethical evaluations of SDS1 in this group, between the AS and GD phases. Opposingly, discussion transcript B shows a group where there were no differences in the evaluation of the peers for the SDS1 during the AS phase, and therefore the peers were not motivated to discuss the evaluations in the next phase.

Most of the chat messages exchanged between the students ranged from 1 to 10 tokens in each SDS (see Fig. 8). In the case of SDS1, messages larger than 60 tokens were found, corresponding to those in bold in the discussion transcript A in Table 4. These are notorious for having greater argumentative and reflexive content, written by two different peers.

Table 4. (a) Chat transcript of group with notorious SDS1 score change (delta 6) among AS and GD phases. (b) Chat transcript of a group with no change of SDS1 scores.

Discussion transcript A	Discussion transcript B
A: Do you think favoritism can be acceptable in this case? B: I agree that the situation doesn't benefit the organizational climate, but anyway, the company is run by the managers as they want, or they are ordered. C: I agree with that, company management is free to do whatever they want behind the scenes. **A: Yes, but it is important that management ensures that the work environment of the company is healthy, and favoritism is likely to generate chaos and employees may perceive the situation as abusive. In addition, although the manager decides what to do, IMHO it is unethical for a new employee to achieve much greater career advancement in much less time than a person who has dedicated his entire career to the company.** A: I agree that management can do what they want, but it does not mean that it is correct. B: But who says the new employees did not deserve the promotion? Isn't it possible at all that they may have just done an outstanding contribution to the company? A: What if it's the opposite?	A: I think our judgments are very similar. B: Yes C: Yes

(continued)

Table 4. (*continued*)

Discussion transcript A	Discussion transcript B
A: Or if all equally contributed to project success? A: What if the new hires did nothing valuable for the company at all? A: There is no way to be sure it is one way or the other. B: Ana is free to go where they value her, or create her own company. C: The one who complaints is not Ana! C: ... but they are work mates anyway, loyal with one another. A: Sure, but no sensible person would simply quit his job because other colleagues feel crushed or abused. C: I believe that an ethical company should ensure a long lasting relationship with its employees. C: Issues such as favoritism can ruin the work environment, and as the case says, the pissed colleagues just want to go elsewhere. C: It is quite possible that the company is not willing to follow ethical rules or principles consistently. A: But suppose that management behavior has consistently fallen into ethically questionable practices, such as favoritism. C: If that is the case, I agree that people are free to leave. **B: The fact that Ana and her friends work for their own interest is the 'engine of the economy'. A company must take advantage of personal interests to reward them and exchange them for their service. If for the company Ana and her team do not generate values that equals the reward (salary and benefits) they receive, sooner or later they will be dismissed. It's a company, not a charity work.** A: I'm still in my position. C: I agree with this. C: But it does not mean that the treatment of the company is unethical. C: If it says that there is recognition for those who were in high positions of the project, and not for the supporting team members. A: If I do not say that you are not right in that, but in this case we are specifying that everyone worked on the special project C: That's it	

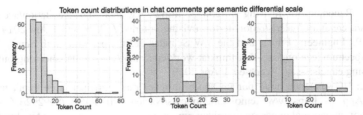

Fig. 8. Token count distributions in chat messages per statement/SDS. (Color figure online)

6   Conclusions and Future Work

In this paper we reported on our initial efforts towards developing a tool for fostering meaningful ethical discussions among engineering students in the classroom. The tool is based on six design principles; namely, the possibility of it being embeddable in a traditional ethics course, support for multidimensional ethical judgments, the anonymity of judgments and interactions, domain independence, device independence and ease of use. A trial with 35 engineering students confirmed that the average student considers the tool offers a very good usability, however, there are still a few aspects in relation to user interface design, mostly about the chat interface, which can be optimized. With regard to the design of the activity, the trial cohort highlighted the convenience of anonymity when discussing ethical cases, as well as the process comprising successive individual and anonymous group work phases.

Analysis of student behavior in the trial activity revealed that ethical judgments tend to be stable across the successive phases. However, judgments tend to change the most in groups where more discussion has been generated. Conversely, in the groups where there is little variation in the ethical evaluation, less discussion is generated and less variation of the ethical judgments. For this reason, we consider that a desirable modification to the activity in the future would be supporting group composition that maximizes the heterogeneity of the students in the groups according to their ethical judgments in the Individual Appraisal phase. We hypothesize this would raise students' interest in discussing the ethical case, and bring greater transactivity [14], along with a greater chance of students varying their ethical judgments as a result of argumentative and reflexive processes.

Finally, it is also necessary to investigate the role of the teacher in the activity. In particular, his/her ability to spur a debate leading to an ethically grounded case resolution, while validating that students recognize the virtues of the resolution reached. It is also necessary to investigate whether the activity can facilitate students' building of ethical schemata, as well as ethical meaning they can transfer to different cases in further ethical discussions as students, or as professionals in the workplace.

Acknowledgements. This research has been funded by CONICYT Fondecyt Initiation into Research grant 11160211, and Fondecyt Regular grant 1161200.

References

1. ABET: Rationale for revising criteria 3. http://www.abet.org/accreditation/accreditation-criteria/accreditation-alerts/rationale-for-revising-criteria-3/. Accessed 1 Apr 2019 (2016)
2. Patel, P.: Engineers, Ethics, and the VW Scandal. IEEE Spectrum, 25th September 2015. http://spectrum.ieee.org/cars-that-think/at-work/education/vw-scandal-shocking-but-not-surprising-ethicists-say. Accessed 1 Apr 2019
3. EMOL: UC suspende hasta por un año a alumnos que participaron en copia masiva por WhatsApp. https://www.emol.com/noticias/Nacional/2016/06/23/809292/UC-suspende-hasta-por-un-ano-a-alumnos-que-participaron-en-copia-masiva-por-WhatsApp.html. Accessed 1 Apr 2019 (2016)

4. Sarangi, S., Sharma, P.: Artificial Intelligence: Evolution, Ethics and Public Policy. Routledge, India (2018)
5. Holsapple, M.A., Carpenter, D.D., Sutkus, J.A., Finelli, C.J., Harding, T.S.: Framing faculty and student discrepancies in engineering ethics education delivery. J. Eng. Educ. **101**(2), 169–186 (2012). https://doi.org/10.1002/j.2168-9830.2012.tb00047.x
6. Sunderland, M.E.: Sci. Eng. Ethics (2013). https://doi.org/10.1007/s11948-013-9444-5
7. Génova, G., González, M.R.: Teaching ethics to engineers: a socratic experience. Sci. Eng. Ethics **22**(2), 567–580 (2016). https://doi.org/10.1007/s11948-015-9661-1
8. Hess, J.L., Fore, G.: A systematic literature review of US engineering ethics interventions. Sci. Eng. Ethics **24**(2), 551–583 (2018)
9. Kohlberg, L., Hersh, R.H.: Moral development: a review of the theory. Theor. Pract. **16**(2), 53–59 (1977). https://doi.org/10.1080/00405847709542675
10. Dillenbourg, P.: Over-scripting CSCL: The risks of blending collaborative learning with instructional design. In: Kirschner, P.A. (ed.) Three Worlds of CSCL. Can We Support CSCL?, pp. 61–91. Open Universiteit Nederland, Heerlen (2002)
11. May, D.R., Luth, M.T.: The effectiveness of ethics education: a quasi-experimental field study. Sci. Eng. Ethics **19**(2), 545–568 (2013). https://doi.org/10.1007/s11948-011-9349-0
12. Bandura, A.: Perceived self-efficacy in cognitive development and functioning. Educ. Psychol. **28**(2), 117–148 (1993)
13. Weinberger, A., Ertl, B., Fischer, F., Mandl, H.: Epistemic and social scripts in computer–supported collaborative learning. Instr. Sci. **33**(1), 1–30 (2005)
14. Weinberger, A.: Principles of transactive computer-supported collaboration scripts. Nordic J. Digit. Literacy **6**(03), 189–202 (2011)
15. Hernández Leo, D., Asensio-Pérez, J.I., Dimitriadis, Y.: Computational representation of collaborative learning flow patterns using IMS learning design. J. Educ. Technol. Soc. **8**(4), 75–89 (2005)
16. Hoffmann, M., Borenstein, J.: Understanding Ill-Structured engineering ethics problems through a collaborative learning and argument visualization approach. Sci. Eng. Ethics **20**(1), 261–276 (2014). https://doi.org/10.1007/s11948-013-9430
17. Binder, P.: The intersection of ethical decision-making modules and classroom response systems in business education. The Future of Education, Florence, Italy. Accessed 9 June 2013 (2013)
18. Butchart, S., Handfield, T., Restall, G.: Using peer instruction to teach philosophy, logic, and critical thinking. Teach. Philos. **32**(1), 1–40 (2009)
19. Node.js. https://nodejs.org/en/. Accessed 16 Mar 2019 (2019)
20. Express.js. https://expressjs.com/. Accessed 16 Mar 2019 (2019)
21. PostgreSQL. https://www.postgresql.org/. Accessed 16 Mar 2019 (2019)
22. EJS. https://ejs.co/. Accessed 16 Mar 2019 (2019)
23. Bootstrap. https://getbootstrap.com/. Accessed 16 Mar 2019 (2019)
24. Tan, J.: Onerous favorites. markkula center for applied ethics, Santa Clara University. https://www.scu.edu/ethics/focus-areas/more/engineering-ethics/engineering-ethics-cases/onerous-favorites/. Accessed 16 Mar 2019 (2015)
25. Bangor, A., Kortum, P.T., Miller, J.T.: An empirical evaluation of the system usability scale. Int. J. Hum.-Comput. Interact. **24**(6), 574–594 (2008)
26. Quanteda. https://quanteda.io/. Accessed 15 Apr 2019 (2019)

Tailorable Remote Assistance with RemoteAssistKit: A Study of and Design Response to Remote Assistance in the Manufacturing Industry

Troels Ammitsbøl Rasmussen[(✉)] and Kaj Gronbak

Department of Computer Science, Aarhus University, Aarhus, Denmark
{troels.rasmussen,kgronbak}@cs.au.dk

Abstract. In this paper we present our findings from interviewing manufacturing employees about their remote assistance practices and requirements to remote assistance technology. We found that their needs were rather heterogeneous regarding mobility, camera setups and location of guidance. We built the prototype RemoteAssistKit (RAK) as a design response to their heterogeneous needs. RAK is a tailorable remote assistance solution, where different mobility modes, camera setups and locations of guidance can be explored and interchanged using a graphical user interface. RAK thus moves some of the design responsibility from the designer to the users, who are empowered to tailor remote assistance to their needs and preferences.

Keywords: Remote assistance · Interview study · Augmented reality · Tailorability

1 Introduction

In an industrial context remote assistance is required in situations where a "worker", typically a machine operator or machine technician, experiences a problem with a machine or piece of equipment and thus calls a "remote helper", typically an experienced colleague. The problem solving activity between the worker and helper is mediated by a communication system, which is either a dedicated remote assistance system or a more general purpose system, such as a video calling application.

In this paper we present our qualitative, empirical findings on remote assistance practices and needs of employees in the manufacturing industry. This is a rare view into the real world practices and needs of a specific group of users of remote assistance technology. Most research on remote assistance make use of lab controlled studies that rarely involve the perspectives of manufacturing employees, who we argue are lead users of remote assistance technology, because

The work reported here is funded by MADE Digital (Project 6151-00006B).

H. Nakanishi et al. (Eds.): CRIWG+CollabTech 2019, LNCS 11677, pp. 80–95, 2019.
https://doi.org/10.1007/978-3-030-28011-6_6

they benefit greatly from advances in the technology. Next, we present our design and implementation of RemoteAssistKit (RAK), which enables users to tailor remote assistance to their needs and personal preferences. RAK lets the users (the workers and helpers) explore mobility (mobile vs stationary user interface), different camera setups (scene camera, head-mounted camera or a combination), and guidance locations (display separate from the task space, heads-up display or AR directly in the task space) without the need for any programming knowledge by making available a graphical user interface with which they can tailor RAK using modular, (mostly) web-based software components that represent the different levels of mobility, camera setups and guidance locations. The motivation behind RAK is twofold. First of all, from interviewing industrial employees at three different manufacturing companies, it is evident that the employees have heterogeneous requirements to remote assistance technology, because of their diverse roles, tasks and environments - no one-size-fits-all. The motivation behind the modularity of RAK is to support their heterogeneous needs. Secondly, the use of camera setups, for instance scene cameras or scene and mobile camera combinations, and the location of guidance, including AR guidance, has not been adequately explored in a real setting outside the lab. Thus, we know little about the adoption of different camera setups and AR for remote assistance in the wild, including the manufacturing industry. RAK enables users to easily explore different configurations of camera setups and guidance locations trial-and-error style, and thus can be used as a research tool to better understand the usability and usefulness of different camera setups and guidance locations in various situations in the wild.

After describing the findings from interviews and RAK, we conclude the paper with a discussion of the limitations of and future work on RAK and its intended use as a tool for further scientific inquiry into remote assistance in the wild.

2   Related Work

In this section we present related work on remote assistance and heterogeneous user needs.

2.1   Remote Assistance

Different interfaces and interactions for remote assistance are typically compared with respect to how well the worker-helper pairs collaborate and perform on a given physical task. This includes comparisons of camera setups [5,8], guidance techniques [6,9] and the location of guidance [2,9].

Different camera setups have different strengths and weaknesses. With a handheld/head-mounted camera the worker can capture close-up machine details from various angles, but the video the helper receives is unsteady and hard to annotate [2]. With a scene camera (camera mounted in the environment) the video is steady and easy to annotate, but at the cost of loss of detail. Researchers have compared a head-mounted camera to a scene camera and found that worker-helper pairs performed best using the scene camera [5]. A combination of scene- and head-mounted camera, where the helper can select between the videos from the two cameras, might seem like the best of both worlds, but so far research on camera combos have not shown any performance benefits over just using a single scene camera [5]. Researchers have also compared different ways of remote controlling the movement of a camera, thus providing the helper with a degree of view independence [10,11]. Lately the use of 360-degree live video for remote collaboration has received some attention [12,14], because it can provide the helper with a view of the task space independent of the worker's orientation. However, the challenge is knowing where other people direct their attention in the 360-degree video.

Early work on remote assistance suggests that providing the remote helper with the ability to use a pointer on shared video of the task space is ineffective, whereas sketching on the video is beneficial, because sketches are representational, i.e. can express complex 3D object manipulations [6]. Kirk et al. [9] compared freehand sketching to unmediated hand gestures on video and found that unmediated representations performed the best. In the same study, Kirk et al. also compared the output locations of the helper's gestures - external monitor vs. projecting gestures on the table surface of the task space - and did not find a significant difference in performance between the locations. In recent years, the helper's guidance techniques have increasingly been explored using augmented and virtual reality [1,2,7,12]. A common approach to AR remote assistance is that the helper uses a PC or tablet to make 2D annotations on live video/images of the task space, and then the worker's AR device interprets and registers the annotations in 3D task space [2,7].

2.2 Heterogeneous User Needs

Tailorability of component-based groupware has received interest within the CSCW community, because *the inter- and intra-individual differences constitute the need for system designs, which can [...] exhibit different behaviour in different usage situations, and accommodate individual and group needs and preferences* [15]. According to Hippel et al. one strategy for addressing heterogeneous user needs is that the manufacturer of a product or service provides the users with a "user innovation toolkit" [16]. A user innovation toolkit partitions product or service development into solution-information-intensive subtasks and need-information-intensive substasks. This allows the users to focus on need-information-intensive subtasks - they know what they want - while the manufacturer focuses on solution-information-intensive subtasks - they know how to produce the users' individual designs. We argue that RAK can be described as a user innovation toolkit with a sparse solution space, because RAK allows users to explore different remote assistance configurations trial-and-error style until they find a configuration that works for them. Providing the users with the means to innovate and customize a product using an innovation toolkit has been shown to improve user satisfaction of products, including security software [3] and consumer watches [4].

The work closest to ours is that by Speicher et al. [14], who created a modular, customizable remote assistance system, 360Anywhere, providing support for multiple collaborators, 360° cameras, projectors, sketching in the 360° video, session persistence and rewind of video features. Their argument for creating the system is similar to ours: they wanted to cater to users' heterogeneous collaboration and augmentation needs. But the challenges they address with the system and the intended use scenarios are different. Their major concern are the challenges of using 360° video and the intended use scenarios are primarily set in an office environment and includes brainstorming and an online lecture. In our work we focus on making the camera setup and location of guidance tailorable to the specific needs of manufacturing employees during remote assistance on physical tasks.

3   Interviews with Manufacturing Employees on Remote Assistance

Over the course of a year we visited three manufacturing companies in Denmark. Company A CNC mills metal molds for internal use in the process of manufacturing of toys. Company B manufactures, sells and services large inline printing machines, which can print on a variety of product packaging. Company C manufactures, sells and services wind turbines. We interviewed two employees from each company. Our contact persons inside the companies selected the employees based on their experience with remote assistance. The interviews were semi-structured and lasted between 21 min–49 min, with an average of 27 min. All employees were male between 25 and 50 years old, and one of the interviews took place on Skype. The employees from company B were interviewed together, hence they are referred to as E3-4. During the interviews, we asked questions about their daily work, current remote assistance practices, problems that required remote assistance, technologies used for remote assistance, mobility needs, and requirements to a remote assistance solution. With these interviews we hope not to generalize, but to show the diversity of tasks that require remote assistance in industry and the heterogeneous requirements to the design of remote assistance technology. For a quick overview between the relationship between employees and companies refer to Fig. 1.

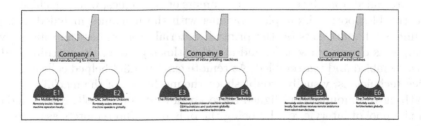

Fig. 1. Overview of company-employee relationship

Employee 1 - The Mobile Helper. E1 was responsible for managing the purchase, implementation and maintenance of CNC machines and additional equipment used in the process of manufacturing metal molds at company A. During the interview he focused on a very important machine, a washing machine specially designed to clean the mold parts between each step in the manufacturing process. Importantly, he described how this was the only washing machine of its kind in the mold factory and thus it was costly whenever it stopped working. He was the main responsible for helping the machine operators fix any problems with the washing machine and he needed to do so quickly. Remote assistance involved remotely accessing the human machine interface (HMI) of the washing machine and video calling the machine operators using FaceTime to see the current state of the machine. The machine operators were not expected to assemble/disassemble parts of the machine, only to be able to operate the machine interface.

Employee 2 - The CNC Software Unicorn. E2 was responsible for the robot-control software on the CNC machines at company A, and globally responsible for remotely helping with software problems on the machines. He was the only person in the company in this position. Thus, if a machine operator in China or Mexico experienced software-related problems with a CNC machine he would call E2. Remote assistance involved remotely accessing the human machine interface (HMI) and video calling to see how the robotic parts of the machine behaved as he executed different software programs. According to E2 most problems could be solved by simply accessing the HMI and talking to the machine operator on the phone (no video communication required), because E2 was very familiar with the software and behaviour of the machine. However, sometimes he would benefit from seeing live video of the machine. Again, the machine operators were not expected to assemble/disassemble parts of the machine, only to be able to operate the machine interface.

Employee 3 and 4 - The Printer Technicians. E3-4 worked for company B, the manufacturer of inline printing machines. These machines are large (several meters long, wide and high) and can print on practically any type of product packaging. E3-4 had experience as service technicians, responsible for installing and servicing printing machines at the customer factories, and as remote experts, which are called upon by either the customers or colleagues, when machines need to be troubleshooted. Example problems with the machines included leakages and undesirable artifacts on the printed material. Sometimes the solution was as simple as cleaning a sensor, and at other times parts of the machine had to be disassembled and reassembled. As remote experts E3-4 helped colleagues, the service technicians, visually troubleshoot the mechanics of the machine to see if everything was mounted or aligned correctly down to every bolt. E3-4 stand out from the pool of interviewees by being the only ones who remotely assisted with problems on their customers printing machines, whereas the other interviewees provided remote assistance on internal machines/equipment. So, pressure was on to find the right solution to a problem with a printing machine as quickly as possible, because downtime of a machine in production was costly for their customers.

Employee 5 - The Robot Responsible. E5 worked for company C and was hired as a skilled worker on the production floor. He recently became responsible for the robot which lubricates bolts for the windmills, but had 8 years of prior experience with robots in manufacturing from a previous job. The robot was the only one of its kind in the company worldwide and, according to E5, he was currently the only one internally with the competencies to program the robot. The robot was popular among the people on the production floor, because it relieved them from having to lube the bolts by hand, which was painful for their hands and shoulders. Sometimes his colleagues wanted to use the robot, when he was not present, for instance he might have a sick day. Because they did not have the same experience and competencies as E5, he had to remotely assist them in the use of the robot, which he accomplished using two separate software programs. E5 could remotely access and control the software on the computer connected to the robot using TeamViewer and send robot programming files to his colleagues on the production floor. He could not however remote control the movements of the robot. Additionally, E5 had installed a webcam in the environment that provided an overview of the robot and could be accessed from a program on his phone.

Employee 6 - The Turbine Tester. E6's job was to test the turbines for faulty electrical circuits and mechanics before they left the factory at company C. He had 8 years of experience as a turbine tester, and before his current job, he worked as an ordinary electrician. E6 used a "test player", a specialized computer, that he connected with cables to a section on the turbine to run tests. The test player contained a program for running tests on different sections on the turbine and would throw an error message if something was wrong with the electrical circuits or mechanics of the section being tested. The error messages did not always explain the exact cause of the error and so it was the testers job to hunt for the cause of the error by checking that cables had been connected correctly and the mechanics are working as expected. Due to E6's experience as a turbine tester, he was tasked with remotely assisting colleagues in other countries, whenever they encountered an error message they did not understand or could not find a cause for. He made use of a video calling app (he used a PC, while his remote colleagues used a smartphone), because he needed to see the turbine to be able to investigate the causes of a particular error message. Often troubleshooting an error involves compared a schematic of electrical wiring to video of the actual wiring.

A limitation of our interview study is that the interviewed employees had most experience in the role of the remote helper and primarily answered questions from their perspective as helpers. However, E5 would sometimes take on the role of the worker, when he needed help from the robot manufacturer.

Fig. 2. Machine operators/technicians at company A, B and C need remote assistance to solve problems with different machines, including large printing machines at company A (left), special washing machine for molds at company B (middle), and bolt-lubing industrial robot at company C (right).

Furthermore, E3-4 had previously held job positions as service technicians, but now - due to their large experience - held management level jobs, and thus would primarily take on the role of the remote helper. This means that these employees should be able to understand the remote assistance needs from the perspective of the worker. In future studies, we would acquire more participants with more extensive experience as the worker (Fig. 2).

4   Interview Findings

The interviews with employees from manufacturing companies revealed that they had heterogeneous needs for remote assistance, but also some needs in common. Below we describe their needs and possible design and research implications.

Need Support for Existing Remote Communication Equipment. First of all, despite the employees different tasks and working environments, all employees had in common that they used software to remotely access the machine interface (VNC Connect, TeamViewer etc.). This granted them access to status information on the machine, sensor data, and in some instances the ability to control certain parts of the machine. Additionally, they all used video communication software, like FaceTime or Skype, on their smartphones or PCs to obtain live video of the current state of the task space. The video feed contains information not available in the machine interface, and vice versa the machine interface contains information not available in the video feed. A design implication may be to combine the two software programs into one program by augmenting the video feed with manipulable sensor data and other status information using augmented reality. Further research is needed to understand which is beneficial to the remote helper: an augmented view of the task space in which he can consume status information and control machine parameters, or the traditional separation between the abstract representation of the machine and video feed.

Need Support for Varying Degrees of Mobility. In E1's case the need for mobility was a result of the importance of a particular machine, the washing machine, and the urgency of reacting to requests for help anywhere at anytime. *E1: I prefer helping them (the machine operators) right away, because it is very important that the washing machine is running, because parts (of a mold) in the washing machine risk getting destroyed, if they stay in there for too long E1: Often I am in the supermarket or picking up the kids (from school), when they (the machine operators) call me.* E5 seemed to enjoy the mobility of the smartphone, because he enjoyed checking the status of the robot at his convenience. He was proud of being in charge of the robot as the only one in company C. Thus, his preference for using a smartphone seems more emotional than rational. *E5: In the morning when I wake up, I have to check the status of the robot (from his phone).* For E6 remote assistance involved comparing a schematic of electrical wiring to live video of the actual wiring. E6 believed it was easier to access schematics on the PC than on the phone and thus preferred to use a PC for remote assistance. *E6: On the PC I have the drawings and I can show them (his remote colleagues) the drawings [...] it will be too difficult to do it on the phone, I think.*

Generally, employees whose main purpose it is to give remote assistance can be expected to be in an office where stationary, powerful hardware for remote assistance is available, including VR and advanced tracking equipment. However, employees that take on remote assistance tasks sporadically throughout their work week, as is the case of all of the interviewed employees, cannot be expected to always be in their office upon a request for help and thus need mobile alternatives. E1's situation at work describes this best. At the time of the interview, he would regularly take part in project meetings at company A. *E1: My current situation at work requires me to be in two places, about 2 km apart, and I would like to have it (remote assistance functionality) on the phone, because I don't bring my computer (to project meetings 2 km from his office).*

As the above accounts show, some employees require to be mobile due to specific circumstances, while others do not. The implications of the mobile helper for the design of remote assistance is the need to explore guidance techniques on tablets/smartphones by taking into account their limited screen real estate, multi-touch and sensory capabilities. Another important thing to consider are the seamless transitions between mobile solutions and stationary solutions with comparatively more computational power, which have not received much research attention. Our prototype RAK handles the transition between a mobile and stationary solution by making use of a device agnostic web application running on both smartphones, tablets and desktops. Furthermore annotations, i.e. the sketches made on a device, is persisted, so when the helper transitions from one device to another, sketches will re-appear.

Need Support for a Variety of Camera Setups. Some of the interviewees had considered or were already using specific camera setups. E5 for instance had taken the initiative to install a scene camera in the robot cell, which he could access remotely from his phone. *E5: I have mounted a web camera inside (the robot cell), so I can see how the robot is positioned right now (from his smartphone).* Thus, E5 could remotely check on the status of the robot, even when no workers were present locally. Upon showing us around on a printing machine in their test facility, E3-4 told us that they had considered to use a small wireless camera by placing it on the printing unit adjacent to the unit undergoing maintenance, while showing the helper's guidance on video from the camera on a tablet/smartphone placed in front of the worker. Thereby, their idea was to make use of the industrial environment to provide the helper and worker with a shared over the shoulder view of the printing machine. E1 mentioned that with a few scene cameras he could capture the most crucial areas on the washing machine, and suggested to use the scene cameras to both live transmit video and record activities in the task space, thereby supporting him in identifying how mistakes were made after the fact. *E1: It would be interesting with constant surveillance of the machines [...] A bunch of cameras in the production that one could log into and use to go back in time, because many of the errors are related to persons making mistakes [...] I know who used the machine last (because of digital logging) [...] but they used the machine in a different way (than intended) and we don't know why a certain error occurred and how the situation was (at the time the error occured) [...] or when the error occurred, because they left the machine to itself"* At the time of the interview, E6 was planning to use a commercial remote assistance solution, where the camera was part of a heads-up display or smartphone, thereby providing the helper with a view through the eyes of the worker. *E6: I am participating in a project right now, which involves the use of a commercial remote assistance solution. We are implementing this in Russia now so I can support them (the turbine testers in Russia). The plan is that I use a laptop and they use glasses (heads-up display) or a phone, whatever they prefer.* E6 would remotely troubleshoot the electrical wiring of turbines, so sometimes he required close-up views of the wiring to compare it to schematics, and therefore using a head-worn/handheld camera made sense. It is evident that many of the employees had already considered and some experimented with the benefits of particular camera setups. Interestingly most of the solutions that were considered or in use included scene cameras, while most commercial solutions today include wearable cameras that capture video from the point of view of the worker either through a handheld smartphone or a head-worn solution. The use of scene cameras in industry raises some questions that have not been answered in current research on scene cameras. Those questions include: "How feasible is a solution, where one or more scene cameras are mounted ad hoc in the environment?", "How time consuming it is to mount one or more cameras ad hoc in the environment?", "How feasible it is to permanently mount scene cameras that covers specific areas of a machine and are the workers concerned about video recording of their activities?", "Does scene cameras capture the areas of the task space in enough detail that the helper can give feedback on the worker's object manipulations, or is a scene camera + mobile camera combo needed?". In RAK we aim to support the experimentation of camera setups by letting the worker choose between a scene camera (webcam), mobile camera (tablet/smartphone camera) or scene+mobile camera setup.

Need Support for Visual Guidance and a Variety of Visual Guidance Locations. The helper providing visual guidance to the worker was believed to be useful, especially to avoid misunderstandings of employees with poor English skills that do not share terminology with the helper. This feature was brought up by both E2 from company A, E3-4 from company B, and E6 from company C. They all remotely assist colleagues in other countries.

E2: There is this communication barrier which limits how well you communicate (with people from China and Mexico) [...] I see some benefits of remote assistance technology, because I can see what you (the machine operator) are looking at, and I can draw something on a screen or show you where to locate something.

E3-4: At the same time you (the worker) show me something with the camera, you are able to see something on your screen, where I've added a layer of information. Often the OEM technician does not know the technical name of the mechanic components [...] their English is primitive [...] I don't always understand what he says.

The employees expressed different ideas on where to locate the guidance in the worker's task space. E2 talked about the possibilities of AR, where guidance is located directly in the worker's task space, but without any notion of the benefits of using AR. Upon showing us around on a printing machine, E3-4 explained that they considered to show the guidance on live video on a tablet/smartphone placed in front of the worker, while the camera, responsible for capturing video of the printing machine, was mounted on the adjacent printing unit behind the worker. E6 was piloting a commercial solution, where guidance was shown on live video on either a handheld smartphone or heads-up display. While they agreed on the usefulness of visual guidance, none of the employees reflected on the benefits and drawbacks of different guidance locations, for instance comparing AR guidance to guidance on video. It is clear from the empirical research on remote assistance - dominated by controlled lab studies - that visual guidance in live video of the task space is helpful during remote assistance, however a clear advantage of using AR guidance has yet to be demonstrated [2,7], especially in the wild. RAK enables users to experiment with different guidance locations and compare non-AR guidance on video and AR guidance during real remote assistance. Hence, in future work we hope RAK can be used to identify the characteristics of real remote assistance tasks, where AR guidance is preferred over non-AR guidance and vice versa.

Create Ownership for Solutions Among Super Users. Some employees (E2 and E5) had in common that they got to modify machines and technology for their work and thus had become the in house experts or super users.

E2: I developed the software for the machines [...] I am responsible for the machines globally, so if somebody has a problem in Mexico, they call me.

E5: I have mounted a web camera inside (the robot cell), so I can see how the robot is positioned right now (remotely from his smartphone) [...] I have numbered each door on the computers (the computers on the robot) [...] I can tell them (his colleagues) "go to door number 1 and take out the controller" [...] I don't have to use the technology (remote assistance solution), but I want to [...] I keep going until it works.

The above accounts provide examples of employees in the manufacturing industry trialing remote assistance solutions on their own premises, and some even create their own remote assistance solutions. E2 and E5 were clearly proud of their position in the companies and the responsibility they had been trusted with to choose, create and modify technology for internal use, including remote assistance technology. This bottom up approach to innovation in the manufacturing industry is exactly what we intend to support on a smaller scale with the tailorability of RAK - rather than have management impose a specific remote assistance solution on the employees. This should make actual users of the technology more accepting of it and increase the likelihood of successful adoption, because of a sense of responsibility and ownership for the technology.

5   Design of RemoteAssistKit

From our interviews with manufacturing employees it became clear that one specific remote assistance solution might not satisfy their heterogeneous needs for mobility, camera setups and guidance locations. That is how we were inspired to design RemoteAssistKit (RAK).

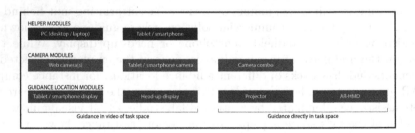

Fig. 3. The modules of RemoteAssistKit. The helper modules, camera modules and guidance location modules can be interchanged and combined in different ways.

With RAK we provide the users the flexibility and power to design their own remote assistance solution by mixing modular, interchangeable software modules to match their task requirements and preferences without the need of any programming knowledge. Thus we move the need-intensive-subtasks of developing a remote assistance solution to the users [16]. RAK consists of three types of modules: helper modules, camera modules and guidance location modules. See Fig. 3 for a conceptual overview. The modules can be combined in different ways and make up different design configurations of RAK, as illustrated in Fig. 4.

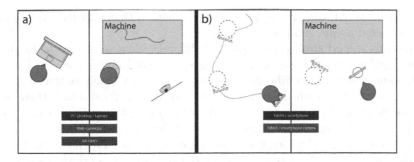

Fig. 4. Two example configurations of RAK seen from a top view. (a) The helper uses a laptop to sketch on live video from a web camera mounted in the worker's task space, while the worker wears and AR-HMD to see the sketches registered in 3D to the task space. (b) The helper is on the move and uses a smartphone to sketch on live video captured from a tablet in the worker's task space, while the worker sees the sketches on the tablet. The tablet is either mounted on a tripod or held by the worker

The interviewed employees had varying needs for mobility. Some helpers are able to answer calls from a worker using the computer in their office, while others, due to the urgency of the call, will need to be able to give help on the go. RAK supports these varying needs for mobility. Currently, two different helper modules are included in RemoteAssistKit. (1) A mobile helper module, which allows the helper to provide remote assistance on the go using a tablet/smartphone. (2) A stationary helper module, with which the helper can use a desktop/laptop PC to provide remote assistance. Both modules make use of a pointer and freehand sketching as the means to provide visual guidance in a shared live video feed of the worker's task space. The interactions for pointing and sketching vary only slightly between the tablet/smartphone and PC implementations due to variations in the input method - touch on mobile device and mouse on PC. Transitions from PC to mobile device or vice versa is supported as annotations are persisted, meaning sketches made on one device will reappear on another device, as long as the same "virtual room" on the server is shared between the worker and helper.

The interviewed employees had varying needs for the camera setup. Some helpers wanted to be able to check on equipment, when no workers were around locally or to view recordings of machine failures, which required the use of scene cameras. Some needed detailed views of a task space area, thus they used a head-worn/handheld camera. In RAK we wish to support the employees' varying needs for and experimentation with camera setups. Therefore, three different camera modules are included in RAK. (1) A web camera module which uses one or multiple web cameras to capture the task space. The web cameras must be mounted as scene cameras in the environment. (2) A mobile camera module, which uses a handheld mobile device (smartphone/tablet) to capture the task space from the front facing or back facing camera. The handheld device may be held by the worker, mounted on a tripod or attached to a machine in the environment, thus acting as a scene camera. (3) A combined webcam+mobile camera module. All camera modules have in common that they live stream video to the selected helper module.

The interviewed employees expressed different ideas on where to locate the helpers guidance in the worker's task space, but did not reflect much on the benefits and drawbacks of different guidance locations. We believe that by getting them to experiment with different guidance locations, it will teach them about their requirements to the location of guidance and how it may differ depending on their remote assistance tasks. Therefore, four different guidance location modules are included in RAK of which two have AR capabilities: (1) An external display module, which shows the helper's guidance (transmitted from the helper module) on live video of the task space (transmitted from the camera module) on an external display. This external display module runs on a smartphone/tablet, so the worker can quickly and easily bring it with him and place it in a way that makes the helper's guidance viewable, while he executes some task on a machine. (2) A heads-up display module, which shows the helper's guidance on live video of the task space on a heads-up display. We used the Mira headset, a head-mounted frame in which a smartphone can be mounted to create a head-mounted display, and we created an application for the headset, which shows video hovering in the left corner of the eye, similar to the experience of using a heads-up display. (3) A projector module, which uses a projector to project the helper's guidance directly onto the task space, as long as the task space is (approximately) a planar surface. The worker is required to follow a calibration procedure to align helper's guidance to the real task space before remote assistance can commence. (4) An AR-head-mounted display module which - as the name implies - uses an AR-head-mounted display (MS Hololens) for displaying the helper's guidance directly in the task space. We make use of the rather simple spray-paint technique [13] to interpret the helper's 2D guidance in 3D, which leaves room for future improvement. The AR-HMD module makes use one or more scene cameras (tablet camera or web camera), and it is the helper's 2D pointing and sketching in the video feed(s) of the scene camera(s) that is interpreted in 3D on the worker's AR device. The interpretation works by aligning a virtual camera to the real scene camera by scanning a marker on the real camera with the AR device. See Fig. 5 for an example of the AR-HMD module combined with the mobile camera module and the stationary helper module.

The helper must select the helper module, and the worker must select the camera and guidance location modules using a graphical user interface. See Fig. 6 for a screenshot of the web based user interface for selecting modules. The user interface connects helpers and workers using the concept of virtual rooms - one helper and one worker per room. A helper/worker can join an existing room or create a new one to start communicating with each other. The helper joins a room with a helper module on a smartphone/tablet or PC, while the worker joins a room with a camera module and possibly a guidance location module on his devices. They select which modules to use in the drop down menus and click the join button next to the modules, upon which they are redirected to the selected module applications.

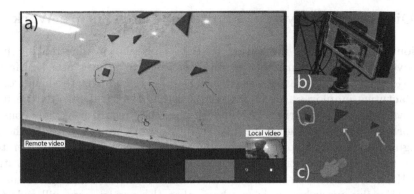

Fig. 5. Example configuration of RAK. (a) Screenshot of the helper's interface. He uses a PC to sketch on live video from a smartphone in the worker's task space. (b) The worker wears an AR-HMD to align a virtual camera to the front-facing camera of the smartphone. (c) Because of this alignment, the worker can see the helper's sketches in AR on the task space, in this case the annotations point to some puzzle pieces on a whiteboard.

Fig. 6. User interface which connects helpers and workers using the concept of rooms. In the example the rooms are named after the problems that require assistance

5.1   Technical Implementation

RAK consists of a distributed set of applications running on the helper's and worker's devices. The two helper modules (mobile and stationary), the camera modules (web camera, mobile camera, combo) and the guidance location modules (external display, projector, head-up display) are single page web applications written in ECMAScript 6 and transpiled to pure JavaScript. Thus, these modules are device agnostic in that they can run in a browser on both a desktop/laptop PC or on a tablet/smartphone. The modules make use of the p5 javascript library for drawing the user interface. Additionally, the AR-HMD guidance location module runs on an MS Hololens and is a Universal Windows Platform (UWP) app written in C-sharp. The helper, camera and guidance location modules need to communicate during setup and when certain events, such as sketching events, occur. This communication is implemented using websockets and a Node.js server. The Node.js server also works as a signalling server for setting up WebRTC video streaming between the helper and camera modules and between the camera and guidance location modules (the latter only applies to the external display and head-up display modules).

6   Discussion of System Limitations and Future Work

Previous work on "user innovation toolkits" has shown that making need-intensive tasks the responsibility of the user leads to greater user satisfaction [3,4]. However more research is needed, where RAK is put in the hands of the manufacturing employees, to understand whether they will take on the need-intensive tasks of configuring RAK, or whether they regard it as time consuming work in an already tight schedule. In future work we put RAK to the test through a design workshop, where manufacturing employees (machine operators, service technicians and remote supporters) explore the different configurations of RAK in a real, familiar industrial use context on real machine problems. By completing this workshop it is our hope that the participants will reflect on their current remote assistance practices, design future practices that matches their needs, and generate knowledge about the feasibility and usefulness of the different design configurations in a real industrial use context - hence answering some of the questions related to remote assistance in the wild, for instance "How feasible is a solution, where one or more scene cameras are mounted in the environment?" and "Are there any industrial tasks where AR guidance is particularly well/ill-suited?".

An important aspect of remote assistance that we did not yet modulparize in RAK is the content of the visual guidance. RAK currently only supports pointing and sketching. In a possible future implementation we would like to modularize the content of the visual guidance providing the helper with the option to choose between sketching or using natural hand gestures. The natural hand gestures have been shown to lead to better performance between worker-helper pairs in controlled studies [9].

7   Conclusion

We have presented our findings from interviewing manufacturing employees about their remote assistance practices and needs. Furthermore, we have presented the design and implementation of the tailorable remote assistance prototype, RAK, which serves as a design response to the at times heterogeneous needs of employees. Especially, employees exhibited heterogeneous needs and preferences for mobility and camera setups due to differences in the problems they assist with and the task environment of the worker. In the future, we plan to use RAK as a tool for further scientific inquiry into questions regarding the helper's need for mobility, and the feasibility and usefulness of being able to configure camera setups and guidance locations during remote assistance in the wild.

References

1. Chen, H., Lee, A.S., Swift, M., Tang, J.C.: 3d collaboration method over HoloLens^{TM} and Skype^{TM} end points. In: Proceedings of the 3rd International Workshop on Immersive Media Experiences, ImmersiveME 2015, pp. 27–30. ACM, New York (2015)
2. Fakourfar, O., Ta, K., Tang, R., Bateman, S., Tang, A.: Stabilized annotations for mobile remote assistance. In: Proceedings of the 2016 CHI Conference on Human Factors in Computing Systems, CHI 2016, pp. 1548–1560. ACM, New York (2016)
3. Franke, N., von Hippel, E.: Satisfying heterogeneous user needs via innovation toolkits: the case of Apache security software. Res. Policy **32**(7), 1199–1215 (2003)
4. Franke, N., Piller, F.: Value creation by toolkits for user innovation and design: the case of the watch market. J. Prod. Innov. Manag. **21**, 401–415 (2004)
5. Fussell, S.R., Setlock, L.D., Kraut, R.E.: Effects of head-mounted and scene-oriented video systems on remote collaboration on physical tasks. In: Proceedings of the SIGCHI Conference on Human Factors in Computing Systems, CHI 2003, pp. 513–520. ACM, New York (2003)
6. Fussell, S.R., Setlock, L.D., Yang, J., Ou, J., Mauer, E., Kramer, A.D.I.: Gestures over video streams to support remote collaboration on physical tasks. Hum. Comput. Interact. **19**(3), 273–309 (2004)
7. Gauglitz, S., Nuernberger, B., Turk, M., Höllerer, T.: World-stabilized annotations and virtual scene navigation for remote collaboration. In: Proceedings of the 27th Annual ACM Symposium on User Interface Software and Technology, UIST 2014, pp. 449–459. ACM, New York (2014)
8. Kim, S., Billinghurst, M., Lee, G.: The effect of collaboration styles and view independence on video-mediated remote collaboration. Comput. Supported Coop. Work **27**(3-6), 569–607 (2018)
9. Kirk, D., Stanton Fraser, D.: Comparing remote gesture technologies for supporting collaborative physical tasks. In: Proceedings of the SIGCHI Conference on Human Factors in Computing Systems, CHI 2006, pp. 1191–1200. ACM, New York (2006)
10. Kuzuoka, H., Oyama, S., Yamazaki, K., Yamazaki, A., Mitsuishi, M., Suzuki, K.: GestureMan: a mobile robot that embodies a remote instructor's actions (video presentation). In: Proceedings of the 2000 ACM Conference on Computer Supported Cooperative Work, CSCW 2000, p. 354. ACM, New York (2000)
11. Lanir, J., Stone, R., Cohen, B., Gurevich, P.: Ownership and control of point of view in remote assistance. In: Proceedings of the SIGCHI Conference on Human Factors in Computing Systems, CHI 2013, pp. 2243–2252. ACM, New York (2013)
12. Lee, G.A., Teo, T., Kim, S., Billinghurst, M.: Sharedsphere: MR collaboration through shared live panorama. In: SIGGRAPH Asia 2017 Emerging Technologies on - SA 2017, pp. 1–2. ACM Press, Bangkok (2017)
13. Nuernberger, B., Lien, K., Höllerer, T., Turk, M.: Interpreting 2d gesture annotations in 3d augmented reality. In: 2016 IEEE Symposium on 3D User Interfaces (3DUI), pp. 149–158, March 2016
14. Speicher, M., Cao, J., Yu, A., Zhang, H., Nebeling, M.: 360anywhere: mobile Ad-hoc collaboration in any environment using 360 video and augmented reality. Proc. ACM Hum. Comput. Interact. **2**(EICS), 1–20 (2018)
15. Stiemerling, O., Cremers, A.B.: Tailorable component architectures for CSCW-systems. In: Proceedings of the Sixth Euromicro Workshop on Parallel and Distributed Processing, PDP 1998, pp. 302–308, January 1998
16. von Hippel, E., Katz, R.: Shifting innovation to users via toolkits. Manage. Sci. **48**(7), 821–833 (2002)

Vision-Based Indoor Positioning (VBIP) - An Indoor AR Navigation System with a Virtual Tour Guide

Hung-Ya Tsai[1(✉)], Yamato Kuwahara[2], Yuya Ieiri[2], and Reiko Hishiyama[1,2]

[1] OSENSE Technology Co., Ltd., Taipei City, Taiwan
hungyatsai@osensetech.com
[2] Graduate School of Creative Science and Engineering, Waseda University,
3-4-1, Okubo, Shinjuku-ku, Tokyo 169-8555, Japan
kuwayama08@akane.waseda.jp, ieyuharu@ruri.waseda.jp, reiko@waseda.jp
http://www.osensetech.com/

Abstract. In this paper, we describe the structure of a Vision-Based Indoor Positioning (VBIP) system which is a pure software solution without any hardware deployment. We conducted an experiment by providing our VBIP system to navigate visitors through three different buildings with a total length over 350 m during Science and Technology Festival 2018 at Waseda University. This large scale experiment pointed out our incomprehensive thinking while designing the algorithm only based on human behavior, and motivated us to remodify our algorithm based on natural features in the environment. We further conducted another experiment and found out that our VBIP system is improved. VBIP system can now reduce the drift error of VIO (Visual Inertial Odometry) to around 1.4% for over 350 m tracking. For the experiment result, we believe that VBIP is one step closer to perfection.

Keywords: Indoor navigation · Computer vision · Augmented Reality

1 Introduction

1.1 Indoor Navigation System

Information regarding to the user position has always been a sensitive but extremely valuable data. This information is widely used in real life application with broadcasting, advertising, recommending, and navigation. If people get lost in an unfamiliar area, they would open a Google map or any other map to localize themselves and find the destination. However, that only works in outdoor but fails in indoor environment since GPS would be seriously affected by shelters and high buildings. Hence, an indoor positioning and navigation system has been a research focus for decades, however, since its complexity, there is no perfect solution yet. Researchers from a wide variety of fields came up with different algorithms trying to solve this problem such like triangulation [1], angle

© Springer Nature Switzerland AG 2019
H. Nakanishi et al. (Eds.): CRIWG+CollabTech 2019, LNCS 11677, pp. 96–109, 2019.
https://doi.org/10.1007/978-3-030-28011-6_7

of arrival (AOA) [2], time of flight (TOF) [3]. Most current methods are based on signals including WiFi [2], beacon [4], RFID [5], therefore require hardware deployment. There are few disadvantages of these hardware-dependent system, for example, they need a huge amount of construction time and cost without any guarantee of the accuracy; they also requires significant maintenance costs since the hardware consumes electricity and needs to replace the battery once in a while. We are fully aware of these shortcomings, hence, we aim to provide a pure software algorithm to solve the indoor localization and navigation problem.

1.2 Augmented Reality

When discussing about a navigation system, people are used to 2D navigation mode. However, we believe there should be a more intuitive way like a virtual tour guide who will always walk in front of you and show you the way. With the upgrade of hardware devices and algorithm improvement, 3D rendering, 3D reconstruction, Visual Inertial Odometry (VIO), camera pose estimation and other heavy computing algorithms now can be calculated real-time on mobile, hence, Augmented Reality (AR) raises lots of interests in research and business domain. Google recently launched a trial regarding to an AR outdoor navigation system which shows the direction arrow, name of the street and the distance in AR, see Fig. 1.

Fig. 1. An AR outdoor navigation system provided by Google.

From our perspective, it proves that our vision of providing an AR indoor navigation system is reasonable, besides that, we further proposed an AR virtual tour guide guiding system to replace the traditional ones with direction arrows. In our other paper, we also proved that the AR virtual tour guide is more intuitive and useful than the original method by conducting a questionnaire after the experiment.

1.3   VBIP

To get rid of hardware dependency, we proposed a pure software based algorithm called VBIP. VBIP, a Vision-Based Indoor Positioning System aims to provide a cross platform, easy-to-use and high-accuracy AR indoor navigation system only with existing features such like visual information and magnetic field. We have achieved a large scale experiment of VBIP at Waseda University during Science and Technology Festival 2018, however, we discovered few problems after the Festival, hence, we modified our algorithms and corrected the calibration model with reasonable methods and gained better experiment results. Our main contribution is that we provided and proved an AR indoor navigation system could actually be used in real cases. In the following paragraphs, we will introduce our VBIP system and show experiment results in this paper.

2   Related Work

2.1   Other Indoor Navigation System

As we mentioned above, people from different fields proposed different methods trying to solve the indoor localization problem. Silke et al. [6] proposed a Bluetooth-based positioning system by approximating the relation between RSSI (Radio Signal Strength Indicator) and associated distance. Frederic and Francois proposed an advanced integration of WiFi and inertial sensors based on a kalman filter and a particle filter to do localization [7]. Yung-Hoon et al. proposed a ray tracing method to reduce the ranging error resulting from the propagation delay and enhance the accuracy of ultra-wideband positioning system [8]. Bekkali et al. proposed a RFID indoor positioning technology based on probabilistic RFID Map and a kalman filter [5]. Even that there are lots of scientists who have dedicated their lives in designing a perfect indoor navigation system, however, there is no perfect solution yet due to the low accuracy.

2.2   VIO

Visual Inertial Odometry (VIO) is widely used in robotic field to estimate a robot location. It requires a sequence of images, and with feature comparison, one can estimate camera motion and generate a coordinate system by analyzing the changes of feature position and inertial measurement units between different images. VIO algorithm conducted in VBIP is based on keyframes and a non-linear optimization as addressed in [9]. Since VIO is an estimated function, it accumulates errors over time. Although scientists proposed different methods such as an EKF-based approach in [10,11] or an extended kalman filter based algorithm [12] trying to reduce the accumulated error, however, the drift error still remains. In our VBIP system, VIO is considered as an extremely important part during both construction and adoption processes, however, in this paper we would not discuss on how to improve VIO but will focus on describing our whole system structure and flow.

3   VBIP System

VBIP is divided into two parts, the first part is constructing an indoor map, and the second part is using the preconstructed map. Our challenge in this event is to provide an AR indoor navigation and guiding system for visitors to know more about Waseda University. VBIP would lead visitors to three specified spots in three different buildings with a total path length over 350 m. Besides that, the experimental environments contain different floors, multiple stairs, doors, overpasses, slopes and numerous people. We believe this experimental environments match the real-world cases, and provide VBIP a solid validation.

3.1   VBIP Construction

There are multiple ways to construct a VBIP indoor map, and each holds different strengths. The professional version may require a 360° camera and a floor plan of the building which will take more time to construct but can provide extra functions and better accuracy. However, due to lack of time and a floor plan, we adopted the easiest and fastest way to construct a VBIP map by using only one smart phone.

The VBIP map construction is simple, we use Visual inertial odometry (VIO) to generate a virtual coordinate system corresponding to the real world coordinate system, meanwhile capture visual features and collect magnetic field simultaneously. Figure 2 shows a screenshot while constructing the VBIP map.

Fig. 2. A screenshot of VBIP construction. The bottom right corner is the created path.

Visual features captured during the construction process would be stored as a sparse point cloud, we recorded each feature with its 3D coordinate (X, Y, Z), color (R, G, B) and a RETOP [13] descriptor which stores the patch information around the feature and would be further used for cross comparison. Due to the copyright issues, we cannot show the point cloud of Waseda University, therefore we show the point cloud of OSENSE Technology instead in Fig. 3. Magnetic field collected during the process would be stored with its coordinate (X, Y, Z) and magnetic intensities (Bx, By, Bz) for fast localization.

Fig. 3. Left image shows the sparse point cloud of OSENSE Technology. Right image shows the corresponding location.

3.2   VBIP Adoption

VBIP adoption can be divided into two states, the localization state and the tracking state. During the localization state, VBIP proposed a two cascaded search algorithm shown in Fig. 4 to fast localize user position and a hybrid tracking algorithm to improve positioning accuracy. However, during the Science and Technology Festival 2018, this proposed algorithm was still under development. Therefore, in our first experiment, we used QR codes instead to fast localize user position. Afterward, we modified our VBIP system by replacing QR code to this proposed two cascaded search, and further implemented a second experiment to see if VBIP system was improved.

In the first cascade, we aim to narrow down the potential user position into a smaller area. It is easier to do that with signal based technology. Signal has its own transmission distance, hence, by analyzing the receiving signal and signal source position, one can obtain a smaller area where user might have high possibility locate. However, VBIP does not rely on any hardware or signal, therefore we proposed using magnetic intensities and a particle filter to roughly localize user position. Particle filter is a pose estimation methodology which uses a bunch of particles and a probability model to update particle positions, with the number of updates, particles will finally converge. Since our probability model is a modified Gaussian distribution which 68% of values will distribute within one standard deviation (σ) away from the mean. Hence, when 68% of the number of particles converge within one standard deviation, we complete the first cascade search. The system flow of this cascade search is shown in Fig. 5.

Fig. 4. A real case of proposed two cascaded search algorithm.

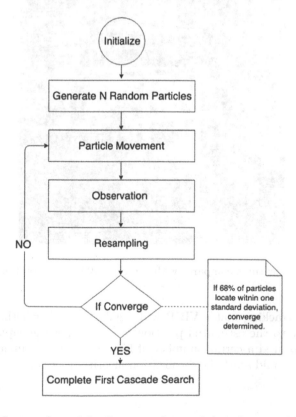

Fig. 5. System flow of the first cascade search based on particle filter.

In the second cascade search, VBIP would extract RETOP descriptors from point clouds within one standard deviation, and further compare with RETOP descriptors captured from current frame. Afterward, VBIP extracts 3D coordinates (X, Y, Z) in world coordinate space from each reference match and 2D coordinates (U, V) of the projection points in pixels from current captured frame. With 3D and 2D information, VBIP can further calculate camera pose by using PnP algorithm. At this point, we complete the second cascade search and successfully localize user position with better accuracy. The details of 3D point cloud comparison and 3D pose estimation will be addressed in details in the following paragraph, the feature comparing result is shown in Fig. 6.

Fig. 6. Current features compares with prestored 3D point cloud in VBIP map.

During the tracking state, VBIP will regularly check whether the tracked position is close to the estimated position by comparing the captured features. Once VBIP captured a certain number of features that lies outside the tracked position, VBIP would start the localization algorithm again.

4   First Experiment Conducted During Science and Technology Festival 2018 at Waseda University

In this experiment, OSENSE Technology designed an application with our VBIP AR indoor navigation system and an interaction game for visitors to know more about Waseda University. Visitors should follow an AR Waseda Bear to three specific spots in three different buildings, once visitors approach the destination, and there will be an AR coin. Collect coins at each destination and answer pop out questions in regards to Waseda University to complete the game. Once the QR code was scanned, an AR Waseda Bear will lead your route and direction by walking on the real path like a virtual tour guide. The AR Waseda Bear will stop at each anchor position on real environment and wait for you, once you come closer enough, the AR Waseda Bear will move to the next anchor position and repeat these actions until you reach your destination as shown in Fig. 7. In general, we could simply adopt VIO on smart phone to reproduce the prebuilt path for the AR Waseda Bear to follow. However, VIO is an estimation methodology with estimation error (drift error), and the error will accumulate over time and vary from time to time. Therefore, achieving a navigation system only by VIO seems impossible, especially for a large scale environment as Waseda University.

Fig. 7. The left image is the AR Waseda Bear waiting for you. The right image is the AR Waseda Bear moving to the next anchor.

Before the event, we conducted several internal tests and found out that there are two main problems we need to solve in order to provide a use worthy AR tour guide navigation system. The most significant problem is rotation drift. The rotation drift problem influences the whole coordinate system and would be the key to success of this AR navigation. The average of the rotation error is under 5°, and a 5° rotation error seems negligible in a short-range path. However, since our path is larger than 100 m, it would cause approximately 10 m error. The other one is scale drift problem. The scale drift problem is particularly noticeable while turning since AR has no sense of actual environment. If the estimated path is shorter than the actual path, the AR Waseda Bear would turn earlier and walk into the wall.

In order to reduce the impact of these problems mentioned above, we proposed a nearest point algorithm based on human behavior. Generally speaking, if there is no rotation drift, the Waseda Bear will stop at real field where users can step on, hence the nearest point would be almost the same as the anchor point, and there will be no modification to the original route. However, if there are some estimation errors that cause the AR Waseda Bear to go outside the actual path, for example, into the wall or outside the bridge, VBIP system would find the nearest point to the drifted anchor. By analyzing each nearest point and anchor point, VBIP system would be able to adjust the drifted route to the actual environment.

After implementing this adjustment algorithm, one can finally follow the AR Waseda Bear to complete the journey and reach its destination. After achieving this goal, we launched our first experiment during Science and Technology Festival 2018. The experiment route and best tester result is shown in Fig. 8.

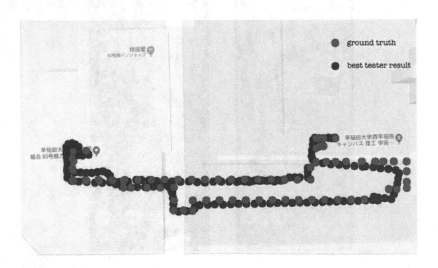

Fig. 8. The navigation ground truth path and the best tester result.

Based on the experimental results in Figs. 9 and 10, we found out that only around 20% of visitors can complete a route with a total length more than 350 m and reach the destination, on the other hand, most of other visitors were lost after hundreds of meters. After analyzing all the data, we summarized several reasons. The most important factors is that there were many people during the festival, so for VIO, the interference noise is serious which directly leads to drift error larger than our internal trials. Besides that, this experiment also pointed out flaws in our nearest point algorithm which is that in a navigation system, the modification of the guidance route should not rely on the user's behavior, but should rely on the facts of the environment. Based on this realization, we further proposed an algorithm that is independent of user behavior but is completely related to the visual features of the environment, and conducted another experiment afterward.

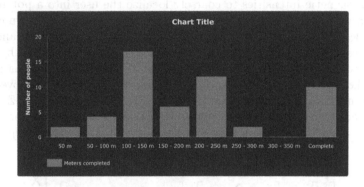

Fig. 9. The experiment result of meter completed by visitors.

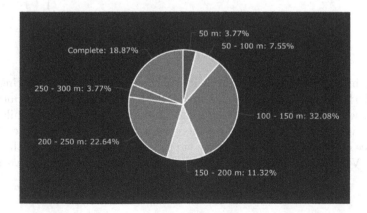

Fig. 10. The experiment result of meter completed by visitors.

5   VBIP System Modification

In order to provide a use worthy AR indoor navigation system, we proposed an intuitive and reasonable hypothesis. We believe that with 3D point cloud comparison and feature coordinate calculation, we will be able to estimate the current user position and eliminate the drift error. However, 3D point cloud comparison is extremely complicated and requires a lot of computing power and a lot of computation time, especially for a large scale environment containing millions of feature points such as Waseda University. Since it is impossible to compare each point at one time, we proposed a two cascaded search mentioned above to fast localize user location. In the first cascade search, we use a particle filter and magnetic intensities to coarsely localize the user into a potential circle with a radius around 5 to 10 m. In the second cascade search, we compare RETOP descriptors of all the points cloud inside the potential circle and uses a Brute-Force matcher to find raw matches. We further refine matches by removing outliers with more than 10% of error. Since RETOP descriptor has 128 bits, raw matches with hamming distance larger than 13 bits will be removed. Once the refine matches are found, we retrieve the 3D coordinate (X, Y, Z) of each reference point and its projection point (U, V). With a known camera matrix, we could calculate the camera pose and heading by the formula in Fig. 11.

$$
s \begin{bmatrix} u \\ v \\ 1 \end{bmatrix} = \begin{bmatrix} f_x & 0 & c_x \\ 0 & f_y & c_y \\ 0 & 0 & 1 \end{bmatrix} \begin{bmatrix} r_{11} & r_{12} & r_{13} & t_1 \\ r_{21} & r_{22} & r_{23} & t_2 \\ r_{31} & r_{32} & r_{33} & t_3 \end{bmatrix} \begin{bmatrix} X \\ Y \\ Z \\ 1 \end{bmatrix}
$$

Fig. 11. A formula for 3D camera pose estimation.

Even this proposed method works, it still consumes a lot of computing power. In order to fast localize user position during the localization state, it is inevitable. However, we believe a cross check should be done only once in a while during the tracking state. In this case, we increase a background thread to do cross check once every 5 s. When the system captured features lies outside the tracked position, VBIP would calibrate the route and remove the cumulative error of VIO.

6   Second Experiment Conducted After VBIP System Optimization

Experiment Result [Experiment 2]

According to the second experiment in Figs. 12, 13 and 14, we found out that almost 80% of the users can now complete the route. The average destination drift of successful visitors is less than 5 m which is only around 1% of the total length (5/350). These experiment results shows our modified algorithm has been greatly improved. However, there are still a few problems remaining, the most influential problem is the 5 second interval. In most of the cases, users would not stray from the right path too much, hence the system could match the same features and calibrate the route. However, in a few cases, users might step on a new path with different visual features, in that case the system could not find matches and the system failed. One solution is to shorten the interval and do cross check frequently, however, it will soon make the phone overheat. In our further research, we will focus on finding a dynamic interval to balance the two factors and maximize the benefits.

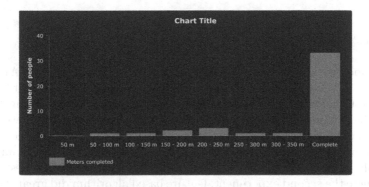

Fig. 12. The experiment result of meter completed by visitors.

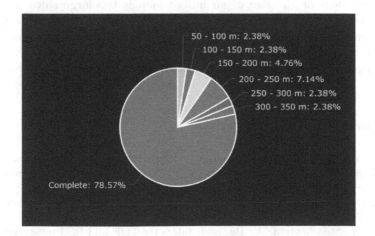

Fig. 13. The experiment result of meter completed by visitors.

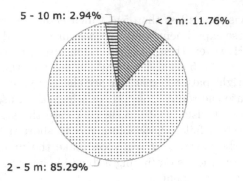

Fig. 14. The experiment result of destination drift by successful visitors.

7 Conclusion

In this paper, we conducted experiments in regards to a large scale AR indoor navigation at Waseda University during Science and Technology Festival 2018. The biggest challenge is to eliminate the drift error in VIO tracking for over 350 m. The first proposed algorithm is based on human behavior, however, due to the diversity of user behaviors, the effect has not improved significantly but rather raised more issues. The second proposed algorithm is more intuitive and reasonable by comparing the visual features and doing a 3D pose estimation. According to the second experiment, feature based algorithm did greatly increase the success rate by around 4 times hence proved our proposed algorithm works. However, there are still a few problems remaining such as the smart phone overheat problem or the size of an indoor map is too large since it contains a great amount of 3D point clouds. Our future work will focus on solving the overheat problem by proposing a dynamic model to determine the time interval between each cross check.

The demo video of VBIP conducted at Waseda University can be found here [14].

References

1. Wang, Y., Yang, X., Zhao, Y., Liu, Y., Cuthbert, L.: Bluetooth positioning using RSSI and triangulation methods. In 2013 IEEE 10th Consumer Communications and Networking Conference (CCNC), pp. 837–842. IEEE (2013)
2. Yang, C., Shao, H.-R.: Wifi-based indoor positioning. IEEE Commun. Mag. **53**(3), 150–157 (2015)
3. Galov, A., Moschevikin, A.: Bayesian filters for TOF and RSS measurements for indoor positioning of a mobile object. In: International Conference on Indoor Positioning and Indoor Navigation, pp. 1–8. IEEE (2013)
4. Kuo, Y.-S., Pannuto, P., Hsiao, K.-J., Dutta, P.: Luxapose: indoor positioning with mobile phones and visible light. In: Proceedings of the 20th Annual International Conference on Mobile Computing and Networking, pp. 447–458. ACM (2014)

5. Bekkali, A., Sanson, H., Matsumoto, M.: RFID indoor positioning based on probabilistic RFID map and Kalman filtering. In: Third IEEE International Conference on Wireless and Mobile Computing, Networking and Communications (WiMob 2007), p. 21. IEEE (2007)
6. Feldmann, S., Kyamakya, K., Zapater, A., Lue, Z.: An indoor Bluetooth-based positioning system: concept, implementation and experimental evaluation, vol. 272 (2003)
7. Evennou, F., Marx, F.: Advanced integration of wifi and inertial navigation systems for indoor mobile positioning. Eurasip J. Appl. Signal Process. **164–164**, 2006 (2006)
8. Jo, Y.-H., Lee, J.-Y., Ha, D.-H., Kang, S.-H.: Accuracy enhancement for UWB indoor positioning using ray tracing. In: 2006 IEEE/ION Position, Location, and Navigation Symposium, pp. 565–568. IEEE (2006)
9. Leutenegger, S., Lynen, S., Bosse, M., Siegwart, R., Furgale, P.: Keyframe-based visual-inertial odometry using nonlinear optimization. Int. J. Robot. Res. **34**(3), 314–334 (2015)
10. Li, M., Mourikis, A.I.: High-precision, consistent EKF-based visual-inertial odometry. Int. J. Robot. Res. **32**(6), 690–711 (2013)
11. Bloesch, M., Omari, S., Hutter, M., Siegwart, R.: Robust visual inertial odometry using a direct EKF-based approach. In: 2015 IEEE/RSJ International Conference on Intelligent Robots and Systems (IROS), pp. 298–304. IEEE (2015)
12. Bloesch, M., Burri, M., Omari, S., Hutter, M., Siegwart, R.: Iterated extended Kalman filter based visual-inertial odometry using direct photometric feedback. Int. J. Robot. Res. **36**(10), 1053–1072 (2017)
13. Huang, J.-Y., Tsai, H.-Y., Tsai, C.-H.: RETOP: a retinal topography keypoint descriptor. In: 2016 IEEE/ACIS 15th International Conference on Computer and Information Science (ICIS), pp. 1–6. IEEE (2016)
14. Tsai, H.-Y.: An large scale indoor navigation demo conducted at Wased University (2018). https://osensetech.blob.core.windows.net/waseda/WasedaDemo.MP4

Developing Hyper-stories in the Context of Cultural Heritage Appreciation

Nelson Baloian[2(✉)], Gustavo Zurita[1], José A. Pino[2], Sergio Peñafiel[2], and Wolfram Luther[3]

[1] Department of Information Systems and Management Control,
Faculty of Economics and Business, Universidad de Chile,
Diagonal Paraguay 257, Santiago, Chile
gzurita@fen.uchile.cl

[2] Department of Computer Science, Universidad de Chile,
Beaucheff 851, Santiago, Chile
{nbaloian,jpino,spenafie}@dcc.uchile.cl

[3] University of Duisburg-Essen, Duisburg, Germany
wolfram.luther@uni-due.de

Abstract. Storytelling has been used as a powerful methodology to design learning activities. By producing their own stories, students learn while developing artifacts, which can be shared with other peer learners generating a rich collaborative learning environment based on constructivism. Digital media and especially hypermedia have been successfully used to support storytelling in learning contexts since it eases the collaborative authoring process and allows for the creation of stories with parallel threads and multiple versions, supporting various viewpoints of the same story. Inspired by the context of learning the cultural heritage of the Armenian cross-stones or Khachkars, we developed a tool in which students can create their own hyper-stories to discuss their different aspects. The tool reflects the inherent attachment of the Khachkars to a geographical location by offering a map on which learners can present the location of the stones. We conducted a preliminary test for answers to our research objectives on the effectiveness of a tool that raises the interest and knowledge of the users in cultural heritage objects, which are located in open-air settings. We also address the tool's usability when using a mobile interface. The results indicate that there is a slight increase in the interest and knowledge of users in objects associated with cultural and historical heritage. The usability of the tool over mobile interfaces was acceptable, although it is necessary to improve certain functionalities.

Keywords: Mobile learning · Hyper-storytelling · Collaboration · Cultural heritage

1 Introduction

Tangible cultural heritage (ruins, ancient churches, vestiges of certain original cultures, etc.) are scattered along various geographical places around the world. Most of them remain in physical locations where they were originally created and have not been

© Springer Nature Switzerland AG 2019
H. Nakanishi et al. (Eds.): CRIWG+CollabTech 2019, LNCS 11677, pp. 110–128, 2019.
https://doi.org/10.1007/978-3-030-28011-6_8

moved to museums for various reasons. Some are impossible or very difficult to transport. There lacks systematic efforts to "discover" and classify them, in addition to a lack of knowledge of their existence. In some cases, only those who live within close proximity to the place know of them. In many cases, the geographical context is important so as to give meaning to the information and knowledge of the historical facts associated with these patrimonies.

Since these heritage sites cannot be taken to museums, a computational tool that is able to take the museum to the geographical places where they are located would contribute to learning more about these places. Our proposed method uses hyper storytelling to make collaborative descriptions of these places, where any person interested in contributing with can generate a unique story, interpret it from various points of view and offer multiple stories that account for a more realistic and vivid way. The developed computational tool will be used to collaboratively describe places of cultural heritage value, as done in similar scenarios applied in other contexts of storytelling activities, [1–4].

The heritage sites around which stories can be built correspond to archaeological sites and the objects they contain. For example, in the archaeological site of Noratus, Armenia, there are patrimonial objects called Khachkars. In Tiahuanaco, Bolivia, there are archaeological vestiges of vessels or containers scattered in the area that have not been registered yet nor classified, and little or nothing is known about them. Videos, photos (from the internet or taken in the same place), links to web pages with complementary information, virtual 3D representations of objects (virtual museums), and georeferentiations of the places where they are located may be used to describe patrimonial objects.

Authors in [5, 6] identified what is known as the problem of "getting lost in hyperspace", which is basically the user's difficulty in building a map or a systematic representation of the structure of the hypertext program and, by extension, the structure of the information it contains. Our approach includes the georeferentiation over maps as a central scaffold that addresses the sense of being lost in a spatial context in a map while creating connections between sites with spatial location.

Several tools for supporting storytelling activities for learning have been developed in the past for students of basic and middle school [1, 7–10]. Most of them implement linear stories, instead of non-linear narratives (hyper-stories) [9, 11], for example, European history for children [9], Australian history [3], natural history of America in Chicago and New York [5]; or for increasing the intercultural awareness in higher education [12]. Narratives can also be used within the design of new technologies to support lifelong learning in a cultural setting [4]. Mulholland and Collins [4] present a tool which comes close to the idea presented in this work which is a media integrated storytelling platform for non-linear digital storytelling, which can be used as a cultural heritage learning platform. However, the authors only consider the descriptions, and not the location factors.

We would like to study whether making hyper-stories raises people's knowledge and interest in heritage and culture. We therefore conducted a preliminary test to obtain first answers to two main research objectives: (1) the effectiveness of the developed tool to raise the interest and knowledge of the users in cultural heritage objects, which are located in open air settings, and (2) the usability of the tool, especially when using a mobile interface.

Users participating in the test were purposely recruited from an engineering Masters degree program. This circumvents a positive bias towards topics of cultural heritage, as would have been the case if we had recruited students from the Humanities. During the test, we focused on users who build hyper-stories "in-situ" by using mobile devices; although thereafter, other users could use the hyper-stories for learning purposes. We consider building hyper-stories as the first step and therefore the most important one.

2 Hyper Storytelling as a Support of Cultural Heritage

Digital storytelling is a powerful teaching tool in the cultural and educational field [13–15], which facilitates the presentation of ideas, communication or knowledge transmission, through the integration and organization of multimedia resources on technological platforms of various kinds, including Web 2.0 tools [2, 3]. Digital storytelling takes advantage of the contributions of content generated by students, through a simple procedure consisting of selecting a topic, performing research on it, writing a script, and developing a story with multiple purposes: descriptive, informative, creative, etc. [13].

The construction and elaboration of stories generates attractive scenarios for learning, in which each student adopts the role of a multimedia content producer [14]. This entails applying the narrative, descriptive and creative capacity of the authors and taking the design of an initial script or storyboard as a starting point. It also implies the development of digital narratives that promote new forms of writing and interpretation of multimedia messages, thus training specific digital skills needed to interact in a technological environment, known as digital literacy of the 21st century [15, 16].

Web 2.0 allows for the development of collaborative spaces that enable users to produce information pills, digital stories and all kinds of stories that can be shared with each other through various social network platforms, using narrative formulas and simple technological tools capable of integrating multimedia resources with great expressiveness and communicative value. From a technical point of view, digital stories are constructed using hypermedia language, which can lead to complex stories, thus requiring careful elaboration of a literary and technical script that integrates the optionality and alternatives that hypertext allows. Increasingly, educational units at elementary, middle school, college and graduate levels, use activities focused on the construction of stories from this perspective, given their characteristics and educational potential, obtaining interesting results [10].

There exists a classification of the most relevant approaches for managing digital storytelling processes in the literature [14, 16], as presented below.

(a) Linear vs. non-linear storytelling types are differentiated based on action sequences of media occurring in the story. Non-linearity enables storytellers to tell more complex stories with different storylines within the same story [5, 9, 11], i.e. Hyper Storytelling. Different points of view on individual media could affect the normal flow of a story. Non-linear stories may be told in several versions with various content sequences [10]. The interactive storytelling process enables storytellers as well as story listeners to make their own decisions actively to determine the subsequent course of the storyline. Dynamic narratives are created by which users can interact at each part.

(b) Collaborative/social storytelling processes can assist in designing the active experience. In particular reference is made to typical web 2.0 environments for narration to define and design multimedia pathways using social features (annotation, collaborative writing, video-sharing, etc.) enabling a continuous improvement of the narrative structure [2].

(c) Mobile/ubiquitous storytelling takes place in a physical environment where the digital natives actually move around and interact with digital content as well as with others using mobile devices and communication technologies. Mobile storytelling is considered a part of the transmedia storytelling, the process where key elements of narration are spread out from various devices like smartphones, tablets, etc. [17].

3   Tool Design Requirements

Based on the previous discussion, we present the requirements for the tool that can support the construction of hyper-stories based on georeferenced archeological artifacts. We exemplify the requirements by a hyper-story constructed around the topic of Khachkars (Armenian cross stones).

R1. Archeological artifacts or sites are the bases for the building blocks of the hyper-stories. Users build a story by adding descriptions, comments, multimedia material, including their 3D representation in a virtual environment and links to other building blocks. To make an association with a film telling a story we call each building block a "scene" of the hyper-story, which has a scenario (the 3D environment) and a (geographic) location where it develops. In our example the core of a scene might be a single or a group of Khachkars.

R2. Each scene should be georeferenced in the place where the artifacts are currently located or where they were originally found. The georeferencing of the archeological objects can be done while the users are at the same place, using mobile computing devices with positioning capabilities, or it can be done remotely on a desktop computer. In our example the scenes were georeferenced at the place where the Khatchkars were originally found.

R3. Archeological artifacts or sites within a scene should have a digital multimedia representation (pictures, videos, animations, etc.) and a 3D model with metadata, which describes them. In our example there is a virtual 3D model of the stone and metadata describing important information like the year of creation, the sculptor who carved it, important ornamental elements it contains, etc.

R4. Descriptions of the objects and archaeological sites will be carried out collaboratively among the participants. Collaborative work can develop synchronously, as well as asynchronously. The use of tags and colors will allow sorting, classifying and grouping the described historical objects and places.

R5. Each scene may have zero or many links to other scenes, which are related to it and may continue the topic or introduce a new hyper-story. This requirement is stated in order to implement a hyper-story with multiple scenes. A link may be labeled with a text in order to describe the relation between the two scenes it connects. Links might be one or bi-directional.

R6. Provide visual support for traversing the multiple linear stories within the hyper-story, through the use of a graph that will show its nodes corresponding to the scenes georeferenced in the map, and where the edges are labeled according to the relationship that the user determines that exists between two nodes. The visual support to go through the hyper-stories will allow the users to specify the interrelations between the scenes. The nodes linkage generates semantics. Examples of this semantics are: sequences of routes, hierarchical ordering, and scenes grouped under specific criteria. The scenes grouping can be achieved by the combined use of colors and links

Regarding **R6**, the interrelations between nodes can generate different semantics associated with each georeferenced scene/node, where each of its combinations can correspond to a story within the hyper-story. The basic semantics associated with the stories that can be generated on the basis of a hyper-story scheme of Fig. 1, can help the user's understanding of the associated semantics. These are:

(a) The first basic relation between scenes (Nodes) is the **arc,** which means after visiting one scene, the ones linked to that should be visited. In Fig. 1, we see that after Node 4, Node 5 should be visited; also, after Node 1.1, Node 1.2 and/or Node 3, AND? Node 2 should be visited. This basic relation may define sets of related scenes according to the paths defined by the links (see section c and d)

(b) The second basic way to relate scenes is specifying a **group of scenes,** which have common characteristics by assigning the same color to them. In Fig. 1 Node 1.2, Node 2 and Node 4 were created with red color, similarly, Node 1 and Node 1.1 in yellow, and 5.1 and Node 5 in green, defining three groups of scenes.

(c) **Ordered traversal** between Node 1 and Node 2: One option would be Node 1, Node 1.1, Node 1.2, and finally Node 2. An alternative path would be Node 1, Node 1.1, and Node 2 - skipping Node 1.2; or Node 1, Node 1.1, Node 1.2, Node 3 and finally Node 2 – (additionally visiting Node 3). Ordered traversal paths emerge when implementing what is known as "depth first" traversing of a graph.

(d) **Hierarchical traversal**: A hierarchical traversing path emerges when implementing a "width first" graph traversal. They are defined by starting from a node (any) and visiting the neighbors (in any order) and then the neighbors of the neighbors recursively. In Fig. 1 we can start from Node 1.2 and then visiting 1.1, 2 and 3 (in any order), after which we can visit 1 and 4, and finally Node 5.1 and then Node 5.

(e) **Labels** on the arc may be used to further refine the ways to relate nodes among them. In Fig. 1 Node 1.2, the link labels relate Node 1, Node 2 and Node 1 among one another. Also, Node 1.2, Node 3, Node 4 and Node 5.1 form another related Node group.

Along with the various ways of implementing interrelations between the nodes, an additional functionality has been added to the graph that allows the user to be shown the possible paths that the links generate between two nodes, without repeating them, and based on the addresses of the edges. To see this functionality, the user must mark two nodes, the start node and the end node, and the implemented functionality will immediately show all possible paths. In this way, a user can go through several possible stories within a hyper-story. For example, in the graph of Fig. 1, if the selected start and end nodes are Node 1 and Node 2 respectively, the possible paths that will be shown to the users corresponding each one to a story would be two, (i) Node 1, Node 1.1, and Node 2; and (ii): Node 1, Node 1.1, Node 1.2, and Node 2.

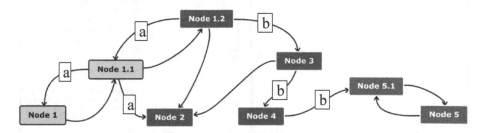

Fig. 1. The graph illustrates the explanation described in the requirement R6, regarding the use of a visual tool to support users in the monitoring of hyper-stories, explaining the different interrelationships and semantics associated with their use. Each Node is associated with a georeferenced scene. (Color figure online)

4 Tool Description

Figures 2 and 3 show some of the main interfaces of the tool. Various sessions can be created where users can contribute.

To implement the **R1** requirement, the tool presents as a central view the world map taken from Google Maps (see the left-hand side view of Fig. 2), on which points, or geometric figures corresponding to archaeological sites are georeferenced for which a description that corresponds to the construction of the story is given, see the right view of Fig. 2. For each georeferencing, users must specify a title, plus the digital artifacts indicated in the **R2** requirement. Each created georeference can be commented on in the description of each georeferencing or in the comments area, which extends the story in a linear and non-linear way; users can add various digital contents specified in the **R3** requirement, such as photos, descriptions that complement the story, links to other web pages (Wikipedia, YouTube, etc.), other related georeferentiations, and virtual 3D representations of objects in virtual Museums. For example, the view on the right of

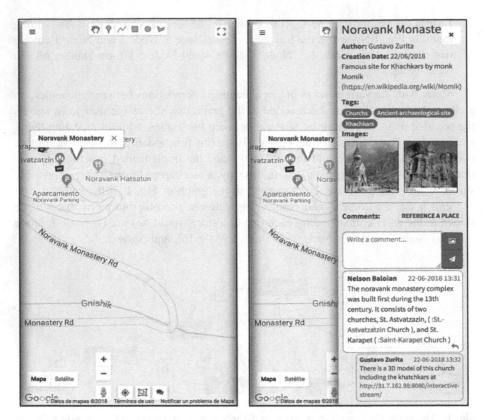

Fig. 2. Screenshots of the tool, seen from the interface of a mobile phone, and showing two different states of the tool, corresponding to one of the sessions in which the students performed the preliminary testing. The screenshot on the left shows the result of having created a new georeferentiation of the site "Noravank Monastery", by using the functions of the buttons that are shown at the top of the interface. The screenshot on the right shows the state in which the interface of the tool changes, after the "Noravank Monastery" site previously created has been chosen. In this last state, the information associated with the site is displayed in a window that overlays the map from the right side of the tool's interface. The information shown corresponds to what was generated and introduced when the site was created: the author of the georeferenced site, the date of creation, its classification labels (Churches, Ancient-archaeological-site and Khachkars), its classification color (blue), links with more information of the site, one or more photos (which can be taken in the same place where the georeference was created or upload remotely). Also, in this state, any user who shares the session can comment on the georeferenced site or read all the comments and their responses that other users have already entered in a collaborative manner. In these comments, it is possible to include links to other georeferenced sites, which allows for the construction of hyper-stories. (Color figure online)

Fig. 3, corresponding to a virtual 3D representation of the church of "St. Astvatzatzin Church" entered by the user "Gustavo Zurita" in the view of Fig. 2 (right).

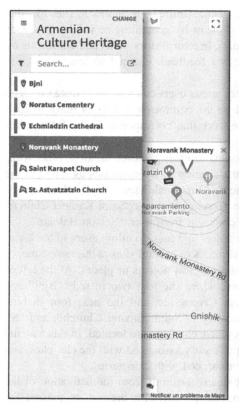 

Fig. 3. The screenshot on the left shows a status of the interface with a list of six previously created archaeological sites, by the users who worked collaboratively in a session entitled "Armenian Culture Heritage". As with the association of labels when a site is georeferenced, the use of colors (associated when the site is created) can also be used to classify them. For this session, the students chose the color red for the first two sites with the purpose of denoting "ancient cemeteries", and the blue color for the following four sites that denote the "ancient churches". This list is displayed in a window that overlaps the map from the left side, by clicking on a button with an icon that contains three lines located in the upper left part of the tool interface. In this state of interface, once you choose one of the sites displayed in the list of the overlaid window, as is the case of "Noravank Monastery" and that is highlighted in blue in the list (whose information is displayed in the state of the interface shown in the screenshot on the right of Fig. 2), it is georeferenced on the map, as seen behind the window on the right side of this interface state. The screenshot on the right shows an activation of another state that shows an interactive 3D view that was associated through a link at the time the site "Noravank Monastery" was georeferenced. (Color figure online)

These hyperlinked extensions can be resources generated by data from the crowd, like Wikipedia or YouTube. In the case of the virtual 3D Khachkar museum, it is a co-curated virtual 3D resource, in which both "the crowd" and Khatchkar experts work together. On the one hand, mobile hyperlinked storytelling helps promote cultural heritage sites by making them part of an interactive story. On the other hand, users who learn about crowd-based 3D museums are potential future contributors to sites like this one, e.g., by taking photographs or scans on-site or by generating or validating sensor metadata for the cultural objects, like GPS data. In return, story paths and comments by mobile users using this tool can be used as a feedback channel to learn about the cultural heritage resource linked therein.

Any user can create a georeferencing, or various users can together create one. The generated stories can be constructed based on the comments that users make to each georeferencing, thus allowing collaborative work that corresponds to the R4 requirement, see Fig. 2 (right).

In the description and comments associated to each georeferentiation, other locations can be georeferenced, which allows the creation of hyper-stories as stated in the R5 requirement; Thus, e.g., the georeferencing "Noravank Monastery", which can be seen in Fig. 2 (right), is associated with the georeferentiations "Saint Karapet Church" and "St. Astvatzatzin Church". Please see comment from user "Nelson Baloian".

Georeferentiations can be organized by colors and tags, to allow users to track and characterize the descriptions of the historical places of several sites at the same time, or to generate multiple stories of the same archaeological objects or places. At the left of Fig. 3, a list of georeferentiations is shown, where the first two in red ("Bjni" and "Noratus Cemetery") correspond to ancient Cemeteries, and the next four in blue ("Echmiadzin Cathedral", "Noravank Monastery", "Saint Kaparet Church", and "St. Astvatzatzin Church") correspond to places where churches are located. In this way the georeferentiations in red allow the building of a story associated with the churches, and the blue ones correspond to another story associated with cemeteries.

Figure 4 shows two views in different states, resulting from the activation of the graph that shows all the scenes of a hyper-story built with the aim to present the museums located at the center of the city of Yerevan. They have been georeferenced on the map using the red color, and with labeled edges that explain the rationale or their associations. These views correspond to the actual work done by three graduate students of the Master program in computer science at the American University of Armenia (see next section for more detailed description of this activity). Figure 4, shows the nodes corresponding to the scenes or nodes of beginning at the "Avetik Isahayakyan House-Museum" and ending at "The Gallery of Mariam and Yeranuhi Aslmazyan Sisters" on the right-hand side of Fig. 4, another more extensive path is depicted, which visits the nodes "Avetik Isahayakyan House-Museum", "Isahakyan Museum", "Hovhannes Shiraz Home and Museum", "Hovhannes Tumanyan Museum", "Silva Kaputikyan House-Museum", and "The Gallery of Mariam and Yeranuhi Aslmazyan Sisters". In the lower part of the view on the right the interface shows the list of all possible trips. In this case, each of these scenes was added and linked in order to advise people while taking a tour of the museums in Yerevan in a convenient order according to their geographic proximity. In another similar session, three other students generated a similar graph, but in that case, students decided to link the museums according to their thematic nature, e.g., by painters, poets or sculptors.

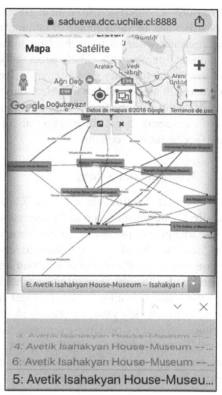

Fig. 4. The screenshot on the left shows a state that displays in the lower half of the interface, the graph that visualizes the links between the stories (or hyper-stories) constructed collaboratively by the students. In this session all the georeferenced sites were associated with the red color, so each node of the graph is displayed in a red rectangle containing the name of the site and connected by black arcs. Specifically, in this graph you can see the selection of a path between the site "Avetik Isahakyan House-Museum" and the site "The Gallery of Mariam and Yeranuhi Aslmazyan" labeled with a prefix "4:" (followed by the list of names of the sites of the chosen route) whose connection arcs are shown in red, and their origin and destination nodes framed with a blue border. The screenshot on the right shows another state of the interface where at the bottom are displayed other possible paths labeled with prefixes corresponding to numbers from "1:" to "5:", which can also be chosen as other routes between the same sites chosen in the screenshot on the left. In this way, a user can choose a route between two sites, choose them in sequence, while they are shown on the map, and in turn open them to access their detailed information, along with the comments built collaboratively. (Color figure online)

5   Preliminary Testing

We conducted a preliminary test to answer our research objectives about the effectiveness of a tool like the one described to raise the interest and knowledge of the users in cultural heritage objects that are located in open-air settings, as well as the usability of the tool, especially when using the mobile interface. Users participating in the test were purposely recruited from an engineering Master degree program in order to avoid a positive bias towards topics of cultural heritage, as would have been the case if we had recruited students from the Humanities. As mentioned in the first section of this document, engineers are clearly better subjects to measure the degree of motivation that the use of the tool can generate, since these students, due to their training, are more interested in aspects of the technical type than the cultural.

Since this was the first testing of the tool by users not involved in its development, we also wanted to get information about the usability of the system to improve its interface in future versions.

5.1 Experimental Setting

We recruited 12 graduate students, 7 male and 5 female, ages 22 to 24 years old, enrolled in the capstone project preparation course in which they learn how to conduct a research project in general. In the frame of this course, this test was a student activity for "learning by doing" on how to conduct an experiment in order to validate hypotheses about the ability of a certain system for fulfilling requirements. The activity started with a 15-min demonstration where the teachers showed how to use the system, and the students composed a small test hyper-story. The teacher then instructed the students to form six groups of two students each and choose a topic related to cultural heritage, giving as possible examples "ancient churches", "modern churches", "museums", "archeological sites", "soviet architecture", "modern architecture" and "monuments". At the end of the session they had to answer a pre-questionnaire (see next subsection for the content).

Fig. 5. A student takes a photograph of the Armenian parliament, which was georeferenced as an example of Soviet architecture.

After this session, the students worked for one week creating the hyper-stories by using the tool in their mobile devices. The students were not told beforehand, which were the research objectives, in order not to bias them.

After the week, the students presented their work to the teacher and the other students explaining what message they wanted to convey with their story. After all groups presented their work, they answered a post-questionnaire, which also included questions for measuring usability. After that they participated in a 30-min focus group.

5.2 Students' Produced Hyper-stories

From the six groups, two chose the Armenian Churches (one with exclusively ancient churches and the other included some new ones), two Monuments and Statues in Yerevan, one example of Soviet Architecture (see Fig. 5), and the last one Galleries and Museums, as their topics for the hyper-story they had to create with the tool, each of them in six different sessions created with the tool.

Table 1 summarizes the main objective characteristics of the created hyper-stories. The table shows a wide range in the value of the parameters considered for this description, which are, apart from the topic itself, the total number of nodes, the number of those which were created while being physically in the place (thus using a mobile device), the number of links, the links semantics, which are the meanings or concepts students used to organize the graph structure with the links and thus the structure of the hyper-story, and the number of photos.

Table 1. Summary of the hyper-stories created by the students according to the number of nodes created (in place and remotely), number of links, links semantic, and number of photos.

Topic	#Nodes remotely	#Nodes in place	#Links	Link semantics	#Photos
Churches, new/old	8	15	29	Hierarchic	60
Statues in Yerevan	2	4	12	A walking tour	20
Statues in Yerevan	5	12	22	A walking tour	34
Soviet architecture	4	8	27	Thematic	10
Galleries & Museums	3	9	18	Thematic	17
Ancient Churches	5	5	8	Location, style, history	13

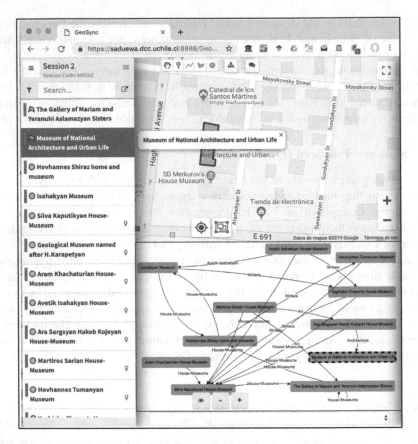

Fig. 6. Screen capture of the interface of the tool executed on a desktop computer, showing the graph of the hyper-story created by a group of students that chose to geo-reference "Galleries and museums", in a session called "Session 2". In the screenshot, a user chose the "Museum of National Architecture and Urban Life" from the list on the left, at the same time that its georeferencing is shown on the map, and its representation in the graph, shown by a represented node by a rectangle with black border of dotted lines. The relationship of this node, with other nodes that correspond to other sites of museums, is denoted through the labeled arcs that leave or enter it. In this graph in particular, the nodes and their arcs between one another, were created to relate museums according to different criteria; that is, this is the basis of the hyper-story constructed. For example, in this screenshot some arcs of the graph associate museums according to their nature; e.g. the type of link semantic is thematic, ("house-museum" means the former house where an artist used to live was converted into a museum after passing away), and others link museums by the type of artists that exhibit their works of art in these museums (mostly writers, one architect and a painter).

Through a review of student hyper-stories we observe various semantics that they associated to the links created among the georeferenced sites. This is not about the label of the link itself, but about how the links were relating to the nodes in general and thus giving a structure to the whole graph (see requirement R6 in Sect. 3). Except for one case, all groups were very consistent in assigning a semantic meaning to the links. For example, Fig. 6 displays the graph for the group that implemented a hyper-story on Galleries & Museums. They related the nodes according to what was the gallery or museum about. Therefore we see that "house-museum" means that it is (also) a house where an artist used to live and was converted to a museum after she passed away. Additionally, there are also links used to relate the nodes by the type of artist, so most of the nodes in the shown part of the graph represent a writer's museum. This means, the "reader" of the hyper-story can traverse it by following a "house-museum" path or a "writers" path.

By contrast, in Fig. 7 the graph shows that nodes are connected hierarchically: There are two nodes representing monastery complexes (Haghbat and Sanahin), as well as single structures belonging to them. The arcs go from the nodes representing single structures to the nodes representing the complex to which they belong.

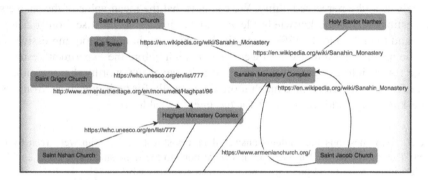

Fig. 7. This figure shows part of the graphic that represents the hyper-history elaborated by the group that georeferenced "Ancient Churches" in a session called "Session 6". The arrows of the arcs were used to indicate the nodes with greater importance; that is, according to the classification of Table 1, the semantics of the links is hierarchical. Specifically, the graph has two central nodes, each representing the complexes of the ancient churches "Haghpat Monastery Complex" and "Sanahin Monastery Complex" to which other arches point, from nodes corresponding to less relevant ancient churches that are part of these complexes.

5.3 Questionnaire Results

To obtain feedback from the students about the perceived utility; i.e., its effectiveness in increasing the interest and knowledge of users in objects associated with cultural heritage found in outdoor environments, we conducted a pre-test and a post-test. Table 2 summarizes the answers of the pre-test. The two questions, "what is your knowledge about the topic?" and "what is your interest on the topic?" are asked to find out if there is any variation before and after performing the activity with the tool, since these are two of the most basic research objectives that we had in mind when conducting the experiment.

Table 2. The table shows the two questions the students answered in a pre-test, and the answer given by each student (labeled with s1 to s12).

	s1	s2	s3	s4	s5	s6	s7	s8	s9	s10	s11	s12	Mean min/max
1 - On a scale from 1 to 10, what would you say is your knowledge about the topic you chose for the experiment?	9	3	5	1	2	4	5	5	6	4	7	9	6.5 1/9
2 - On a scale from 1 to 10, what would you say is your interest on the topic?	10	5	7	4	8	5	7	7	7	5	8	9	7.75 4/10

In the post-test, besides the same two questions of the pre-test, we included three more related to the perceived utility. We can note that the mean value of the answers to the questions about the knowledge level and the interest level rose from 6.5 to 7.6 (17%) and from 7.75 to 8.3 (7%) respectively, which might not be too impressive. This might be because the initial values were already high before the experiment, especially the one for the interest (second) question. It is however noteworthy that the minimum answer for both questions rose much more dramatically for both questions, from 1 to 4 for the knowledge and from 4 to 7 for the interest (Table 3).

Table 3. Two questions the students answered in a post-test, and the answer given by each student. The identification s1 to s12 does not correspond to the same student in Table 2 with the same ID since the post and pre-test were performed anonymously.

	s1	s2	s3	s4	s5	s6	s7	s8	s9	s10	s11	s12	Mean min/max
1 - On a scale from 1 to 10, what would you say is your current knowledge about the topic you chose for the experiment?	9	9	6	7	8	8	6	4	8	9	9	8	7.6 4/9
2 - On a scale from 1 to 10, what would you say is your current interest on the topic?	9	9	8	7	8	9	7	8	8	9	10	7	8.3 7/10
3 - On a scale 1 to 10 please indicate if you enjoyed performing the activity (1 not at all, 10 yes, I fully enjoyed it)	10	6	8	4	6	8	10	10	10	10	10	8	8.4 4/10
4 - On a scale from 1 to 10, what would you say is the ability of developing hyper-stories to raise interest in the topic the hyper-story is about	10	7	7	5	7	6	6	6	4	8	10	7	6.9 4/10
5 - On a scale from 1 to 10, what would you say is the ability of developing hyper-stories to implement an "open air" Museum?	10	7	9	5	5	8	7	5	7	9	9	9	7.5 5/10

For evaluating the usability of the system we applied the System Usability Scale (SUS) test, which has been widely used for more than 30 years as a "quick and dirty" but effective and reliable instrument [18, 19]. This instrument requires a minimum of 12 participants that also matched our sample. The test consists of 10 questions that are answered according to the Likert scale, of which 7 measure the usability and 3 measure how easy it is to learn to use the system. The output of this test is a number between 0 and 100, which does not correspond to a percentage, but is interpreted in the following way:

- 80.3 or higher means a high level of usability.
- Around 70 signifies that the usability of the system is acceptable, but can be improved.
- 51 or under signifies the HCI of the application should be redesigned in depth.

Table 4 shows the outcome of the SUS questionnaire, which indicated that the interface is acceptable, but can be improved.

Table 4. The table shows the answers given by the students for the SUS questionnaire. The value on the Rate column was computed for the odd numbered question by subtracting 1 from the mean values. For the even numbered question, the mean value vas subtracted from 5. The total SUS value was computed by adding all the rates and multiplying this number by 2.5 [18].

		s1	s2	s3	s4	s5	s6	s7	s8	s9	s10	s11	s12	Mean	Rate
1	I think that I would like to use this system frequently	5	3	2	2	3	2	2	2	4	4	4	4	3.1	2.1
2	I found the system unnecessarily complex	1	2	2	2	2	1	3	3	1	1	1	2	1.8	3.2
3	I thought the system was easy to use	5	5	2	2	4	5	2	2	4	4	4	4	3.6	2.6
4	I think that I would need the support of a technical person to be able to use this system	2	1	1	2	1	1	5	4	1	2	5	3	2.3	2.7
5	I found the various functions in this system were well integrated	4	3	2	3	5	2	3	3	3	4	5	5	3.5	2.5
6	I found there was too much inconsistency in this system	1	3	2	3	2	4	4	4	3	2	3	4	2.9	3.1
7	I would imagine that most people would learn to use this system very quickly	5	4	2	3	5	4	5	2	5	5	3	4	3.9	2.9
8	I found the system very cumbersome to use	1	3	2	4	1	3	5	3	2	2	2	1	2.4	2.6
9	I felt very confident using the system	5	3	3	2	5	4	1	3	4	4	5	4	3.6	2.6
10	I needed to learn many things before I could get going with this system	5	1	2	3	1	1	3	2	1	1	1	1	1.8	3.2
	Total SUS														68.75

After the students completed the questionnaires, a brief focus group session was held centered on two simple questions: What are the main positive and negative characteristics of the tool?

Regarding the positive aspects, they mentioned very prominently and almost unanimously that the possibility of linking georeferenced sites differentiates this tool from others that are publicly available. They especially appreciated the "view functionality" resulting from the creation and linking of georeferenced, sites that we are referencing as a graph in this article (see Figs. 6 and 7). The members of the two groups, which developed hyper-stories around monuments in Yerevan, commented that this tool could be effectively used for supporting tourists visiting the city if used in a crowdsourcing modality. This aspect is especially interesting, since it shows that the tool is effective in terms of being used in places where historical or archaeological sites are located, thanks to the mobile devices they used. The above is supported by the results shown in Table 1, where from a total of 80 georeferenced nodes, 66.25% correspond to georeferenced nodes "in place" and 33.75% to remotely georeferenced nodes.

Most negative aspects were related with some bugs that they discovered while using the tool, like photos being cropped or rotated when uploading them, and that they had to first enter Google maps independently of the tool in order to activate the GPS functionality of the tool when using it with mobile devices. They also missed the possibility of editing the content of the nodes after being published in order to complete them or correcting some wrong information. Some students also mentioned the idea of having the possibility of linking nodes with undirected arcs, so that it is possible with just adding one link to go indistinctly from one node to the other. This hints at the fact that the usability could be improved after fixing the bugs.

6   Conclusions

The developed tool allows the museum to be taken to the geographical places where archaeological objects belonging to different cultural patrimonies are located through the hyper-storytelling. It also allows users to create linear and nonlinear historical descriptions in a collaborative way, focused on the location of archeological artifacts.

According to the reviewed literature, there is no other proposal similar to ours in which users based on georeferencing, associated with cultural historical sites, can perform collaborative hyper-stories.

With the proposed tool, one can also describe intangible heritage objects, which are associated with specific historical places. For example, the explanation on why the Khachkars were built with certain characteristics can be described for certain regions of Armenia, although their vestiges are not even present nowadays. By hyper-linking co-curated and virtual 3D resources, the awareness of mobile users about the existence of virtual replicas of intangible objects can be raised and they can get access to these resources.

The results of the preliminary testing to answer the achievement of the two research objectives regarding the tool developed indicate that there is a slight increase in the interest and knowledge of users in objects associated with cultural heritage found in outdoor environments. Regarding this result, it is noteworthy that the users are students of Engineering Sciences, who initially may not have interest in historical and heritage sites as social science students may have. This guess may be confirmed with future inquiry.

Concerning usability of the tool on mobile interfaces, we can say that it was acceptable (68, 75 points over 100). It is necessary to improve certain functionalities, being the most relevant: loading the photos taken "in-situ", and the creation of links between georeferenced nodes directly over the visual view of the graphs.

Furthermore, from our general observation of the preliminary testing, and according to [1], the tool: (a) enhances collaborative storytelling, (b) supports collaborative work and (c) ensures a sense of authorship of the stories in a mobile scenario. These are aspects of future work that we will address with more tests and a variety of final users.

Acknowledgments. This research was funded by support from the Chilean Government through Comisión Nacional de Investigación Científica y Tecnológica–CONICYT and the Fondo Nacional de Desarrollo Científico y Tecnológico–Fondecyt Regular project number 1161200.

References

1. Liu, C.-C., et al.: Collaborative storytelling experiences in social media: influence of peer-assistance mechanisms. Comput. Educ. **57**(2), 1544–1556 (2011)
2. Cao, Y., Klamma, R., Martini, A.: Collaborative storytelling in the web 2.0. In: Proceedings of the First International Workshop on Story-Telling and Educational Games (STEG 2008) at ECTEL. Citeseer (2008)
3. Smeda, N., Dakich, E., Sharda, N.: Digital storytelling with Web 2.0 tools for collaborative learning. In: Collaborative Learning 2.0: Open Educational Resources, pp. 145–163. IGI Global (2012)
4. Mulholland, P., Collins, T.: Using digital narratives to support the collaborative learning and exploration of cultural heritage. In: Proceedings of the 13th International Workshop on Database and Expert Systems Applications, 2002. IEEE (2002)
5. McLellan, H.: Hyper stories: some guidelines for instructional designers. J. Res. Comput. Educ. **25**(1), 28–49 (1992)
6. Conklin, J.: Hypertext: an introduction and SurvevJ. Computer **20**(9), 17–41 (1987)
7. Garzotto, F., Herrero, E., Salgueiro, F.: One tool-many paradigm: creativity and regularity in youngsters' hyperstories. In: Aylett, R., Lim, M.Y., Louchart, S., Petta, P., Riedl, M. (eds.) ICIDS 2010. LNCS, vol. 6432, pp. 44–49. Springer, Heidelberg (2010). https://doi.org/10.1007/978-3-642-16638-9_8
8. Dreon, O., Kerper, R.M., Landis, J.: Digital storytelling: a tool for teaching and learning in the YouTube generation. Middle Sch. J. **42**(5), 4–10 (2011)
9. Garzotto, F., Forfori, M.: Hyperstories and social interaction in 2D and 3D edutainment spaces for children. In: Proceedings of the Seventeenth Conference on Hypertext and Hypermedia. ACM (2006)
10. Soffer, Y., et al.: The effect of different educational interventions on schoolchildren's knowledge of earthquake protective behaviour in Israel. Disasters **34**(1), 205–213 (2010)

11. Spaniol, M., Klamma, R., Sharda, N., Jarke, M.: Web-based learning with non-linear multimedia stories. In: Liu, W., Li, Q., W.H. Lau, R. (eds.) ICWL 2006. LNCS, vol. 4181, pp. 249–263. Springer, Heidelberg (2006). https://doi.org/10.1007/11925293_23
12. PM Ribeiro, S.: Developing intercultural awareness using digital storytelling. Lang. Intercult. Commun. **16**(1), 69–82 (2016)
13. Niemi, H., et al.: Digital storytelling for 21st-century skills in virtual learning environments. Creat. Educ. **5**(9), 657 (2014)
14. Gaeta, M., et al.: A methodology and an authoring tool for creating complex learning objects to support interactive storytelling. Comput. Hum. Behav. **31**, 620–637 (2014)
15. Robin, B.R.: Digital storytelling: a powerful technology tool for the 21st century classroom. Theory Pract. **47**(3), 220–228 (2008)
16. Cao, Y., Klamma, R., Jarke, M.: The hero's journey-template-based storytelling for ubiquitous multimedia management. J. Multimed. **6**(2), 156–169 (2011)
17. Jenkins, H.: Transmedia storytelling and entertainment: an annotated syllabus. Continuum **24**(6), 943–958 (2010)
18. Brooke, J.: SUS-A quick and dirty usability scale. Usability Eval. Ind. **189**(194), 4–7 (1996)
19. Brooke, J.: SUS: a retrospective. J. Usability Stud. **8**(2), 29–40 (2013)

A Method for Automated Detection of Cultural Difference Based on Image Similarity

Mondheera Pituxcoosuvarn[1]([⊠]) [iD], Donghui Lin[1] [iD], and Toru Ishida[2]

[1] Department of Social Informatics, Kyoto University, Kyoto, Japan
mondheera@ai.soc.i.kyoto-u.ac.jp, lindh@i.kyoto-u.ac.jp
[2] School of Creative Science and Engineering, Waseda University, Tokyo, Japan
toru.ishida@aoni.waseda.jp

Abstract. In intercultural collaboration, the lack of a common ground, typically evidenced by language differences, can result in misunderstandings. Many times, team members do not realize that a misunderstanding exists during the collaboration. One solution is to identifying the words that have a high probability of causing misunderstanding. However, it is difficult for people to identify those words, especially for monolingual and monocultural people, as they have never experienced the language and culture of the other party. Many researchers have been trying to identify cultural differences using survey studies but the resulting coverage is limited, requires excessive effort, and can yield bias. In this paper, we propose a novel method that applies an image comparison technique to an image database to automatically detect words that might cause misunderstanding. We test our method on 2,500 words in a Japanese-English concept dictionary called Japanese WordNet. This paper provides explains the results gained. We also discuss the use of the proposal and visualization as a support tool to enhance intercultural workshops.

Keywords: Intercultural collaboration · Multilingual communication · Image similarity

1 Introduction

For organizations, diversity provides vast benefits. Diversity of top management can strongly improve innovativeness and firm performance [15]. Besides top management diversity, racial diversity in the general workforce is also connected to increased sales revenue, more customers, bigger market share, and greater relative profits [6]. From these studies, we can infer that, cultural difference, which is diversity in the cultural backgrounds, is important and beneficial for organizations and teams. It could lead to a broader range of ideas and some of those ideas could lead to promising innovations.

However, language differences and cultural differences are significant issues in intercultural collaboration. Even though diversity has many advantages, it

© Springer Nature Switzerland AG 2019
H. Nakanishi et al. (Eds.): CRIWG+CollabTech 2019, LNCS 11677, pp. 129–143, 2019.
https://doi.org/10.1007/978-3-030-28011-6_9

also raises difficulties in communication. With different cultural and language backgrounds, communication and collaboration become challenging. Nowadays, support tools and services are available for multilingual communication [10]. Machine translation (MT) is now available and helps to offset translation problems when there is no bilingual human or translator around. Various MT embedded chat systems have also been developed to support communication across languages. Unfortunately, MT is not perfect and can cause difficulties in communication, including misunderstanding due to mistranslation, cause conversation breakdown [13], and difficulties in establishing mutual understanding [16], etc. The absence of a common ground can result in misunderstanding, and it might take time for the participants to realize the misunderstanding unless he/she has been deeply engaged in both languages and cultures or knows the team members very well. An attractive solution is extend MT systems such they can identify likely causes of misunderstanding.

Therefore, the purpose of this paper is to propose a baseline method to automatically detect words that could cause misunderstanding when the team members speak different languages. We utilize an image comparison technique to detect these words. Because people with different language background sometimes see things differently [4], images from existing databases can be linked back to the languages and keywords which would allow us to identify the cultural differences. As far as we know, this is the first study to base the automatic detection of cultural differences on image comparison.

The outputs of this method can be used to support intercultural design workshops and MT-mediated communication. Potential cultural differences can then be visualized or the MT system can warn the user that the word used has a high probability of triggering a misunderstanding.

2   Motivation

2.1   Motivating Scenario

Obviously, multilingual communication is more difficult than monolingual communication. The differences in cultural backgrounds can yield even more problems if no common ground exists between the parties. Our previous work [14] reported collaboration difficulties among children during a workshop. Briefly a block of clay was shown to the children and they were asked "what does this looks like". A Japanese participant said it looked like 'red bean paste' but the children from other countries did not understand, since red bean paste in their culture looks different. The problem was solved by finding images of Japanese red bean paste, and showing those images to the other children. In this case, even if MT output was correct, this problem still exists because the team members have different backgrounds. Fortunately, they realized that they did not fully understand each other after a moment, so they could resolve the misunderstanding. Failure to identify misunderstanding rapidly delays the collaboration significantly and might lead to failure. In many cases, people do not realize that there is misunderstanding happening during the conversation, instead they think they understand but, they do not. Our solution is to create a tool that can detect cultural differences and thus possible misunderstandings. The prior study found that the children had different mental images due to their diverse cultural backgrounds, the problem was solved by searching for images in their language and share them with the other children, so they finally understood each other. From this case, we would like to investigate if the difference or the similarity of images can link us back to the cultural difference or give us information about cultural background.

2.2   Cultural Difference and Images

Cho and Ishida [2] referred to the detection of cultural difference as detecting semantic difference based on the culture definition of Geertz [5], which defines culture as "a historical transmitted pattern of meanings embodied in symbols". They said that it can be viewed as 'a pattern of interpretation' or 'a pattern of semantic'. Our method is designed to detect semantic difference in two languages and thus could be viewed as cultural difference. We expect it to be used as a tool to predict misunderstanding that could happen. The children's workshop indicated that the world could look different through the language glass. Besides the event, Deutscher [4] gave a lot of interesting examples of how different language speakers see the world differently. One example provided is that the historical evidence of ancient people shows no reference/usage of blue color, not because they saw less color than we do, but because blue is extremely rare in nature, so there was no need to find a name for this color. He also mentioned that some languages have no word for 'time', and some languages use four cardinal directions instead of 'left' and 'right'. It is reasonable then to assume that people with different language backgrounds might have different images in their mind and might have different thoughts when presented with the same word or the translation of the same word. Nowadays, there are databases of images with annotations in various languages and many image search tools are available. If these images and their keywords satisfy users by providing good images for the keyword input in different languages, we could use the image database as a tool to identify cultural difference. For instance, the word '団子' (dan-go), which means Japanese sweet dumpling made of rice flour, can be translated into 'dumpling', however, when we look for images of '団子' and 'dumpling' the results are totally different. Even though the translation of this word is not wrong, Japanese speakers and English speakers have different mental images when presented with these two words, as shown in Fig. 1. From this example, we can infer that an annotated image database covering the different languages can help us identify cultural differences between or among the speakers of different languages.

3   Related Work

3.1   Cultural Difference Detection

Cultural difference detection Groups of researchers have been studying and identifying cultural difference. Most of them collect data using cross-national surveys

Fig. 1. Samples from images of '団子' (dan-go, Japanese sweet) (left) and 'dumpling' (right)

and then analyze the survey results. For example, Hofstede's cultural dimension [7] is a well-known model of culture. Yoshino [17] also conducted a cross-national survey and compared the social values, ways of thinking, and other attributes. The results from these studies are interesting, but it seems impossible to apply the results to achieve real-time detection.

Cho et al. [3] studied the cultural difference in pictogram interpretations and its pattern. They did a web survey to understand the difference in pictogram interpretation in the U.S. and Japan. They found that, 19 of 120 pictograms were judged to have culturally different interpretations. They also found three patterns of the interpretation difference including, "two cultures could share the same concept but with different perspectives", "two cultures partially share the concept", and "two cultures do not share any concept".

Yoshino et al. [18] proposed a method for cultural difference detection in Wikipedia. The initial dataset is created by examining words and phrases with different meaning and usage in Japanese and Chinese by 18 Japanese students and five Chinese students. They proposed a flow of judgements based on the initial dataset. They evaluated four judgements as being successful in assessing cultural difference, including, "The article is not explained from a global viewpoint", "While the Japanese Wikipedia version of the article mentions Japan, the Chinese version does not.", "Existence of a defining statement, categorization by country name, and reference to origin or target country.", and "Neither country name is mentioned in either language version of Wikipedia."

Existing works on cultural difference identification and detection have been conducted within specific areas of use. Moreover, the need for human judgement is inevitable. Accordingly, this paper focuses on developing a method that can automatically detect cultural differences present in a broad range of domains.

3.2   Support Tools for Heterogeneous and Intercultural Team

In interdisciplinary and cross-cultural collaboration, the team members have various backgrounds and if they are not aware of it, difficulties in collaboration can arise. A group of researchers [11] proposed a support tool to create awareness of the bias in design teams. Their goal was to make each member be aware of her/his own interpretation of a topic while understanding and respecting the other team members' viewpoints. Their process includes asking each member to make a bias card by choosing three pictures for a topic, together with text (up to 140 characters), and sharing the cards among team members.

Their proposed tool can help create mutual understanding among the members. However, topics must be selected and the same process must be performed repeatedly. By comparison, our proposal can create mutual understanding without the need for topic assignment and eliminates the need for repetitive checks.

4   Method

To resolve the problem mentioned in Sect. 1, we introduce a method that can detect possible misunderstanding when communicating across languages by comparing images that are associated with keywords in different languages. We chose to use image comparison for several reasons. First, images are well linked to language and culture, as explained in Sect. 2. Second, it is often said that "A picture is worth a thousand words". Images contain information that might not be present in a dictionary. Finally, since image databases and image search engines are available, it is more convenient and less time consuming to use them together with an image comparison technique to automate the detection of possible misunderstanding. Figure 2 shows the overall procedure used to compute the similarity of a word and its translation in another language. If the similarity is low, there is more possibility of misunderstanding when those words are used in cross-culture and cross-language communication.

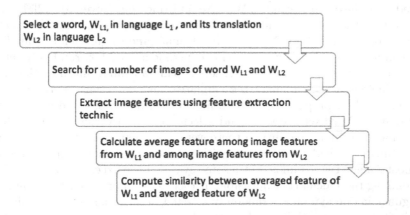

Fig. 2. Similarity calculation procedure.

First, a word, W_{L1} is selected in language, L_1. Its translation in language L_2 is W_{L2}. We look for a certain number of images in an image database or in the put of an image search engine for both words. The number of images should be sufficiently large, since many images may not well represent the keywords. Ideally, all the images linked to a word should be similar, but in many cases the images are rather diverse. For example, when the keyword is 'lion', the image results are mostly pictures of lions. But, when the keyword is 'zoo', the image results could include pictures containing different kinds of animals. If we only chose one image for the word 'zoo', we might get only the image of a lion, which does not well represent 'zoo' but has high similarity to the word 'lion' instead. To calculate similarity, after randomly selecting images, an image processing technique is used to extract features of all images for word W_{L1} and word W_{L2}. Feature extraction is a dimensional reduction process so the original image data can be simplified and processed. The features extracted from the images for the same word are averaged and compared with processing results for the other word. It is also possible to compare every extracted feature but this would take too long time and consume large amounts of computation resources. Lastly, the similarity between the two averaged features is computed. This similarity usually ranges from 0 to 1. A lower similarity indicates a bigger difference between the images and thus a higher chance of misunderstanding.

5 Experiment

We conducted an experiment to examine the proposed detection method. The selection of the data source and tools used were based on simplicity, and they could be adjusted or replaced with other resources or services for better accuracy. The software for this experiment, was written in Python.

The system computed the similarity between words in English and Japanese using words from Japanese WordNet [9], a Japanese-English lexical database, created from the original English WordNet of Princeton University [12]. In Word-Net, lemmas, the dictionary form of words, are linked to sets of synonyms called synsets. For Japanese WordNet, Japanese lemmas and English lemmas are linked to the same synset. We conducted this experiment on 2,500 randomly-selected noun synsets. Around half of the synsets Japanese lemma linked to the synset, so it is impossible to calculate the similarity for those synsets. Based on the detection method proposed in Sect. 4, first, we randomly selected a synset from the Japanese WordNet database and selected one or two lemmas in each language, based on its availability. If there were more than two lemmas, we run the same similarity calculation program with ten images for each lemma and choose the most similar two lemmas. Since some synsets have excessive number of lemmas making the calculation infeasible, if there were more than five lemmas for a language in one synset, we randomly selected just five lemmas and calculated the similarity among them to find two lemmas for the next step of calculation. The reason behind this is when there are too many lemmas, some lemmas have slightly different, boarder, or more specific meaning than the others, so we attempt to find the two most similar lemmas that can strongly represent the synset in each language.

For this experiment, we downloaded 30 images for each word if there was one lemma per language and 15 images for each word if there were two lemmas,

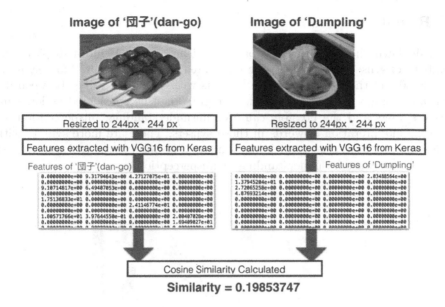

Fig. 3. An example of feature extraction and image comparison process

with Google Image Download API[1]. The images were resized to 224 pixels × 224 pixels for feature extraction. To extract image features, we used one of the most popular tools, VGG16[2] from Keras. The software transformed visual information of the image into a vector space. The result of feature extraction was a vector that contains 4,096 feature values for each image. An example of feature extraction and comparison is shown in Fig. 3. After that, averaged features were calculated. The synsets with two lemmas had their averaged features calculated from both lemmas.

Several similarity measures can be used, but for simplicity, we used cosine similarity, one of the most common methods of comparing vectors. Given A is the feature vector for one word and B is the feature vector for its translation, cosine similarity was calculated as follows:

$$similarity = \cos(\theta) = \frac{\mathbf{A} \cdot \mathbf{B}}{\|\mathbf{A}\|\|\mathbf{B}\|} = \frac{\sum_{i=1}^{n} A_i B_i}{\sqrt{\sum_{i=1}^{n} A_i^2}\sqrt{\sum_{i=1}^{n} B_i^2}} \tag{1}$$

We iterated the program 2,500 times on Windows servers. The calculation took several days since it involved around 150,000 images and heavy computation loads.

---

[1] https://github.com/hardikvasa/google-images-download.
[2] https://keras.io/applications/#vgg16.

6   Result

We calculated the similarity of words in 2,500 synsets. Figure 4 displays the numbers of synsets grouped by the calculated similarity result. Most synsets, almost 60% of the synsets, contain lemmas with similarity values between 0.7 and 0.9. Synsets with similarity lower than 0.6 can be considered as low similarity synsets and the possible cause of misunderstanding, misperception, or different interpretation of words in those synsets. There are more synsets with high similarity than synsets with low similarity, because in the real world, most words do not cause misunderstanding or misperception.

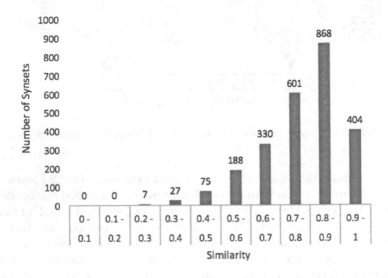

Fig. 4. The Histogram of word similarity in synsets

Figure 5 displays typical examples of synsets with similarity values lower than 0.6 and higher than 0.6. The similarity values are rounded to four decimal places. Each synset used for the calculation contained one to two lemma(s) in English and one to two lemma(s) in Japanese.

The images under each lemma are chosen just to demonstrate the meaning of the lemma and represent overall images to the reader. Some images in the table are not used in the real calculation, but are similar to those images that were used in the calculation. These images are displayed for the reader understanding, because most images downloaded in our experiment are not permitted to be publicly reused.

From Fig. 5, it is obvious that synsets with high similarity contain more similar images from its lemmas. For synset 04317175, the word 'stethoscope' and '聴診器' (stethoscope) refer to the same object and so give the same interpretation to the reader. Synset 13490343 also has high similarity but slightly lower than the synset of word 'stethoscope'. Images of all the words in this

Similarity		Synset Data	English lemma 1	English lemma 2	Japanese lemma 1	Japanese lemma 2
Low	0.2731	10913871 {william_cowper, cowper, クーパー}	william cowper 	cowper 	クーパー (Mini Cooper) 	-
	0.3660	00269674 {makeover, リフォーム}	makeover 	-	リフォーム (reform) 	-
	0.5024	07491476 {amusement, 御楽しみ, 娯しみ, 楽しみ, 御楽, お慰み, 慰み, 御楽み, 御慰み, 楽しび, 面白さ, お楽しみ, 愉しみ, 興}	amusement 	-	娯しみ * (recreation, playfulness) 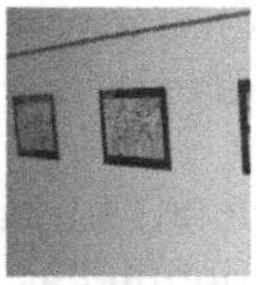	お慰み * (recreation) 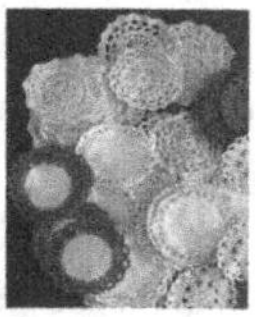
High	0.7632	07673397 {oil, vegetable_oil, 植物油}	oil 	vegetable oil 	植物油 (vegetable oil) 	-
	0.8396	13490343 {growth, 成長, 進化, 発展, 進歩, 発達, プログレス, 発育}	growth 	-	成長 (growing) 	進歩 (progress, improvement)
	0.9677	04317175 {stethoscope, 聴診器}	stethoscope	-	聴診器 (stethoscope) 	-

* Real image results contain various styles of images that are different from this example.

Fig. 5. Example of synsets with high and low similarity from the result

synset, including 'growth' '成長' (growing) and '進歩' (progress, improvement), yield similar images and they have similar meaning. But, since these words are abstract nouns, the images are slightly different. For example, images for all those 3 words contain images of small trees, in addition to graphs with upward arrow and figures representing evolution and development. Synset 07673397 contains the words 'oil', 'vegetable oil', and '植物油' (vegetable oil); it has slightly lower similarity than the first two synsets. However, the word 'oil' has broader meaning than the other two words so it yielded images of drilling rigs and oil in containers.

To detect the cultural difference and misunderstanding due to different language and backgrounds, we focus on synsets with low similarity. Synset 10913871 has remarkably low similarity. The reason for the similarity result between 'Cowper', 'William Cowper' and 'クーパー' (Mini Cooper) could be the nature of language. Because Japanese language has relatively few phonemes, many words derived from foreign language can be written in Japanese character but they are pronounced differently from the original words. Both 'Cowper' and 'William Cowper' are person's names but 'クーパー' is pronounced 'Kuu-Paa'. It is the homophone of 'cooper' in Japanese which makes most people think of Mini Cooper, i.e. the car made by the automobile marque called Mini. When an English speaker person uses the word 'Copwer', without any further explanation, a Japanese speaker might misunderstand that the speaker is talking about cars.

Synset 00269674 involves two words: 'makeover' and 'リフォーム' (reform). 'Makeover' is defined as "the process of improving the appearance of a person or a place, or of changing the impression that something gives" [8]. But when it is used in English, people will think about a personal makeover, usually involving make up and change in appearance. Image results from this word mostly include picture of women before and after a beauty makeover. Whereas 'リフォーム', in a Japanese dictionary, is defined as: (1) Revise, improvement (2) To remake, to resize or redesign clothes, to renovate building(s). The main image created by a Japanese is usually related to building renovation. Images of this word are usually images of a renovated room.

Synset 07491476 links 'amusement', '娯しみ' (recreation, playfulness), to '娯慰み' (recreation). The Oxford Advanced Learner's Dictionary defines 'amusement' as "the feeling that you have when something is funny or amusing, or it entertains you" and "a game, an activity, etc. that provides entertainment and pleasure". The images of this word show mostly pictures of amusement parks and rides. The word '娯しみ', and '娯慰み' are rarely used in daily life. They have similar meaning to 'amusement' in terms of fun and pleasure, but their use is different and more complex. '娯しみ' is not included in standard dictionaries but are used by only some groups of people. However, its adjective, '娯しい', exists in dictionaries describing the feeling of fun and enjoyment. The kanji, Chinese character used in Japanese language, '娯' means recreation and pleasure. The images of '娯慰み' are related to ink painting magazines and painting exhibitions since they are used as magazine names and exhibitions. The image results are much different from each othes, since this word is ambiguous and intangible. A few images from '**お慰み**' are related to handmade objects and craftwork due to the usage of this word. Even though the meaning of this word is mainly about fun and recreation, this word can be explained as "To create enjoyment, give people pleasure". Unlike the other words in this synset, this word involves personal pleasure. It is also often used conditional, for example "it will be fun, if I succeed".

6.1 Pattern of Low Similarity Synsets

From the results of our experiment, low similarity has a few reasons that cause. Synsets with low similarity could lead to misunderstanding and different interpretations between English and Japanese speakers. When we look at the synsets with similarity lower than 0.6, we find two interesting causes related to cultural difference.

First, a word and its translation have the same meaning but represent different images in the languages. Because of the different backgrounds, language and culture, people look at a word and its translation differently.

Second, words in one language can have more specific or broader meaning than in the other. The cases in this category includes:

1. Broader meaning in one language - When the word in one language has broader meaning, it might yield a greater variety of images.
2. Several homonyms in one language - When one word has several meanings it could confuse people even for native speakers. Some of the meanings might include slang or a negative interpretation compared to its translation.
3. Specific noun in one language, i.e. name of famous person, brand name, product name, company name - When a word is used as a specific noun, such as a product name, in one area, many people will think about the product instead of the original meaning of that word.

7 Discussion

7.1 Visualization of the Cultural Difference

Existing work [11] raise the possibility of sharing images and short texts made by each team member in design workshops to help mutual understanding and own bias. Here, we would like to present an alternative tool to be used in the same situation. The key advantage of our tool is that the information to be shared can be created automatically using data output by the proposed cultural difference detection method. Using visualization can help team members realize the difference and understand each other better; Fig. 6 is an example. This graph can be shown to the team member together with the images already downloaded for the calculation. When the word 'makeover' is mentioned, we grow the tree graph from the root nodes for a few levels and investigate the neighbor nodes using data from Japanese WordNet. In this graph, we use 0.6 and 0.75 as thresholds to determine node color. We use green for similarity values of 0.75 and above (high similarity nodes), yellow for values between 0.6 and 0.75 (medium similarity). Yellow nodes might contain different interpretations of words or concepts where the difference is not obvious enough to cause misunderstanding but caution in advised. Red nodes are for words with similarity under 0.6; they have high possibility of causing misunderstanding. The hierarchy of this tree is based on the relationships in WordNet. The upper nodes are words with broader meaning than its lower originating node, or a hypernym of the lower node. Lower nodes are words with more specific meaning than their upper nodes, i.e. a hyponym of the upper node. In a workshop, such as a brainstorming workshop for an advertising idea, when the English speaker mentions 'makeover', the Japanese member might look at the translation and think about it as 'reform' and assume that the discussion is about 'reform' not 'makeover'. The automated system can warn and display this tree to the participants. Since, this tree seems to fit the images from Japanese speaker's side, the Japanese can use it to confirm their meaning and the English speaker can see what Japanese speaker thinks about this word since this word is about reconstruction, fixing, and improvement, given that the upper nodes have fair or high similarity.

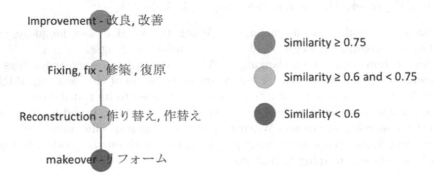

Fig. 6. An example of visualization of cultural difference (Color figure online)

7.2   Application of the Result

The results from our detection method can be used in MT-mediated communication. When a word used in the translation process, i.e. in a chat system, is identified as a low similarity word in our database, we can warn the team members and offer the word tree and related images to them. Even for intercultural workshops or intercultural design workshops that are conducted in one language, it is still useful to warn the team about possible misunderstandings when there is non-native speaker in the team. We can also apply this warning implementation in computer mediated communication between native and non-native speakers. The result can be used as reference for culture and language studies as well. It can be modified and used as an additional tool in existing language learning research, for example to help identify false friends, words in two languages that look or sound similar but differ significantly in meaning [1] in language studies.

7.3 Limitation

Besides cultural differences low similarity is sometimes the consequence of imperfect translation of the language resource. Low similarity can also be caused by technical errors, for instance, few images are available for download. We note that abstract nouns are one of the problems our method has difficulty with, since they are not linked to unambiguous images.

7.4 Future Direction

Our current method requires a combination of different tools so its accuracy also depends on the effectiveness of those tools, including image comparison tool, and the accuracy of the lexical database or the MT system. Since this paper does not focus on the accuracy of similarity in this paper, we can improve accuracy by changing the tools and method used, for example, using different methods to select words in the same synset, using different image comparison methods, using different similarity measures, etc. The threshold of the low or high similarity can also be adjusted and studied in the future for more accurate prediction. Future work could combine the use of dictionaries and other language resources for better translation of each lemma and it could allow us to identify abstract nouns and treat those lemmas differently.

We plan to include a confidence measure of the calculation by looking at the variety of images from one lemma. If one lemma yields wildly different images, the quality of the calculation in the next step might be degraded.

We also plan to implement and evaluate the visualization tool. Comparing word trees that include similarity data is also interesting. We might be able to see the relationship between low similarity nodes form the similarity of the roots.

8 Conclusion

Our main contribution of this paper is to present a novel method to automatically detect cultural difference, and possible misunderstanding, or possible misinterpretation of words. We aim to use it for MT-mediated communication and intercultural workshops. We believe that, this is the first work to apply image comparison to the identification of cultural differences. Since existing works [3,7,17,18] mostly studied and identified cultural difference using the survey method, they can only study cultural differences across specific culture pairs. It also is too expensive and too slow. The proposed method achieves our goal of detecting possible cultural differences, misunderstandings, and misinterpretations in intercultural collaboration automatically. As such, it can be used in broader areas of study and does not need human effort.

We investigated our method by applying it to Japanese WordNet. We looked for dissimilarities between sets of images that represent words in English and Japanese using an existing image database and automated image comparison. We conducted an experiment on 2,500 synsets and presented some of our results in this paper. Low similarity can be due to different images being linked to a word and its translation, resulting from the different backgrounds. The second cause is the unequal meaning assigned to words in each language. For example, when words in one language have several meanings and when one meaning in one language is used as a specific noun, including name of commercial brands, companies, or people.

Acknowledgments. This research was partially supported by a Grant-in-Aid for Scientific Research (A) (17H00759, 2017–2020) and (B) (18H03341, 2018–2020) from Japan Society for the Promotion of Science (JSPS).

References

1. Abou-Khalil, V., Ogata, H., et al.: Learning false friends across contexts. In: LAK 2018: 8th International Learning Analytics and Knowledge (LAK) Conference. Association for Computing Machinery (ACM) (2018)
2. Cho, H., Ishida, T.: Exploring cultural differences in pictogram interpretations. In: Ishida, T. (ed.) The Language Grid. Cognitive Technologies, pp. 133–148. Springer, Heidelberg (2011). https://doi.org/10.1007/978-3-642-21178-2_9
3. Cho, H., Ishida, T., Yamashita, N., Inaba, R., Mori, Y., Koda, T.: Culturally-situated pictogram retrieval. In: Ishida, T., Fussell, S.R., Vossen, P.T.J.M. (eds.) IWIC 2007. LNCS, vol. 4568, pp. 221–235. Springer, Heidelberg (2007). https://doi.org/10.1007/978-3-540-74000-1_17
4. Deutscher, G.: Through the Language Glass: Why the World Looks Different in Other Languages. Metropolitan Books, New York (2010)
5. Geertz, C.: The Interpretation of Cultures, vol. 5019. Basic books, New York (1973)
6. Herring, C.: Does diversity pay?: race, gender, and the business case for diversity. Am. Sociol. Rev. **74**(2), 208–224 (2009)
7. Hofstede, G.: Cultural dimensions in management and planning. Asia Pac. J. Manag. **1**(2), 81–99 (1984)
8. Hornby, A.S., Cowie, A.P.: Oxford Advanced Learner's Dictionary, vol. 1430. Oxford University Press, Oxford (1995)
9. Isahara, H., Bond, F., Uchimoto, K., Utiyama, M., Kanzaki, K.: Development of the Japanese WordNet. In: Sixth International Conference on Language Resources and Evaluation (2008)
10. Ishida, T., Murakami, Y., Lin, D., Nakaguchi, T., Otani, M.: Language service infrastructure on the web: the language grid. Computer **51**(6), 72–81 (2018)
11. Mattioli, R., Ferraris, S.D., Ferraro, V., et al.: Mybias: a web-based tool to overcome communication issues and foster creativity in heterogeneous design teams. In: DS 93: Proceedings of the 20th International Conference on Engineering and Product Design Education (E&PDE 2018), Dyson School of Engineering, Imperial College, London, 6th–7th September 2018, pp. 271–276 (2018)
12. Miller, G.: WordNet: An Electronic Lexical Database. MIT Press, Cambridge (1998)

13. Pituxcoosuvarn, M., Ishida, T.: Multilingual communication via best-balanced machine translation. New Gener. Comput. **36**(4), 349–364 (2018)
14. Pituxcoosuvarn, M., Ishida, T., Yamashita, N., Takasaki, T., Mori, Y.: Machine translation usage in a children's workshop. In: Egi, H., Yuizono, T., Baloian, N., Yoshino, T., Ichimura, S., Rodrigues, A. (eds.) CollabTech 2018. LNCS, vol. 11000, pp. 59–73. Springer, Cham (2018). https://doi.org/10.1007/978-3-319-98743-9_5
15. Talke, K., Salomo, S., Rost, K.: How top management team diversity affects innovativeness and performance via the strategic choice to focus on innovation fields. Res. Policy **39**(7), 907–918 (2010)
16. Yamashita, N., Inaba, R., Kuzuoka, H., Ishida, T.: Difficulties in establishing common ground in multiparty groups using machine translation. In: Proceedings of the SIGCHI Conference on Human Factors in Computing Systems, pp. 679–688. ACM (2009)
17. Yoshino, R., Hayashi, C.: An overview of cultural link analysis of national character. Behaviormetrika **29**(2), 125–141 (2002)
18. Yoshino, T., Miyabe, M., Suwa, T.: A proposed cultural difference detection method using data from Japanese and Chinese Wikipedia. In: 2015 International Conference on Culture and Computing (Culture Computing), pp. 159–166. IEEE (2015)

FootstepsMixer: A Tool to Express Multiple People's Footsteps in a Footstep Transmission System for Awareness Support

Hiroki Echigo[✉][ID], Masakatsu Kanno, Kana Matsu, Taira Endo,
and Minoru Kobayashi[ID]

Meiji University, 4-21-1 Nakano, Nakano-ku, Tokyo, Japan
{hiroki.echigo,masakatsu.kanno,matsu.kana,taira.endo}@koblab.org,
minoru@acm.org

Abstract. Recently, the number of people living in single-person households has increased. Although the numbers of sensor-based services that monitor personal safety are increasing, they do not provide the feeling of living in a multi-person household. In this study, we attempt to realize a system that shares the sounds of a distant family household, thereby creating the impression that the family household is nearby. Using this system, we devised a method to express people's activity in a remote location and evaluated the system experimentally. We considered multiple-footstep expression methods and based on experimental results, identified the most suitable method. Herein, we propose a "FootstepsMixer," a tool that expresses the actions of multiple people using the optimal footstep expression method. With this tool, users can easily express footsteps in an exaggerated manner and can set the number of people and the maximum volume of each footstep. We also consider what type of motion expression can be realized using the proposed tool.

Keywords: Awareness support · Footsteps · Mixer

1 Introduction

Living in a family household, we are constantly surrounded by ambient sounds, such as your mother cooking in the kitchen, your sister going up and down the stairs, or your father working on his computer. Alone in your room, you can imagine what your family members are doing without seeing the source of those sounds. These sounds often provide reassurance and happiness; however, when you live alone away from your family, you cannot hear such sounds because of work or college. We can sense the activities and liveliness of the family members because of these sounds. Herein, "liveliness" refers to the degree of vigor of the person; if you hear footsteps of your sister going upstairs quickly, you understand

© Springer Nature Switzerland AG 2019
H. Nakanishi et al. (Eds.): CRIWG+CollabTech 2019, LNCS 11677, pp. 144–158, 2019.
https://doi.org/10.1007/978-3-030-28011-6_10

that she is vigorous, and if you hear slow footsteps, you understand that she might be exhausted.

The number of one-person households is increasing globally [1]. According to the Organisation for Economic Co-operation and Development (OECD), the number of one-person households is expected to grow in all the OECD countries for which projections are available [2].

Some people who are unable to live with their families owing to various circumstances sometimes feel sad and nervous. To solve this problem, we attempted to realize a system that shares the real-life household sounds of a distant family, creating the impression that the family is nearby (see Fig. 1). Among the various possible sounds, we focused on footsteps because footsteps differ from person to person, and we considered that the sound of footsteps easily represented the liveliness of a family living away.

To achieve this goal, we are developing a system that satisfies the following requirements.

- It enables us to feel the liveliness and activity of a family living away.
- It enables us to share a sense of space with remote partners, while protecting the privacy. (This is in a trade-off relation with the first point.)

Initially, we implemented a microphone and loudspeaker-based system that recorded and reproduced footstep sounds. We found a way to express footstep sounds that could, to some extent, sound like a single person walking around on a floor above the listener. However, the initial system could not effectively express the activities and liveliness of multiple people.

In this paper, we explore various ways of expressing footstep sounds and find a method to reproduce footstep sounds that let remote family members feel as though they were in their family home. To facilitate this investigation, we propose a tool that we refer to as "FootstepsMixer." Using this tool, we search for an optimal footstep expression method. In addition, we consider what type of motion can be expressed using the proposed tool.

2 Related Work

2.1 Awareness Communication

Considerable research has focused on awareness of remote areas [3–8]. For example, Dourish et al. [3] proposed systems called Portholes that arranged still images captured at regular intervals at various points on a single screen such that people at multiple remote points can see at any time. Robert et al. [4] proposed a system called the Video Window System that employed a large super wide screen video, and that keeps video and audio connected to remote rooms at all times. These systems [3,4] can convey a sense of the entire space; however, there are significant privacy concerns.

Ishii et al. [5] proposed the ambientROOM, which was an interface to transmit information variably in the background of awareness. It conveyed the motion

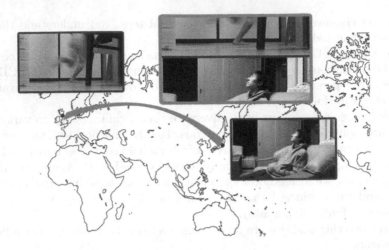

Fig. 1. Image of the proposed system. Our goal is to realize a system that shares the sound of footsteps from the household of a distant family to create the impression that the family is nearby.

of people and animals from remote areas in a surrounding environment using various display media, such as water, light, and shadows. Siio et al. [6] proposed a system called Peek-A-Drawer that automatically transfers photos in drawers to remote locations and shares the contents of the drawers. In addition, Meeting Pot, a system that conveys the scent of brewed coffee to a remote place, has been proposed. Rowan et al. [7] proposed a system called Digital Family Portrait that shares family life with elderly relatives who live in remote areas by connecting via portraits. Although these systems [5–7] can provide a sense of sharing aspects of life while preserving privacy and awareness, they share a limited space and do not fully share the living space. Tsujita et al. [8] proposed a system called SyncDecor that synchronizes furniture used in daily life, such as a trash can whose opening and closing is synchronized with a remote area and a lamp whose brightness is synchronized with a remote area. Although these are highly sensitive to privacy, they are shared only in limited spaces such as drawers, portraits, and pots, and it is difficult to say that they share the sense of life completely.

2.2   Stereophonic Sound

Many studies have attempted to reproduce stereophonic sound based on three clues, i.e., time gap, volume, and phase and change of frequency responses. In the groupware system developed by Cohen et al. [9], the positions of participants in a virtual meeting room are associated with the positions of sound sources. Here stereophonic sound was used to construct an acoustic environment in a virtual conference space in the conference. The system developed by Seligmann et al. [10]

shows participants' activity by arranging not only voice but also keyboard strikes and clicks on the space.

These previous studies indicate that the use of stereophonic sound in a virtual space can provide clues about human actions and a feeling of being near to others. Reproducing stereophonic sound is difficult and requires specialized equipment. In the current study, stereophonic sound does not need to be reproduced perfectly because the purpose is to convey the movement of people in remote places. The goal is to express rough movement and liveliness by the strength of the sound heard via a speaker.

3   Footstep Expression Methods

In this section, we describe the method of expressing footsteps. When footsteps are recorded using a stationary microphone, the volume decreases sharply as the distance between the microphone and the source of the footsteps increases. This sudden change hinders the smooth expression of footstep movement and adjusting the sound like smoothly moving footsteps is difficult. To overcome this difficulty, we developed a method to express the movement of footsteps by mixing and connecting prerecorded footstep sounds. We investigated several ways to express footsteps and conducted experiments to compare them.

3.1   Footstep Expression Models

The four footstep expression models investigated are listed in Table 1. Figure 2 shows how the volume changes over time for Model 1, Model 3, and Model 4. In Fig. 2, the horizontal axis represents time, and the vertical axis represents sound intensity. Model 1 is a raw recording of the sound of moving footsteps using a microphone. The method used in the initial system described in Sect. 1 is used to record this model. Models 2–4 are synthesized reproductions of footstep sounds generated by repeating a single footstep sound while gradually changing the volume. Model 2 (not shown in Fig. 2) is produced by imitating the loudness change of Model 1. Model 3 is designed to test a gradual change in the loudness of footsteps. Here, the loudness decreases linearly up to $-18\,$dB in 2.91 s. The change of loudness over time is expressed as follows.

$$G = -\frac{600}{97}t(= -\frac{18}{2.91}t) \tag{1}$$

Here, G is volume in decibels (dB) and t is time in seconds. The method represented by Model 4 changes volume twice as fast as Model 3; thus, the volume reaches $-18\,$dB in half the time taken by Model 3. The relation between G (dB) and t (s) in Model 4 is shown below.

$$G = -\frac{1200}{97}t(= -\frac{18}{1.455}t) \tag{2}$$

Decibels are represented using a logarithmic scale; thus, they must be represented by a power factor. The relation between G (dB) and Power is expressed as follows.

$$G = 20 \log_{10} Power \tag{3}$$

Table 1. Experimental conditions.

Model	Example
Model 1	Footsteps recorded with microphone
Model 2	Footsteps imitating Model 1
Model 3	Footsteps changed gradually
Model 4	Footsteps changed gradually in half the time of Model 3

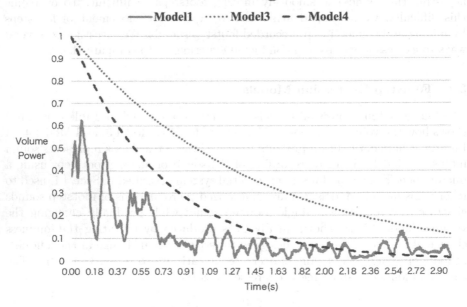

Fig. 2. Comparison of Model 1, Model 3, and Model 4.

3.2   Experiment

The experiment was performed to identify the best model from Models 1 to 4. The best model should not sound as if the people in remote areas are moving momentarily and should not feel like several people are walking. The meaning "moving momentarily" refers to the feeling when a person in a remote area teleports or jumps between footsteps playback devices. In addition, the footsteps in the experiment are one person's footsteps; thus, the feeling that several people are walking is not suitable.

Participants. Twenty college and graduate students volunteered to participate in the experiment. The participants included fifteen males and five females, and ranged in age between 22 and 25 years. Prior to conducting the experiment, the participants were asked the question, "Do you have experience of hearing footsteps from the upper floor in an apartment, or a house?" 85% of the participants answered "Yes."

Experimentation Space. The experimental space was a square (2.61 m per side). This size is sufficiently large for participants to understand the movement of footsteps. We installed four footstep playback devices on poles at the corners of the square space. The footstep playback devices were placed facing downward at a height of 2 m from the floor.

Procedure. The participants listened to the playback of the four types of footstep sounds listed in Table 1 individually. Participants answered the questionnaire for each Model (see Table 1). Table 2 lists questions and options the range of potential responses. The participants were told in advance that they would hear footsteps; however, they were not told how many people's footsteps they would hear. In Table 2, Q1, Q2, and Q4 were evaluated on a seven-point Likert scale. The Latin square method was used in consideration of the influence of the order on the results. After the experiment, we told the participants in the experiment that footsteps sound you heard is of a single person and the participants were asked the questions shown in Table 3. The experimental environment is shown in Fig. 3.

3.3 Results

Results of Questionnaire. For "Q1. Did you feel that it was footsteps?," all models received scores of 5 or more. There was no significant difference between the four models. Figure 4 shows the results for "Q2. Did this footstep make you feel that people in remote areas were moving momentarily?" Here, two of the four models were selected, and the Wilcoxon signed-rank test was performed. A significant difference was confirmed at a 5% level between Model 2 and Model 3 and between Model 2 and Model 4. In Model 2, the participants who responded that they felt that people in remote areas were moving momentarily (answered by 5 or more) had the following opinions.

- "It seems that footsteps were generated in an unnatural place."
- "It sounds like footsteps moving from the right front to the left back in an instant."
- "It seems that footsteps were interrupted on the way."

Table 2. Questionnaire

No.	Question
Q1	Did you feel that it was footsteps? (1. Not at all. - 7. Very much.)
Q2	Did this footstep make you feel that people in remote areas were moving momentarily? (1. Not at all. - 7. Very much.)
Q3	Please enter the reason for your response to Q2
Q4	Did you feel like several people were walking? (1. Not at all. - 7. Very much.)
Q5	Please enter the reason for your response to Q4

Table 3. Questionnaire administered after the experiment.

No.	Question
After-Q1	Which one model felt most realistic liveliness? (first, second, third, fourth, about the same)
After-Q2	Please enter the reason for your response to After-Q1

Fig. 3. Experimental environment. Participants sat at the center of the experiment space and answered questions while listening to footsteps output sequentially from multiple devices counterclockwise.

Figure 5 shows the results for "Q4. Did you feel like several people were walking?" Two of the four models were selected, and the Wilcoxon signed-rank test was performed. A significant difference was confirmed at a 5% level between Model 1 and Model 4. In addition, a significant difference was confirmed at a 1% level between Model 2 and Model 4. In Model 4, the participants who responded that they did not feel that several people were walking (answered by 2 and fewer) had the following opinions.

- "I felt that the footsteps were moving continuously."
- "I felt that one person was walking around."
- "I felt only one person's footsteps."

Q2.Did this footsteps make you feel that people in remote areas were moving momentarily?

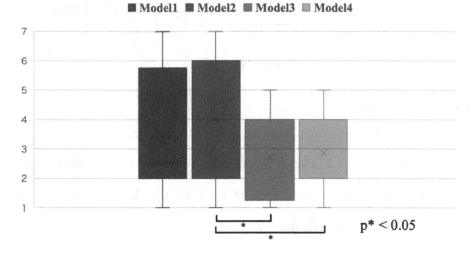

Fig. 4. Q2 results.

Results of After Questionnaire. Figure 6 shows the result for "After-Q1. Which one model felt most realistic liveliness?" The number of participants who answered Model 4 was the greatest (50% of the total number of participants). The reasons provided for selecting Model 4 were as follows.

- "Movement of footsteps was easy to understand and there were no elements that felt particularly unpleasant."
- "I felt that one person was walking around."
- "There were few overlapping footsteps sounds."

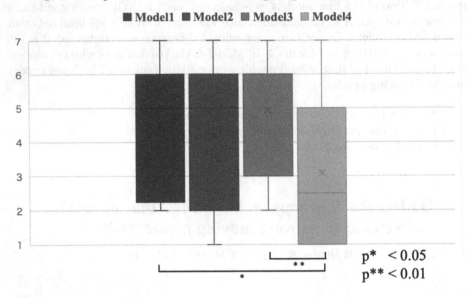

Fig. 5. Q4 results.

3.4   Best Model

The results provided in Sect. 3.3 are summarized as follows.

- Compared to Model 2, Models 3 and 4 did not sound like moving instantaneously.
- Compared to Models 1 and 3, Model 4 did not feel that some people were walking.
- Model 4 felt most realistic liveliness.

Notably, the reason for these results was the difference in volume of the first 1.455 s (half of 2.91 s). According to Fig. 2, the volume up to 1.455 s is in the following order: $Model3 > Model4 > Model1 (\approx Model2)$. In the case of Model 3, the volume power is greater than 0.3 in 1.455 s; thus, the footsteps sounds overlap with the footsteps sounds of the next speaker, thereby appearing like there are several people. Conversely, in the case of Model 1, the volume power is smaller than 0.2 for about the first 0.7 s; thus, it does not sound like movement between the speakers, but it sounds like a different person is walking. Therefore, Model 4 is considered to be the best among four models. In the follow, we describe FootstepsMixer, the tool we developed a tool to express footsteps of multiple people based on Model 4.

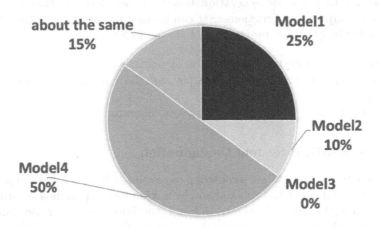

After-Q1. Which one model felt most realistic liveliness?

Fig. 6. Results of questionnaire administered after the experiment (see Table 3).

4 FootstepsMixer

4.1 Problems Expressing Footsteps of Multiple People

According to Sect. 3, when transmitting a single person's footsteps to a remote space, it is possible that listener felt realistic liveliness because of the impression that he/she is nearby. However, when transmitting multiple people's footsteps to a remote place, balancing the volume of each footstep is problematic. In this study, we needed to transmit a sense of liveliness as well as motion, but when multiple people's footsteps are played simultaneously from a single playback device, there is a possibility that sound cannot be discerned as footsteps. In addition, it may be necessary to change the mixing balance depending on the number of people in the remote space. To address these problems, we developed the FootstepsMixer tool that expresses the movements of multiple people. In the following sections, we describe FootstepsMixer's features and system configuration.

4.2 FootstepsMixer Features

Initially, the FootstepsMixer user sets the number of "walkers" in the space. To generate an audio stream to be played from one of the system speakers, FootstepsMixer calculates the positions of the walkers based on the walking speed defined in the system, calculates the intensity of each walker's footsteps based on the distance between the walker and the speaker, generates the footstep sound by repeating a single prerecorded footstep, and mixes the footstep sounds of the walkers at an intensity that corresponds to each of the walkers. Note that the intensity is calculated based on Model 4. The implemented system has four speakers, and this calculation and generation of sound based on a prerecorded footstep is repeated for each of the speakers.

In addition to the basic generation based on the Model 4, FootstepsMixer includes some adjustment functions that can be used to express multiple walkers' footsteps effectively. These functions include the following.

- The user can set footstep exaggeration (weighting).
- The user can set the number of people and the maximum volume of each footstep.
- The user can preview how each of the speaker sounds.

4.3   FootstepsMixer System Configuration

A screenshot of FootstepsMixer's control panel is shown in Fig. 7. FootstepsMixer can generate footsteps of multiple walkers by mixing footstep sounds according to their position in the space. As shown in Fig. 7, the FootstepsMixer user interface is divided into three areas, i.e., Floor Area, Sensor Select Area, and User Select Area.

Floor Area. The square frame in this area indicates the space in which the footstep transmission system can be used. This area plays a role like an execution screen; however, the user cannot set anything in this area. The four circles in the square frame represent the speakers. Here we refer to the speakers as "sensors" to indicate that they represent the audio sensors (microphones) at the remote site. As the user select a given sensor in the Sensor Select Area, the corresponding circle is displayed in dark blue and the corresponding circle for the sensors not selected are displayed in light blue. The user can set the number of walkers in the space in User Select Area; human-shaped icons representing the number of walkers are displayed in the square frame. In Fig. 7, the number of walkers is set to three. The human-shaped icons move in the square frame at random speeds.

Sensor Select Area. In this area, the user can select one of the sensors to playback the sound. Only one sensor at a time can be selected. In Fig. 7, Sensor1 is selected; therefore, in the Floor Area, the upper left circle is displayed dark blue, and the audio stream corresponding to Sensor1 is played back.

User Select Area. In this area, the user can set the intensity of exaggeration (i.e., weighting), the number of walkers, and the maximum volume of each walker's footsteps. To facilitate the differentiation of closely located multiple walkers, the system makes one of the footstep sounds louder than the others. Notably, the intensity of exaggeration refers to the extent to which the footsteps of the walker closest to the sensor are louder than other footsteps.

The algorithm used to calculate the percentage of exaggeration is explained in the next section. The number of walkers (one to five) can be selected. The user can hear footsteps for the selected number of walkers and can set the maximum volume of each footstep. Volume can be from $-18\,$dB to $0\,$dB. The mixed footsteps change dynamically each time the user changes the setting, and the user can adjust the setting based on a preview playback.

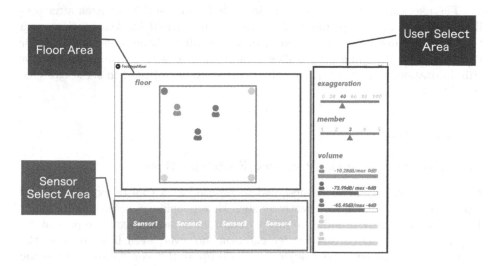

Fig. 7. FootstepsMixer. (Color figure online)

4.4 Algorithm

Here, we will explain the algorithm with and without exaggeration.

Based on the results given in Sect. 3, we use the footstep expression method of Model 4. The number of walkers who create footsteps is represented as $n(1 \leq n \leq 5)$. When the distance between sensors is L (pixel), the distance between the sensor and the foot is d_n(pixel), and the maximum volume is M_n(dB). The volume $G(d_n, M_n)$ can be expressed as follows.

$$G(d_n, M_n) = -36\frac{d_n}{L} + M_n \qquad (4)$$

The equation representing d_n(pixel) with the coordinates $(sensor_x, sensor_y)$ of any sensor in the Floor Area and the coordinates of the human-shaped icon $(human_x, human_y)$ is as follows.

$$d_n = \sqrt{(sensor_x - human_x)^2 + (sensor_y - human_y)^2} \qquad (5)$$

When the number of walkers is set to two or more, this algorithm compares the distance between the sensor and the walkers, and exaggerates the footsteps of the walker closest to the sensor. When w is the exaggeration rate ($0 \leq w \leq 1$), the volume $G(d_n, M_n)$ is expressed as follows.

$$G(d_n, M_n) = \begin{cases} -36\frac{d_n}{L} + M_n & (d_n = minD) \\ (-36\frac{d_n}{L} + M_n)\frac{1}{w} & (else) \end{cases} \tag{6}$$

Here, a set of $d_n (1 \leq n \leq 5)$ is represented as D.

The user can adjust the exaggeration rate in the User Select Area after pre-listening to the footstep sounds. However, in the current implementation, each time the distance between the sensor and the walker changes, it takes time for the system to determine the walker closest to a sensor. To compensation for this limitation, the exaggeration rate w can only be adjusted in six stages (see Fig. 7).

5   Discussion

5.1   Further Use of the Proposed FootstepsMixer

Currently, FootstepsMixer is designed to be used as a tool to explore ways of expressing footstep sounds effectively such that people can sense remote members of their family. Finding a way to control the sound would represent an improvement of the current implementation; however, even if we do not, the tool is can realize our initial objective. To support this contention, we provide the following two scenarios.

Scenario A: Father Wants to Know About the Life of His Two Daughters Who Live at a Distant. Due to an unavoidable circumstance related to his work, the father lives separately from his family (his wife and two daughters). To know that they are doing okay, the father wants to hear his daughters' footsteps rather than those of his wife. Thus, he sets the volume of footsteps of his daughters to be louder compared to that of his wife. Even if the daughters' footsteps are heard simultaneously, he does not perceive the sound as noise; therefore, he sets the system not to exaggerate.

Scenario B: Grandmother Wants to Know the Life of Her Family. A grandmother is living separately from five family members, i.e., her daughter, daughter's husband, and three grandchildren. She wants to know about her grandchildren's every day. Therefore, she sets their footsteps to be louder than those of her daughter or her daughter's husband. However, the sound is a bit noisy because her grandchildren run a lot. Consequently, to compensate for the noisiness, she set the footsteps to exaggerate, which allows her to perceive her grandchildren's liveliness.

5.2 Exaggeration Rate

In the current implementation, the degree of exaggeration was limited to six stages (0%, 20%, 40%, 60%, 80%, 100%). The purpose of this study is to enable people who are listening to the footsteps to understand the liveliness and activities of people in remote areas. Therefore, we assumed that a fine adjustment of the degree of exaggeration was not necessary. However, it is still necessary to consider whether six steps are appropriate. In addition, we recognize that we need to develop a better exaggeration algorithm.

5.3 Limitation

The newly developed FootstepsMixer allows the user to set parameters to control the simultaneous playbacks of multiple walkers' footsteps. The current system limited to a setting in which sensors are placed at the corners of a square. Based on feedback from actual users, it will be necessary to provide additional setting options, including a different arrangement of sensors.

6 Future Work

6.1 Application to Footstep Transmission System

We intend to apply the proposed method to a footstep transmission system that records the activity of people at a remote site and reproduces their footstep sound. This system will transmit data about people's position captured by the foot activity recording device, such as position sensors, and will play footstep sounds based on the position data.

6.2 Long-Term Experiment in an Actual Residence

We need to perform experiments using the footstep recording transmission system in an actual home. By conducting experiments over a long period, we would like to investigate how much awareness can be felt based on footstep activity in a home. Using the tool in an actual home may reveal previously unidentified problems and identify ways to improve the proposed tool.

7 Conclusion

In this study, we attempted to realize a system that shares the living sounds of a household of a distant family to create the impression that the household is nearby. To date, we have not been able to express the activity and liveliness of several people; therefore, we proposed the FootstepsMixer tool that expresses the activity of several people using the footstep expression method we devised. Using this tool, users can easily express footsteps exaggeratingly, and can set the number of people and the maximum volume of each footstep. In future, we would like to apply this tool to a footstep transmission system and conduct long-term experiments in an actual home.

Acknowledgements. This work was supported by JSPS KAKENHI Grant Number JP18K11410. The authors would like to thank Enago (www.enago.jp) for the English language review.

References

1. Chamie, J.: The Rise of One-Person Households. IPS. http://www.ipsnews.net/2017/02/the-rise-of-one-person-households/. Accessed 20 Apr 2019
2. OECD: THE FUTURE OF FAMILIES TO 2030 A Synthesis Report. OECD (2011)
3. Dourish, P., Bly, S.: Portholes: supporting awareness in a distributed work group. In: Proceedings of the SIGCHI Conference on Human Factors in Computing Systems (CHI 1992), pp. 541–547. ACM, New York (1992). https://doi.org/10.1145/142750.142982
4. Robert, E.K., Robert, S.F., Barbara, L.C.: The VideoWindow system in informal communications. In: Proceedings of the 1990 ACM Conference on Computer-Supported Cooperative Work, CSCW 1990, pp. 1–11. ACM, New York (1990). https://doi.org/10.1145/99332.99335
5. Ishii, H., et al.: ambient- ROOM: integrating ambient media with architectural space. In: CHI 1998 Conference Summary on Human Factors in Computing Systems, CHI 1998, pp. 173–174. ACM, New York (1998). https://doi.org/10.1145/286498.286652
6. Siio, I., Rowan, J., Mima, N., Mynatt, E.: Digital decor: augmented everyday things. In: Graphics Interface 2003, pp. 159–166 (2003). https://doi.org/10.20380/GI2003.19
7. Rowan, J., Mynatt, E.D.: Digital family portrait field trial: support for aging in place. In: Proceedings of the SIGCHI conference on Human Factors in Computing Systems, CHI 2005, pp. 521–530. ACM, New York (2005). https://doi.org/10.1145/1054972.1055044
8. Tsujita, H., Tsukada, K., Siio, I.: SyncDecor: appliances for sharing mutual awareness between lovers separated by distance. In: CHI 2007 Conference Proceedings and Extended Abstracts, Conference on Human Factors in Computing Systems, pp. 2699–2704. ACM, New York (2007). https://doi.org/10.1145/1240866.1241065
9. Cohen, M., Koizumi, N., Aoki, S.: Design and control of shared conferencing environments for audio telecommunication. In: Proceedings the International Symposium on Measurement and Control in Robotics, Society of Instrument & Control Engineers, pp. 405–412 (2005)
10. Seligmann, D.D., Mercuri, R.T., Edmark, J.T.: Providing assurances in a multimedia interactive environment. In: Proceedings of the SIGCHI Conference on Human Factors in Computing Systems, CHI 1995, pp. 250–256. ACM, Denver (1995). https://doi.org/10.1145/223904.223936

Speech Speed Awareness System Slows Down Native Speaker's Talk

Tomoo Inoue[(⊠)] and Wei Liao

University of Tsukuba, Tsukuba, Ibaraki 3058550, Japan
inoue@slis.tsukuba.ac.jp

Abstract. Conversation between native speakers and non-native speakers is not always easy. Non-native speakers sometimes feel hard to understand what native speakers talk because of their speaking speed. Even kind native speakers who speak slower in the beginning often get back to their "natural" speed unconsciously after a while. Although non-native speakers may ask a native speaker to repeat what they cannot catch, participants of the conversation would become uneasy for too often request of repeating, which may also reduce productivity of the conversation or the meeting. In this paper, we study how conversation between native and non-native speakers is conducted regarding speech rate, how the introduction of a speech speed awareness system could alleviate this communication problem. The system recognizes speech rate in real-time and makes participants aware when their speech rate is too fast for non-native speakers.

Keywords: Second language conversation support · Speech speed · Non-Native speaker support

1 Introduction

We have more chances of conversation in second languages than ever recently, but conversation between native speakers (NS) and non-native speakers (NNS) is not always easy. The conversation is often unbalanced when NS communicate with NNS.

The reasons of NNS listening and understanding difficulties in second language communication have been investigated in numerous studies. According to the investigation on the factors affecting NNS listening by Bloomfield et al. [1], NNS listening is affected by listener's factors such as working memory and fluency of language, and speaker's factors such as word length, complexity, pose and the speech rate. Speech rate (SR) is an element of the speaker's factors. It is known that it may cause difficulty in the NNS listening when the average SR of the NS becomes fast [2, 3]. However, these did not investigate the real-time SR change of NS. Also, a speech speed awareness system to alleviate this communication problem has been developed, which recognizes the speech rate in real-time and make the participants aware when the speech rate is too fast [4], but its effect has not been published yet.

The purpose of this research is to support conversation by NS and NNS. First, it was examined if increase in the SR of the NS causes understanding difficulty of the NNS in actual second language conversation. Then the proposed speech speed

© Springer Nature Switzerland AG 2019
H. Nakanishi et al. (Eds.): CRIWG+CollabTech 2019, LNCS 11677, pp. 159–171, 2019.
https://doi.org/10.1007/978-3-030-28011-6_11

awareness method, which notifies the NS (and NNS) when his/her SR is too fast, and which expects spontaneous SR adjustment by NS [4], was investigated by the WOZ system.

2   Related Work

2.1   Problems of NNS Listening in Second Language Conversation

In the context of second language conversations by NS and NNS, conversational imbalance is often seen due to NNS listening and understanding problems. According to Ikegami, the general process of listening is a series of processing in which the working memory receives the spoken speech information, instantaneous processing is performed, and lead to the understanding of the information. The series of information processing differs depending on NS and NNS. In the case of a native language, processing from sound perception to word/phrase recognition is performed automatically and unconsciously. However, when NNS processes a non-native language, the process is consciously performed and takes more time [5].

In an investigation of factors affecting NNS listening, Bloomfield et al. pointed out the listener element of working memory, language fluency, and the speaker elements of paragraph length, complexity, pause, and SR. It is also suggested that the SR, which interacts with other factors, may lead to difficulties in NNS listening [1].

Goh surveyed on NNS listening. It showed variety of reasons that NNS felt difficulty of understanding in conversation with NS. They are as follows: lack of vocabulary, cannot recognize the words you know, cannot imagine even if you listen to words, cannot keep up the flow of conversation, the next part is gone while thinking about the meaning of the previous words, appearance of unexpected words could lead to confusion, and if something went wrong they would not be able to understand the following parts, or they would forget the part they heard earlier while listening [6].

In this study, we conducted experimental research to investigate the SR change of NS and NNS incomprehension in second language conversation. We collected the video of the experiment as objective data, as well as the subjective comments like these previous studies.

Regarding the behaviors in second language conversation, when NNS are unable to catch the words of NS, they tend to ask for a repeating. But it becomes psychological burden for NNS if they ask many times [7]. In addition, NS are unconscious of their fast-talking even when they notice their partners are NNS [8]. They may speak slowly at first, but fasten their SR unconsciously. Also known is that SR tends to change dramatically in daily conversation [9]. Thus SR is an important factor.

2.2   Speech Rate and NNS Listening

SR is known to affect the listener's comprehension, which is an important factor especially in second language conversation.

Griffiths conducted an experiment of second language listening. NNS listened the text recorded at three levels of SR of fast (200 wpm), normal (150 wpm), and slow (100 wpm), and were tested their comprehension. The text recorded by fast SR significantly reduced the comprehension of NNS, but normal and slow SR had no significant difference on the influence on NNS listening comprehension [2]. Zhao prepared listening materials in normal SR, those in different SR, and those that NNS could freely control their SR, let NNS listen to each listening material, and investigated SR and NNS listening comprehension. It was shown that NNS often adjusted to a slower SR than normal SR when he/she could control it, resulting in better comprehension [3].

In the context of second language learning, normal and slow SR for NNS are effective for speech comprehension. However, it is not true that the slower the SR the better the listening comprehension. There is an optimal SR by NNS that helps understanding. Hayati divided 62 English learners into 2 groups, and distributed natural SR listening materials and slow SR listening materials to each group. The learners participated in English classes with the same content. They were given a pre-test before listening and a post-test two weeks later to measure their listening comprehension. As a result, both groups improved their listening comprehension, but the group receiving the natural SR listening material showed more progress [10].

Also, in a study on the effects of SR and noise on NNS listening, Jones et al., prepared a fast SR (155 wpm) and a normal SR (178 wpm) instructions of a banking product by using a text-to-speech system. A comparative study was performed using those and also those with a background noise. As a result, it was found that NNS listening comprehension had little to do with the noise. It was also shown that the understanding rate of the content decreased in the fast SR instructions [11].

Matsuura et al. investigated the influence of SR on NNS listening in an accented second language. It was shown that Japanese learners of English learn more efficiently by listening at a slower SR of accented English than by listening at the usual SR [12].

2.3   Second Language Conversation Support

Various methods and systems have been proposed to support conversation in a second language.

Inoue et al. proposed an NNS conversation support method that considered the burden of the NNS in conversation. During the second language conversation including the NNS in a remote setting, the NS inputs keywords and key phrases of the conversation from the keyboard and shares them on the NNS screen. The method was shown to have the effect of increasing understanding of the conversation and increasing the participants' mutual understanding [13].

Okamoto et al. developed a face-to-face cross-cultural communication support system to compensate for the differences in knowledge brought by the cultural background of different countries. This was a system that presented related information of the nouns in a conversation, which was retrieved by the Web. From the evaluation experiment, it was shown that presenting images, explanatory information in the native language, related nouns, and related images about the nouns spoken during the conversation to the user may support the dialogue [14]. However, due to the accuracy of speech recognition, the accuracy of the presented information may not be sufficient.

Fukushima et al. developed an interface that allowed different language debaters to input words in various languages, which were translated into a common language of the discussion in real time by a multi-lingual translation server [15]. Although it could improve the accuracy of the discussion, it needed extra workers for text input besides discussion participants.

This research focuses the SR of NS in second language conversation. and supports it by a method that The proposed system detects the SR of NS in real time, and when the SR is judged to be too fast, notifies it to the participants as an awareness sign.

2.4   Conversation Support by Speech Rate Conversion

A SR conversion systems have been developed to solve the listening problem of the fast SR voice. Fujitsu developed a SR conversion technology that detected the voice interval and the silent interval, and extended the voice interval while shortening the silent interval, so that the SR of the receiving voice could be reduced. As a result of evaluation experiment on participants of all ages, it was confirmed that it increased the ease of listening regardless of the listener's age when the SR of the receiving voice is fast [16]. Kiyoyama et al. proposed a SR conversion method based on expansion and contraction including silent sections, and developed a small SR converter aimed at improving voice broadcasting service for the elderly [17].

A change in SR has the effect of improving the ease of listening in general, but SR conversion could cause time lags in free conversation scenes, and may cause a sense of discomfort in synchronization. In order to examine the influence of the difference between the speaker video and the speech on the word intelligibility, Tsumura et al. prepared a pair word stimulus of one phoneme difference in each mora out of 4 mora words, conducted a word intelligibility experiment under the conditions of "video only," "voice only," and "audio + video;" and examined whether audio-visual integration occurred at each mora position. As a result, when word speech was expanded to 400 ms or more and video with normal speed was added, it was found that the word intelligibility might be affected [18].

Therefore, this research does not apply SR conversion technology. Instead, we try to support listening of the conversation by the method that the speaker spontaneously speaks slowly by informing when the SR of NS is too fast.

3   Experiment on NNS Comprehension of NS Speech

We conducted a face-to-face conversation experiment using NS and NNS as a pair. During a 10-minute free conversation, when the NNS felt difficulty in the NS utterance, he/she pressed the hand-held button to record the time.

It has been pointed out that the complexity and pause of the words and the SR may cause listening difficulties in NNS, but when NS and NNS talk, the real-time SR change of NS is NNS It is unclear what kind of influence it has on understanding.

3.1   Participants

The participants were 15 pairs of Japanese NS (Japanese students) and Japanese NNS (international students) who met for the first time, for a total of 30 participants.

NS was a person who used Japanese as a native language, and NNS could speak Japanese (N2 or more) but not so fluent as NS, who sometimes felt incomprehension.

NNS was asked to make self-introduction and daily conversation with NS for about 5 min, and his/her Japanese level was confirmed based on the behavior when the NNS is troubled [19], asking the NS to listen back during the conversation, silencing to the NS utterance, or making a troubled expression or gesture.

3.2   Apparatus and Setup of the Experiment

The layout and the setup during the experiment are shown in Figs. 1 and 2. NS and NNS sat face to face at a distance of 120 cm.

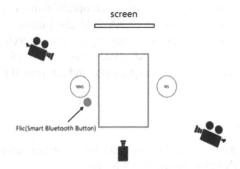

Fig. 1. Layout of the experiment.

Fig. 2. Snapshot of the experiment.

In order to keep track of when NNS felt misunderstanding, we handed Shortcut Labs' Bluetooth-connected push-button device Flic only to NNS (Fig. 3). By using the provided software development kit, the Rasberry Pi 3Model B with Bluetooth connection can record the time when Flic was pressed in a text file.

Fig. 3. Bluetooth-connected push-button device Flic.

3.3 Procedure of the Experiment

NNS was told to press once when NNS was incomprehensible in the conversation with NS, and handed the hand-held button. NNS held the button under the desk so NS would not notice. NS wore a microphone and recorded his speech. The experiment was videotaped. The pair talked freely for 10 min. After that, NNS and the experimenter watched the video recording of the conversation, and confirmed the timing of pressing the button and the reason.

3.4 Collected Data

The acquired data are the video and audio recording of the experiment, and the time log of the unrecognized utterance by the NNS button.

Time and Reason of Unrecognized Utterance. The experimenter with the NNS himself/herself, while playing back the video shot, confirmed to the NNS whether the timing recorded in the text file with the hand-held button matched the timing of the unrecognition, and corrected any mistake. We also identified the reasons for each of the incomprehension (based on the surveys of Bloomfield et al. [1] and Goh [6]). An excerpt is shown in Fig. 4.

#	#	Logged time	Incomprehension part	Reason
Pair13	1	16:06:47	"Stratum"	Unknown word
	2	16:07:09	"Information-related"	Too fast speech
	3	16:07:36	"···vertical···"	Too fast speech
	4	16:07:47	"Would you like it with your mouth"	Too fast speech
	5	16:07:56	"Sichuan"	Late recognition
	6	16:09:21	"Regent"	Unknown word
	7	16:09:34	"I want you to get stuck"	Unknown word/phrase
	8	16:10:46	"Is swimming in your school classes"	Too fast speech

Fig. 4. An excerpt from the sheet of time and reason of incomprehension in conversation.

3.5   Processing of the Collected Data

Labeling NS Utterance and NNS Unrecognition. For the experimental video data with a total of 150 min of speech from 10 min per the pair, the NS speech segment and the NS speech segment where NNS had incomprehension were labeled in the following procedure.

(1) Using the multimodal data annotation tool ELAN, we cut out the speech segments divided by silence of more than 200 ms.
(2) After automated processing by ELAN, manual inspection and correction were performed. Non-verbal speech segments such as laughter, cough and sigh were excluded from the speech segment.
(3) In order to analyze the speech rate of NS, only the speech segments of NS were left.
(4) Every segment of NS speech was transcribed.
(5) We identified and labeled NS speech segments that NNS could not catch (Fig. 5).

Fig. 5. NS speech segments that NNS could not catch were labeled.

Calculation of SR of NS. Although the SR to listen was constant in the conventional study of SR of NS and NNS understanding, the actual speech does not always go at the same speed. Marushima measured speed changes during speech and showed that the speed of natural speech was constantly changing [9]. Therefore, in order to investigate the relationship between SR and the degree of comprehension of the utterance content, it is considered necessary to investigate the SR in the vicinity where the incomprehension arose and the change thereof.

In the experiment, it was found that the button press of the NNS occurred during or immediately after the incomprehensible speech (Fig. 6). Therefore, with regard to the SR of NS at the time of incomprehension, we calculated two SRs in the speech segment that became incomprehensible and the speech segment immediately before that, and examined the change. The SR was defined using the number of syllables per second in the speech segment.

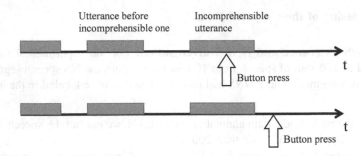

Fig. 6. Button press of the NNS occurred during or immediately after the incomprehensible speech.

3.6 Result

The Reasons of NNS Incomprehension. The reasons of NNS incomprehension of NS speech are shown in Table 1.

Table 1. The reasons of NNS incomprehension of NS speech.

Factor	Reason	# Occurred
Hearer's	Lack of vocabulary	37
	Slow recognition and response to the comprehensible words	25
	Could not keep up with the flow of conversation	2
	Stuck in the previous word	2
Speaker's	Too fast SR	18
	Loudness, crispness	5
Composite	Includes too fast SR	6
	Not include too fast SR	7
Other	Did not hear	1
	Do not know	12
Total		115

From the total of 115 incomprehensible speech segments in 150 min of conversation, 24 cases were because of too fast SR of NS, which comprises 21% of all the incomprehensible cases.

Therefore alleviating the problem of fast SR of NS will contribute to better NNS comprehension.

Change of SR of NS. The change of SR of NS when NNS faced incomprehension was analyzed. Seventy-five cases were used from the total of 115 cases. The cases by the reasons clearly unrelated to the SR, which were "unknown vocabulary" and "did not hear," were excluded. The cases that could not transcribe were also excluded. The SR of the speech segment that became incomprehensible and that of the speech segment immediately before that were shown in Fig. 7. The SR of NS speech that NNS could not hear was an average of 7.85 syllables/second (SD = 1.96), and the SR of NS speech just before its incomprehension was an average of 7.15 syllables/second (SD = 2.14), showing the significant difference (t(74) = 2.231, p < .05). This shows that the increase of SR of NS during conversation actually occurs when NNS faces incomprehension of NS speech.

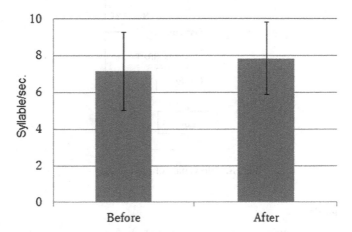

Fig. 7. Change of NS speech speed when NNS incomprehension occurred.

4 An Experiment of Speech Speed Awareness Method

4.1 Speech Speed Awareness Method

Considering the influence of SR in the second language conversation that NS fast-forward is one of the factors that make NNS' comprehension difficult, a method to inform NS fast-forward in real time and encourage spontaneous adjustment of NS has been proposed [4]. In this method, the NNS is assumed those who can make conversation to some degree with the second language used, but who is not as fluent as NS. It is often the case in international business settings in recent years, and thus this assumption is realistic.

4.2 Speech Speed Awareness System by WOZ

The Speech Speed Awareness system by WOZ method was designed, and its effect was evaluated. The flowchart diagram of the system is shown in Fig. 8. To study the effect of the method, WOZ system was used to avoid the influence on the result of other factors than the method such as accuracy of speech recognition.

The system displayed the red screen with the text "TOO FAST" when SR of NS becomes faster than the preset speed that NNS felt comfortable. Its display turned green with the text "GOOD" when SR of NS becomes slower.

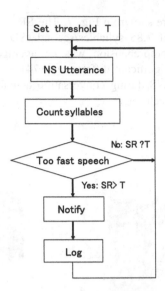

Fig. 8. Flowchart of the system.

4.3   Participants

The participants were 20 pairs of Japanese NS (Japanese students) and Japanese NNS (international students) who met for the first time, for a total of 40 participants.

NS was a person who used Japanese as a native language, and NNS could speak Japanese (N2 or more) but not so fluent as NS, who sometimes felt incomprehension.

NNS was asked to make self-introduction and daily conversation with NS for about 5 min, and his/her Japanese level was confirmed based on the behavior when the NNS is troubled [19], asking the NS to listen back during the conversation, silencing to the NS utterance, or making a troubled expression or gesture.

4.4   Procedure

NNS prepared the threshold SR of notification by the system, by listening sample speeches of various speed and choosing comfortable one. NS wore a microphone and recorded his/her speech. The experiment was videotaped. Each NS and NNS pair talked 5 min. The experiment is shown in Fig. 9. The acquired data were the video and audio recording of the experiment.

4.5   Processing of the Collected Data

For the experiment video data with a total of 100 min of speech from 5 min per a pair, the NS speech segment and the screen notification section by the system were labeled in the following procedure.

(1) Using the multimodal data annotation tool ELAN, we cut out the speech segments divided by silence of more than 200 ms.

Fig. 9. Snapshot of the WOZ system experiment.

(2) After automated processing by ELAN, manual inspection and correction were performed. Non-verbal speech segments such as laughter, cough and sigh were excluded from the speech segment.

(3) In order to analyze the SR of NS, only the speech segments of NS were left.

(4) We identified and labeled the screen notification sections.

(5) NS speech segments before and after the screen notification were transcribed (Fig. 10).

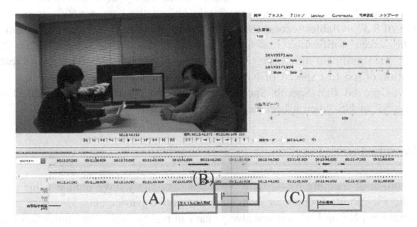

Fig. 10. Labeling a screen notification section and NS speech segments before and after that. (A) NS speech before the screen notification, (B) The screen notification, (C) NS speech after the screen notification.

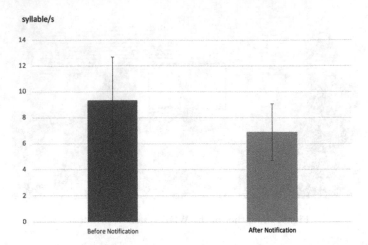

Fig. 11. Change in NS speech speed by the screen notification of too fast NS speech.

4.6   Result

The change in SR of NS by the screen notification of too fast NS speech was analyzed. Fifty-three cases were used from the total of 63 cases in the total of 100 min. conversation. The cases that the experimenter (wizard) made wrong judgement of SR over threshold were excluded. The SR of the speech segment immediately before the screen notification and that of the speech segment immediately after that were shown in Fig. 11. The SR of NS speech immediately before the screen notification was an average of 9.37 syllables/second (SD = 3.35), and the SR of NS speech immediately after the screen notification was an average of 6.87 syllables/second (SD = 2.18), showing the significant difference (Z = −5.759, p = 0.000 < .05). This shows that the notification of too fast speech of NS actually prompted NS slow down.

It was proved that Speech Speed Awareness system by WOZ was effective in reducing SR of NS when it became too fast for NNS.

5   Conclusion

Conversation or meeting by NS and NNS could possibly have unique value considering the viewpoints brought in from such diversified participants. However, conversation between NS and NNS is not always easy in reality. NNS sometimes feel hard to understand NS talk because of their speech rate. In this paper, we study conversation between NS and NNS regarding SR of NS. The first experiment revealed that dynamic SR change of NS actually occurred and that it caused incomprehension of NNS. The second experiment indicated the introduction of a speech speed awareness system, which made aware of SR of NS to him/herself, could actually slow down SR of NS.

The effect by the implemented speech speed awareness system will be investigated in the future. Also, influence on NNS comprehension and mutual understanding between NS and NNS will be investigated.

References

1. Bloomfield, A., et al.: What makes listening difficult? Factors affecting second language listening comprehension. Maryland Univ College Park (2010)
2. Griffiths, R.: Speech rate and NNS comprehension: A preliminary study in time benefit analysis. Lang. Learn. **40**(3), 311–336 (1990)
3. Zhao, Y.: The effects of listeners' control of speech rate on second language comprehension. Appl. Linguist. **18**(1), 49–68 (1997)
4. Jing, Y., Tomoo, I.: A speech speed awareness system for non-native speakers. In: Proceedings of the 19th ACM Conference on Computer Supported Cooperative Work and Social Computing Companion (CSCW 2016 Companion), pp. 49–52 (2016)
5. Ikegami, M.: The relationship between the stage of development of student's listening comprehension skills and the effects of pauses and speech speed. Stud. Lang. Lit. **32**(1-1), 59–88 (2012)
6. Goh, C.C.: A cognitive perspective on language learners' listening comprehension problems. System **28**(1), 55–75 (2000)
7. Yanagimachi, T., Nagano, K., Enai, M., Baba, N.: Communication Problems and Solutions for International Students Speaking in Japanese. Jpn. Soc. Eng. Educ. **61**(4), 43–47 (2013)
8. Sakuma, A.: Various aspects of crosscultural communication: concerning elements other than language. Bull. Nagoya Bunri Univ. **3**, 13–21 (2003)
9. Marushima, A.: Perception of gradually changing speech rate. Res. Exp. Phon. Linguist. **4**, 1–21 (2012)
10. Hayati, A.: The effect of speech rate on listening comprehension of EFL learners. Creat. Educ. **1**, 107–114 (2010)
11. Jones, C., Berry, L., Stevens, C.: Synthesized speech intelligibility and persuasion: Speech rate and non-native listeners. Comput. Speech Lang. **21**(4), 641–651 (2007)
12. Matsuura, H., et al.: Accent and speech rate effects in English as a lingua franca. System **46**, 143–150 (2014)
13. Hanawa, H., Song, X., Inoue, T.,: Keyword generation by native speaker is quick and useful in conversation between native and non-native speaker. In: Proceedings of the 2017 IEEE 21st International Conference on Computer Supported Cooperative Work in Design (CSCWD 2017), pp. 145–150 (2017)
14. Okamoto, K., Yoshino, T.: Development and evaluation of face-to-face intercultural communication support system using related information of nouns in conversation. J. Inf. Process. **52**(3), 1213–1223 (2011)
15. Fukushima, T., Yoshino, T., Kita, C.: Development of non-native language user support system PaneLive at face-to-face discussion using common language. IEICE Trans. Inf. Syst. **J92-D**(6), 719–728 (2009)
16. Togawa, T., Otani, T., Suzuki, K.: Speech enhancement technology, speech rate control technology. J. Inst. Electron. Inf. Commun. Eng. **96**(11), 874–881 (2013)
17. Seiyama, N., Imai, A., Mishima, T., Takagi, T., Miyasaka, E.: Development of a high-quality real-time speech rate conversion system. Trans. Inst. Electron. Inf. Commun. Eng. **J84-D-II**(6), 918–926 (2001)
18. Tsumura, K., Tanaka, A., Sakamoto, S., Suzuki, Y.-i.: Effect of audio-visual asynchrony by speech-rate conversion on word recognition. IEICE Tech. Rep. **105**(479), 103–108 (2005)
19. Ozaki, A.: Use and avoidance of clarification requests by Brazilians in Japanese contact situations. Jpn. J. Lang. Soc. **4**(1), 81–90 (2001)

A Comic-Style Chat System
with Japanese Expression Techniques
for More Expressive Communication

Junko Itou[1(✉)], Kazuho Matsumura[1], Jun Munemori[1], and Noboru Babaguchi[2]

[1] Wakayama University, 930, Sakaedani, Wakayama 640-8510, Japan
itou@wakayama-u.ac.jp
[2] Osaka University, Suita, Osaka 565-0871, Japan

Abstract. This paper proposes a comic-style chat interface that incorporates expression techniques of Japanese manga. Characters used in graphical chat systems can express a variety of visual information. The format of a comic is also used as a visual interface to express a user's states of mind or aspects. However, there is a problem that it is difficult to select drawings or the other components of comic, that match the emotion a user wants to express. By incorporating the techniques of Japanese manga, this paper attempts to explain how to create a screen with a simple reading order and a visual that easily conveys the selected emotions. The results of the experiment showed that the proposed system is superior to prevalent chat systems in conveying user's states of mind.

1 Introduction

This paper proposes a comic-style chat interface that incorporates the expression techniques used in manga, that is Japanese comic. A wide range of information is visualized and conveyed to the reader of a Japanese manga. This information is not limited to attribute information of characters that can be represented in a single drawing, such as gender, age, and appearance; it also includes, for example, the characters' visual line direction, various symbols arranged within the screen, the adjustment of the brightness of the screen, the way the background is drawn, the way these elements are combined, and the way the frames are lined up on a two-dimensional surface. By incorporating these techniques, this paper attempts to explain how to create a screen with a simple reading order and a visual that easily conveys the selected emotions.

In the field of communication over networks, there have been many proposals for graphical dialog interfaces that combine drawings and characters represented by 2D/3D models [1–4]. Some of the useful aspects of interfaces that convey information visually include assisting the understanding of the message content, improving affinity and motivation, and facilitating the interaction between users. Drawing is said to be another language of human beings; a communication medium using vision [5].

© Springer Nature Switzerland AG 2019
H. Nakanishi et al. (Eds.): CRIWG+CollabTech 2019, LNCS 11677, pp. 172–187, 2019.
https://doi.org/10.1007/978-3-030-28011-6_12

The characters used in graphical dialog systems act as agents for users, to express their moods and intentions. Such information cannot be conveyed in a traditional text chat message. However, as long as the characters have their "faces", users are required to control the appropriate facial expressions of the character in order to avoid misleading their interlocutors. It is burdensome for users to manually choose various emotions for each message while chatting [6]. We consider ways to reduce this burden.

In systems that represent interlocutors using avatars, the appearance of the avatar makes them appear human. These systems do not consider the possibility of reading back through the dialog at a later time [7]. Some of systems that use avatars to display information do not consider the interaction between the provider and the receiver of information [3]. As dialog interfaces that leave a record of the conversation, these systems have room for improvement.

In addition to avatars, the format of a cartoon is also used as an interface to visualize information or conversations [8–12]. This makes it easier to grasp the contents of message. However, such systems have problems whereby the objects that users can operate are limited or it is difficult to understand the order of message: it is visually monotonic, owing to which the operation becomes burdensome.

This paper proposes a chat interface that incorporates the techniques of expression used in manga. The system implements a screen that is easy to understand in terms of the order of message, and attempts to convey selected emotions for visual comprehension. The main contributions of this study are as follows. The chat interface makes it possible for chat users to express emotions more easily and richly than existing systems. In addition, the chat interface makes the chat conversation more exciting and enjoyable.

This paper is organized as follows: in Sect. 2, we will describe the problems about existing tools to output comic style records and related chat systems to support conveying nonverbal information. In Sect. 3, we explain how our system supports emotional chat. We will show the experimental result on whether users can add nonverbal information to chat messages intuitively in Sect. 4. Finally, we will discuss some conclusions and our future steps in Sect. 5.

2   Related Works on Transmitting Nonverbal Information

2.1   Images in Communication Support Systems

Pictographs and stamps are used as pictures on cellular phones and instant messengers. There are various types of pictographs, such as those expressing emotional states, or depicting animals, plants, and buildings. Images also can be used to complement the meaning of text in communication services such as LINE[1], Twitter[2], and Skype[3]. The images are used with the object of emphasizing a particular sentence or intention. In these tools, it is possible to create one

---

[1] LINE: Free Calls & Messages, https://line.me/en/.

[2] Twitter. It's what's happening, https://twitter.com/.

[3] Skype: Free calls to friends and family, https://www.skype.com/en/.

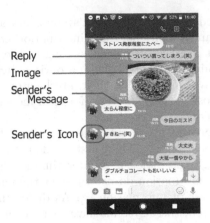

Fig. 1. An example of LINE messages.

meaningful work by using a series of images. On the other hand, the arrangement of the posted images is limited to the arrangement lined up in the vertical space, with no further combinations of graphical expression possible. It is impossible to combine more graphic representations. Figure 1 shows an example of LINE messages.

2.2 Communication Support Systems with Graphical Interface

A number of tools have been developed to support online communication on chat applications, instant messengers, and online games. Users can employ avatars as their agents in these systems. An avatar has a human-like body that can easily express the user's emotions as well as emoticons and pictographs can. In systems that represent emotions with an avatar, users can exchange their intentions easily. However these systems do not consider the possibility of looking back on the dialogue at a later time. Also, systems that use avatars to display information do not consider the interaction between the information provider and receiver. As dialogue interfaces that leave a record of the conversation, these systems still have room for improvement.

Besides avatars, the format of a comic is also used as a visual interface. Comic Chat is a system in which the users talk in a comic-like format with a variety of characters [7]. Every time the user sends a message, a square frame is displayed in sequence from the left to right. The characters, speech balloons, and backgrounds selected by user are drawn in the frames. The user can also use an emotion selection circle on the bottom-right of the input screen to specify an emotion and its degree. When a message is sent, the character with the selected emotion and a balloon with the text inside are displayed in the square frame along with the background. The character's position within the frame, the shape of the balloon, and the perspective are automatically defined. The positions of the balloons and the characters are fixed at the top and the bottom of the frame, respectively. In this system the composition is limited to a pattern that represents the characters from the side. As the shape of the frames are limited to squares of equal size, the interface makes it difficult to grasp the direction of the dialog, the elapsed time, and the development of the narrative. The circular interface of facial expression selection has problems as well, as it is difficult to identify the expression strength accurately.

Comic Diary is a system using which it is possible to write a diary in the format of a comic [8]. The user can save and share personal experiences and records in a format with excellent readability. The system automatically creates a story with an introduction, development, and a conclusion, based on the user's historical behavioral data. The system selects the most suitable parts of comics from a material database. The creation process of a diary is very easy. On the other hands, the user cannot become involved in the creation of the plot or the selection of the comic-related parts, such as the expressions of the characters' emotions. The shape and size of the frames are fixed as in Comic Chat, and the number of frames is limited to no more than 12.

Thawonmas et al. proposed a system that summarizes the behavior of 3D online game players in a comic format based on the game log [9]. It divides the play content into multiple sections based on actions and events within the game, such as dialogs between players and switches of viewpoints. It sorts events within the sections into multiple frames, defines the shapes and sizes of the frames, and creates a comic using them in many formats. Based on the frame composition and layout, the player can comprehend the storyline, the elapse time, and the rhythm. In this system, the screen images and balloons, captured at automatically defined times, are simply laid out in the frames. It is not possible to add other symbols or information to explain a given situation. For this reason, it is not possible to express customized messages that the player might want to convey.

AVACHAT is a comic style communication interface [11]. The avatar agents communicate in the virtual worlds and the 3-D word balloons are displayed above their head. When an agent speaks "loudly", the chat text is placed in a bigger balloon with a bigger bolder font. Comic Live Chat [12] also display transmitted texts in a balloon below the image of the sender. These systems express the remark as a balloon around a person in the chat screen. However, they do not consider the size and the placement of frames, and background effect.

Some systems have been proposed that automatically transform a video into a comic book. Tobita's system [13] allows users to control the frame size and the position by simple manipulations. Chun's system focuses on the placement of balloons in a frame. The system optimizes the positions of balloons considering not only the reading order but also the relationships between the balloons and their owners. However, a mechanism for expressing emotions is not implemented in these systems.

As mentioned above, systems with interactive interfaces that use drawings require visual improvement. Manga applied in some systems uses many elements to visually represent the characters' facial expressions and the situations they encounter. These include the direction of a character's visual line, various symbols and patterns arranged in the background, the shapes of the speech balloons, and frame arrangements. This paper aims to create a system that incorporates these techniques to express user emotions in a format that is visually easy to understand, instead of simply lining up the frames. The system also reduces the burden on the user due to the inputs for emotions.

3   Manga-Style Chat System

3.1   Components of Manga

Our goal is to develop a chat system that incorporates representations from manga, so that the layout of text and the drawings convey information over and above the text content. Manga has many rules to visually represent and transmit information.

Manga consists of drawings within a space delimited by thick lines called a frame. It is possible to convey a variety of information using the layout of the drawing, the text, and the frames. We discuss the main elements and techniques of expression for visual representation and communication used in manga.

The basic element of manga is the frame. A frame is composed of a drawing of characters as well the background, speech balloons, patterns, and symbols drawn on many layers of dots, lines, and texts. The thick lines that indicate the position of the frame form a rectangular shape, and may take on other polygonal shapes as well depending on the content to be represented. These frames lined up on a 2D place form the structure of a manga. The frames have temporarily connected contents, and are arranged in a manner that guides the reader from one scene of the story to the next. The layout and the change of frame size also represent the elapse time or temporal and spatial breaks. Evenly lining up frames of the same size represent a uniform time flow.

Figure 2 shows a typical example of frame arrangement in Japanese manga. The reader starts reading from the frame on the right end at the top to the left at the same level. When the left end is reached, the reader moves to the frame on the right end of the level immediately below and reads it to the left. By adjusting the size and shape of the frames and guiding the reader's eyes in an irregular way [14], it is possible to express emotions better. It is also possible to express the spread of space and the atmosphere of the given place, time, and tempo. This way of expressing movement through frame arrangement and frame composition is a technique unique to manga, as is the drawing method [15].

A speech balloon represents the character's speech. The serifs are written in balloons. Most shapes of the balloons used in American comics are used to explain actions, such as shouting and thinking, rather than to express the characters' psychological condition. The use of fonts and balloons of varied sizes is a technique that originated in Japan [16].

In Japanese manga, the background is simplified, and contains symbols that represent the characters' psychological states. The reader can divine the situation from the volume of the drawing, or the impression of light and darkness afforded by the drawing itself.

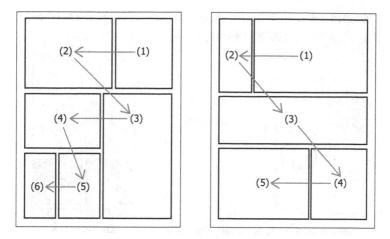

Fig. 2. The typical sequence of frames in Japanese manga.

3.2   Design Policy

We use a variety of techniques of expression used in manga to improve the user's experience of the interface.

– To avoid the impression of monotony and a lack of change, our system employs a composition that views the dialogue by two characters from above or from below. The user can also change the size of the frame to make it easy to understand the time flow.
– To reduce the burden of selecting and entering the appropriate avatars or emoticons, we limit the types of representations available. Prevalent systems that allow the selection of emotions offer an interface with several types of emotions [7,17]. We also narrow down the types of emotions that are frequently expressed in conversation, and limit the selectable emotions to reduce burden.
– The system allows users to combine various manga elements instead of narrowing down the number of emotions. Balloons drawn with rounded lines give a soft and calm impression. When combined with sharp lines, they convey a sense of aggressiveness and urgency. A particularly famous symbol called "manpu" in Japan consists of a line in the shape of a drop. Sweat marks, very different from the shape of actual sweat, are used as to represent an emergency or confusion. In addition to sweat, the shapes of lights and bubbles, fog, blue veins, and bandages adorn drawings in a frame. We incorporate these drawing techniques into the proposed chat system.

3.3   System Overview

The proposed system consists of PHP, Apache and JavaScript with jQuery. JavaScript determines the frame image to be displayed on the clients' screens

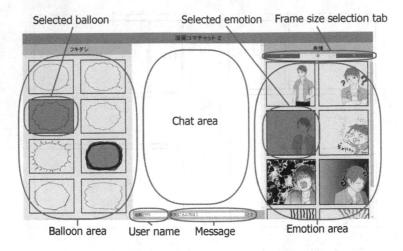

Fig. 3. Overview of the proposed system.

Fig. 4. An example of a screen on a smartphone.

based on the input data including the text message, the size of the frame, the shape of the balloon and the emotion. The input data is sent to the web server that is running PHP. The server sends the data to each client and the clients draw a new frame on the screen using JavaScript.

The proposed system consists of a server and clients connected to a network. When a user starts the system, a window comes up as shown in Fig. 3. The main space displays frames with pictures and chat messages. Users enter chat messages and select the sizes of frames from the upper right tab. They click the illustration of the relevant emotion and the balloon; the system then determines the position of the new frame and draws it along with the message, the balloon, and the character.

Users can access the system from their smartphones or their personal computers. Figure 4 shows an example of a screen on a smartphone.

Fig. 5. Characters in the proposed system.

3.4 Emotions of Characters

Preliminary Research. An overview of the two characters of manga is provided in Fig. 5. Users can choose a character, but two users cannot use the same character at a time. These characters can represent eight kinds of emotions: "Joy", "Surprise", "Sadness", "Thinking", "Neutral", "Doubt", "Confusion", and "Laughing". These eight kinds of emotions were adopted based on the results of preliminary research involving college students who used online communication tools every day.

The preliminary research was carried out in two steps. We classified the emotions used in daily conversations into 10 categories, with reference to the four types of emotions used in related systems [17], the eight basic emotions of Plutchik's wheel of emotions [18], and the six basic emotion of Ekman [19]. From messaging exchanged through tools in daily conversations with the experimenter, two sets of conversation sentences were extracted for each emotion for a total of 20 sets. We handed papers with the 20 sets printed on them to 16 participants and asked them to answer questions about the kinds of emotions they selected for each conversation sentence. The answer choices were the above 10 types of emotions and "Others", and multiple answers were possible. When there was no corresponding emotion, the participants were allowed to describe reasonable, customized emotions in a free description field. Based on the results of this survey, we selected the eight emotions to be used in our system.

Characters. We drew illustrations to be used in the proposed system using mainly the character's facial expressions, actions, manpus, background, and effect lines. We adopted the techniques of expression frequently used for drawings in manga to express each emotion. We adjust the brightness, balloon shape, and representation of symbols within the frames for each emotion.

Fig. 6. An example of arranged frames.

In the frame showing the emotion "Joy", a woman raises the corners of her mouth, narrows her eyes, and moves her hands to express her pleasure. Short, thin lines are drawn on the background outward from the character. The background is drawn to represent the appearance of energy.

In the emotion "Surprise", a man has his eyes and his mouth open wide. The straight lines drawn around the character and the raised shoulders express the movement that tends to occur when one is surprised. The background effect called lightning flash represents the magnitude of the impact.

In the frame showing the emotion "Sadness", the character expresses a morose appearance with wrinkles between the eyebrows, tears, and a stunned disposition. It expresses dark feelings, with the manpu representing black, dull feelings and a background that becomes darker as it approaches the character.

The frame expressing "Neutral" does not use special signs in the background.

Many short lines are arranged around the character in the frame for "Thinking". This method gives the impression to readers that the character is shrouded in thought. It has been reported that persons sometimes take their gazes from their interlocutor when they are thinking what to say [20, 21]. We use this observation on the character in thought.

It is possible to generate frames expressing various emotions by combining speech balloons with the drawings of characters.

3.5   Arrangement of Frames

The system inserts a new frame to the right of a row when the row has no frame. When the row has one frame to the right, a new frame is placed to the left and a new row is inserted below the given row. An example of the insertion of multiple frames is shown in Fig. 6.

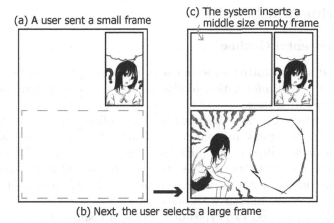

Fig. 7. Insertion of an empty frame.

Fig. 8. Four kinds of combinations involving a text, a balloon, and an emotion.

When a user sends a message with an emotion, the display of the sent message varies depending on the size of the empty space. Figure 7 shows an example of the insertion of an empty frame. When a large frame is transmitted in the presence of empty space, or when a middle frame is transmitted in a small empty space, it does not fit the size of the empty space. The system automatically inserts an empty frame into the empty space and displays the sent frame in a new row.

When users enter a text without choosing a balloon, it is not drawn in the frame. When they do not select an emotion, the character is not drawn. Four types of frames can be created: a text-only frame with no balloon and no character, text within a balloon frame, a character and a text frame, and a combination of text, a balloon, and a character. Figure 8 shows examples of the combinations of text, a balloon, and an emotion.

The system automatically determines the size of the frame for which no emotion is selected. The reason for introducing such a mechanism lies in reducing the burden on the user. When the users emphasize the tempo of their conversation, it is not necessary to select the size of frames at the time of sending a message. When users do not select emotions, the frame size is automatically adjusted according to the empty space of the row.

4   Experimental Results

4.1   Experimental Outline

We conducted a comparative experiment to investigate whether users can intuitively add nonverbal information to chat messages in our system, and if it can reduce the burden on users.

The participants of our experiment were 16 college students accustomed to handling keyboard inputs and online communication. They had all also used emoticons in daily online communication. They were divided into eight pairs and asked to chat while sitting in separate rooms to prevent direct conversations. They were informed in advance about the identity of their conversation partner. The participants were familiar with one another.

The participants used two types of systems, a comparative system and the proposed system. The comparative system was LINE, one of the most popular online communication tools. LINE allows communications through text and multimedia images. A text message is shown herein in a balloon-shaped text box, along with a timestamp and a mark to indicate that the message had been read. New messages are inserted under old ones in the same window. LINE does not allow users to send an image and a text message at the same time. Therefore, text balloons and images are lined up in the vertical chat space.

We instructed each pair of participants to chat for 10 min using each system. Four pairs used the proposed system first and other four first used LINE to account for the influence of order. In both systems, no restrictions were imposed on the subjects with regard to using these systems. The topics of conversation of the participants were the following two themes: a movie and a drama, and an animation that they had recently. At the end of the experiment, we asked the participants to answer some questions.

We denote the experiment that used the proposed system by exp_J and that which used LINE by exp_L. The result of the questionnaire are shown in Table 1. Each number signifies the number of participants who selected the given point on a five-point scale.

4.2   Expression of Nonverbal Information

As shown in Table 1, the participants' assignment of scores for item (i) for the proposed system was higher than that for LINE. There was a significant difference between exp_J and exp_L on the Mann-Whitney U test ($p = 0.01$). One participant described a comment in the free description field of exp_L, as follows: "I could supplement my emotions and intentions by adding a matched image to a text message after sending the text message". Other participants said of the proposed system that the expressions were excellent, and the drawings supported the smooth expression of their emotions and intentions. We concluded that the drawings and images were useful for expressing nonverbal information in both systems. Owing to the significant difference in the test and the scores, the proposed system was found to better express user emotions and intentions than LINE.

Table 1. Results of questionnaire survey.

Questionnaire item	Exp.	Calculated value					Med.	Mode
		1	2	3	4	5		
(i) I could express my emotions or intentions well through my messages	exp_J	0	0	2	9	5	4.0	4
	exp_L	0	2	6	7	1	3.5	4
(ii) I could understand emotions or intentions from my interlocutor's messages	exp_J	0	0	1	6	9	5.0	5
	exp_L	1	0	9	6	0	3.0	3
(iii) I had a sufficient number of emotions to choose from	exp_J	1	3	2	6	4	4.0	4
	exp_L	2	2	5	5	2	3.0	3, 4
(iv) I felt burdened while choosing emotions	exp_J	1	6	3	5	1	3.0	2
	exp_L	1	5	2	5	3	3.5	2, 4
(v) The drawings made the conversation more exciting	exp_J	0	0	1	3	12	5.0	5
	exp_L	1	2	8	4	1	3.0	3
(vi) It was easy to understand the flow of conversation	exp_J	0	2	3	4	7	4.0	5
	exp_L	0	0	5	9	2	4.0	4
(vii) The size control function of frames helped express emotions and intentions		0	2	3	9	2	4.0	4
(viii) The select function of the balloon shapes helped express emotions and intentions		0	0	3	8	5	4.0	4
(ix) There was a sufficient number of balloon shapes to choose from		0	0	1	12	3	4.0	4

With questionnaire items (vii) and (viii), we sought to determine whether changes to frame size and balloon shape helped participants express themselves better in the proposed system. We obtained a median and a mode of 4.0 for both items. In the free description field, the participants wrote the following answers:

- "The size control function of the frames was useful when I wanted to emphasize my message".
- "I could encourage my partner's next messages by leaving an empty space using small- or middle-sized frames".
- "I enjoyed our conversation because I could select balloons according to my messages and thus express my intentions".

These results also show that changes to frame size and balloon shape were useful for expressing nonverbal information.

Some participants reported finding the distinction between a small and a medium frame convenient. However, they hesitated to use a large frame because it made their respective expressions appear too strong. It is thus necessary to consider the appropriate sizes of frames.

4.3 Transmission of Nonverbal Information

Questionnaire item (ii) shows the evaluations of the received messages. The values for item (ii) for the proposed system exceeded those for LINE, and there was a significant difference between exp_J and exp_L in the Mann-Whitney U test ($p < 0.001$).

In the free description field, the participants claimed that the proposed system had made it easy to understand their expressed emotions and intentions through the drawings and the frame sizes. Another participant stated: "I understood the contents of the messages more easily by adding the balloons and facial expressions". Changes in frame size and expressions using shapes of balloons were thus helpful in interpreting nonverbal information. This showed that the participants were able to read situations more intuitively using the proposed system.

It cleared that in conversations using the proposed system, it was easier for users to understand the information and the flow of the conversation than when using LINE.

4.4 Number of Emotions and Selection of Nonverbal Information

Users were allowed to use 88 drawings in exp_L and only eight in exp_J. The results of values for item (iii) for both systems in Table 1, showed no significant difference. We obtained a median and a mode of 4.0 for the proposed system. While the proposed system allows for only eight emotions, the system was assessed to be comparable in terms of performance to LINE. We concluded that our system satisfied users as much as LINE in expressing emotions even if it allowed for considerably fewer drawings.

As discussed in Sect. 4.2, we assumed that changes to frame size and balloon shape were useful for expressing nonverbal information. Moreover, item (ix) had a median and a mode of 4.0 for the proposed system as well. The number of usable shapes of the balloons was considered sufficient to express the participants' emotions.

There was little difference in results between the two methods on item (iv). The large number of emotions in LINE increased the burden on participants to choose the appropriate emotion. Some participants reported feeling stressed from having to choose the size of the frame every time and scrolling the screen for large frames in the proposed system. We need to improve such features of the interface as the display and selection procedures.

4.5 Influence on Conversation

A clear difference between the two systems was observed for item (v). The proposed system had higher scores, with a median and a mode of 5.0, than LINE. There was a significant difference between exp_J and exp_L on the Mann-Whitney U test ($p < 0.01$). It was confirmed that the proposed system can thus encourage conversation through its drawings. For item (vi), the values for both systems

Table 2. The numbers of sent messages, character drawings, and balloons.

	Exp.	Total	Average
The number of sent messages	exp_J	237	14.8
	exp_L	412	25.7
The number of sent drawings	exp_J	219	13.7
	exp_L	49	3.1
The number of sent balloons	exp_J	209	13.1
The number of empty frames	exp_J	32	2.0

were similar with no significant difference. It was thus equally easy to understand the order of frames and messages, and to follow the flow of conversation in both the proposed system and LINE.

Table 2 shows the number of messages sent by all participants, and the characters and the balloons drawn. We rounded the average numbers to one decimal place. The number of sent drawings for exp_J did not include the empty frames.

The drawings and balloons in the proposed system were continually used in comparison with those in exp_L. In the survey, we obtained the following opinions from one participant: "I used the LINE stamp at key points as supplement. The drawings in the proposed system are easier to use repeatedly as a means of expressing emotions, as a text and drawings are a set, and it is easy to understand at first sight". We considered that the high visibility of information was one reason for the high evaluation scores for the proposed system, as mentioned in Sect. 4.2.

The number of sent messages was smaller in the proposed system than LINE because the task the user was required to select many items in order to send a message, such as the size of the frame and the emotion. The arrangement of frames influenced the sense of passing time and the flow of conversation. The number of empty frames was very small for the number of exchanged messages. In the free description field, the participants reported wanting to fill up the empty space in the chat area. We think that they felt uncomfortable about empty spaces and accordingly adjusted the sizes of the sent frames. Thus, further consideration of how to utilize empty spaces is needed.

We did not verify how much the difference between the emotion expressed by the sender and the emotion interpreted by the receiver was present in this experiment. One of the reasons is that the label of the selected emotion and the emotion actually expressed may not always match. For example, if a sender inputs an angry text on the emotion of "Joy", the receiver may interpret the message as angry even if the label is "Joy". We read the logs and checked whether there were unnaturally interpreted answer. As a result, no such unnatural communication was found. In the future, it is necessary to objectively investigate the difference in the interpretation of the sender and the receiver from the perspective of the interlocutor, and the perspective of the third person.

5   Conclusion

In this paper, we proposed a chat system that incorporates expressions from manga to convey emotional information intuitively and appropriately. The system displays input texts, drawings containing characters expressing emotions in a background, and a balloon chosen by the user. By repeatedly exchanging frames, users can understand the flow of conversations. They can also easily convey their intentions and understand those of their interlocutors.

We performed experiments to compare the proposed system and with the LINE chat system. The results of a questionnaire and analysis of log data showed that the proposed system can express and convey user intentions and emotions more easily and comprehensibly than LINE. Although the number of sentences exchanged in our experiments was small, the users felt that the conversations were exciting. The participants were required to select some components to send a message. Using this as measure, we concluded that the burden on users imposed by our system was equivalent to that imposed by LINE. In future research, we intend to enable our system to allow users to select more components of conversations and consider the use of empty spaces.

In this interface, emotions can be exchanged properly in daily conversations. However, users may use different emotions in serious discussions. It may not be suitable for use of this interface in such a situation. In this paper, we designed only two patterns of characters. Also in the experiment, the conversation by two persons was the object of the verification experiment. Therefore, it is unclear how the conversation is affected when the system is applied to three or more persons' conversations. It is necessary to increase the number of characters and verify whether it is possible to understand the order of conversation or whether it is possible to understand the other person's emotion from the messages expressed by manga.

Acknowledgments. This work was supported by JSPS KAKENHI Grant Number 16K00371.

References

1. Cassell, J., et al.: Embodiment in Conversational Interfaces: Rea, CHI-99, pp. 520–527 (1999)
2. De Carolis, B., Pelachaud, C., Poggi, I., De Rosis, F.: Behavior planning for a reflexive agent. In: Proceedings of International Joint Conference on Artificial Intelligence (IJCAI 2001), pp. 1059–1066 (2001)
3. Fukuhara, T., Chikama, M., Nishida, T.: Supporting an experiment of a community support system: community analysis and maintenance functions in the public opinion channel. In: Proceedings of the First International Conference on Communities and Technologies (C&T 2003), pp. 347–367 (2003)
4. Tanaka, T., Fujita, K.: Secretary agent for mediating interaction initiation. In: Proceedings of the First International Conference on Human-Agent Interaction (iHAI2013), II-p5 (2013)

5. Nishida, T.: Social intelligence design for web intellifence. In: Zhong, N., Liu, J., Yao, Y. (eds.) Web Intelligence, pp. 419–437. Springer Science & Business Media, Berlin (2003)
6. Itou, J., Hoshio, K., Munemori, J.: A prototype of a chat system using message driven and interactive actions character. In: Proceedings of the 10th International Conference on Knowledge-based Intelligent Information & Engineering Systems (KES 2006), pp. 212–218 (2006)
7. Kurlander, D., Skelly, T., Salesin, D.: Comic chat. In: Proceedings of the 23rd Annual Conference on Computer Graphics and Interactive Techniques (SIG-GRAPH 1996), pp. 225–236 (1996)
8. Sumi, Y., Sakamoto, R., Nakao, K., Mase, K.: ComicDiary: representing individual experiences in a comics style. In: Borriello, G., Holmquist, L.E. (eds.) UbiComp 2002. LNCS, vol. 2498, pp. 16–32. Springer, Heidelberg (2002). https://doi.org/10.1007/3-540-45809-3_2
9. Thawonmas, R., Shuda, T.: Comic layout for automatic comic generation from game log. Proc. Int. Fed. Inf. Process. (IFIP) **279**, 105–115 (2008)
10. Park, S., Ji, S., Ryu, D., Cho, H.: A new 3-Dimensional comic chat environment for on-line game avatars. In: Proceedings of International Conference on Digital Game and Intelligent Toy Enhanced Learning (DIGITEL 2008), pp. 18–22 (2008)
11. Park, S., Ji, S., Ryu, D., Cho, H.: AVACHAT: a new comic-based chat system for virtual avatars. In: Proceedings of the ACM Symposium on Virtual Reality Software and Technology (VRST 2008), pp. 27–29 (2008)
12. Matsuda, M., Tanev, I., Shimohara, K.: Comic live chat communication tool based on concept of downgrading. In: Proceedings of Instrumentation, Control and Information Technology (SICE 2010), pp. 2775–2778 (2010)
13. Tobita, H.: DigestManga: interactive movie summarizing through comic visualization. In: Proceedings of the ACM Conference on Human Factors in Computing Systems (CHI 2010), pp. 3751–3756 (2010)
14. Negoro, M., Soga, M., Taki, H.: Verification of relation between eye motion, impression and control method for reader's eyes flow in comics. In: Proceedings of the IEEE International Conference on Intelligent Computing and Integrated Systems (ICISS 2011), pp. 265–270 (2011)
15. McCloud, S.: Understanding Comics: The Invisible Art. Kitchen Sink Press, Northampton (1993)
16. Hoributi, S.: How did the Japanese MANGA became popular in America (Moeru Amerika Beikokujin ha ikanishite MANGA wo Yomu youni nattaka) (In Japanese), NikkeiBP (2006)
17. Itou, J., Motojin, Y., Munemori, J.: Development and application of Manga-style chat system aiming to communicate nonverbal expression. In: Proceedings of the 16th International Conference on Human-Computer Interaction (HCII2014), pp. 423–434 (2014)
18. Plutchik, R.: The multifactor-analytic theory of emotion. Psychology **50**, 153–171 (1960)
19. Ekman, P., Friesen, W.V.: Unmasking the Face: A Guide to Recognizing Emotions from Facial Clues. Prentice-Hall, New Jersey (1975)
20. Beattie, G.W.: Sequential patterns of speech and gaze in dialogue. Semiotica **23**, 29–52 (1978)
21. Kendon, A.: Some functions of gaze direction in social interaction. Acta Psychologica **26**, 22–63 (1967)

Work-in-Progress Papers

Modeling of Non-verbal Behaviors of Students in Cooperative Learning by Using OpenPose

Eiji Watanabe[1]([⊠]) [iD], Takashi Ozeki[2], and Takeshi Kohama[3]

[1] Konan University, Kobe 658-8501, Japan
e_wata@konan-u.ac.jp
[2] Fukuyama University, Fukuyama, Hiroshima 729-0292, Japan
[3] Kindai University, Kinokawa, Wakayama 649-6493, Japan

Abstract. In this paper, we discuss the modeling for the interactions between non-verbal behaviors of "teaching/learning" students in the cooperative learning. First, we adopt the positions eyes, face and hands detected by OpenPose [7] as a skeleton detection algorithm by a single camera. Next, we propose a modeling method for non-verbal behaviors based on neural networks. Furthermore, we discuss the modeling results for the interactions between non-verbal behaviors of students based on the internal presentations in the above models.

Keywords: Cooperative learning · Student · Non-verbal behavior · Modeling · Neural network · OpenPose

1 Introduction

The cooperative learning is an effective approach which aims to understand the content as the group with helping each other. In the cooperative learning, students teach other students and vice versa. It is becoming one of the hot topics to be researched [1]. The object of the cooperative learning is to improve the cooperation of the group and the understanding for given contents. Moreover, in [2], the following fundamental factors to be effective among the learning group which is listed as follows; (i) mutually beneficial cooperation, (ii) roles and responsibilities of the individual, and (iii) stimulatory interaction. However, one teacher can not grasp the cooperation and understanding of multiple groups and can not evaluate the above fundamental factors in real time. Therefore, it is important to construct methods for the estimation of the cooperation and the understanding in the group based on the non-verbal behaviors [3,4]. On the other hand, a conceptual model TSCL (Tabletop-Supported Collaborative Learning) has been proposed for understanding of the collaborative learning process [5].

The authors have already discussed the relationship between non-verbal behaviors and understandings of students in the cooperative learning [6]. However, non-verbal behaviors of "teaching/learning" students are represented by

H. Nakanishi et al. (Eds.): CRIWG+CollabTech 2019, LNCS 11677, pp. 191–201, 2019.
https://doi.org/10.1007/978-3-030-28011-6_13

the facial size detected by the camera and the exact direction of the facial movement has not been discussed. In this paper, we discuss the modeling for the interactions between non-verbal behaviors of "teaching/learning" students in the cooperative learning. First, we adopt the positions of eyes, face, and hands detected by OpenPose [7] as a skeleton detection algorithm by a single camera. Next, we propose a modeling method for non-verbal behaviors based on neural networks [10]. Furthermore, we discuss the modeling results for the interactions between non-verbal behaviors of students based on the internal presentations in the above models.

2   Detection of Non-verbal Behaviors of Students in Cooperative Learning Environment

2.1   Non-verbal Behaviors

In this paper, we treat the learning environment using a whiteboard and a table as shown in Fig. 1. In this learning environment, we have to consider two cases; (Case-1) using a whiteboard and (Case-2) not using a whiteboard. In Case-1, the "teaching" student standing in the front of a whiteboard explains and writes the content in a whiteboard. At the same time, other "learning" students sitting around a table take their notes, look at the whiteboard and listen to the explanation. In this case, the role "teaching/learning" of each student is clear. In Case-2, all students sit around a table and they teach and learn with each other by the explanation, listening and taking notes. In this case, the role "teaching/learning" of each student is unclear.

(a) Case-1   (b) Case-2

Fig. 1. Non-verbal behaviors of "teaching/learning" students in cooperative learning.

2.2   Detection of Non-verbal Behaviors by OpenPose [7]

In this learning environment, we can detect the following non-verbal behaviors; (i) writing on the whiteboard, (ii) the explanation to "learning" students, listening to "teaching" student, and (iii) taking notes by using OpenPose [7].

OpenPose can detect a human body, hand, facial, and foot keypoints (in total 135 keypoints) on single images as follows;

- Body: "Neck", "Shoulder", "Elbow", "Wrist", $\cdots$
- Face: "Nose", "Eye", "Mouth", $\cdots$
- Hand: "Finger", "Palm", $\cdots$

2.3   Detection of Non-verbal Behaviors in the Case of Using a Whiteboard

In this case, the "teaching" student in the front of a whiteboard has the following behaviors; (i) writing the content on a whiteboard, (ii) explanation to "learning" students as shown in Fig. 2(a). On the other hand, the "learning" students surrounding a table have the following behaviors; taking notes and listening to the explanation as shown in Fig. 2(b). Therefore, in this case, we use some body parts "Neck", "Eye", and "Finger" for the detection of each behavior as follows; (i) writing the content on a whiteboard, (ii) explanation to "learning" students, (iii) taking notes and listening to the explanation. Here, we define the positions $\boldsymbol{p}^{WB}(t)$ of some body parts for non-verbal behaviors of "teaching" students in the front of a whiteboard as follows;

$$\boldsymbol{p}^{WB}(t) = (x_{Neck}(t), y_{Neck}(t), x^L_{Eye}(t), y^L_{Eye}(t), x^R_{Eye}(t), y^R_{Eye}(t),$$
$$x^L_{Hand}(t), y^L_{Hand}(t), x^R_{Hand}(t), y^R_{Hand}(t))^T, \tag{1}$$

where $(x_{Neck}(t), y_{Neck}(t))$ denotes the coordinates of "Neck". $(x^L_{Eye}(t), y^L_{Eye}(t))$ and $(x^R_{Eye}(t), y^R_{Eye}(t))$ denote the coordinates of "Left Eye" and "Right Eye" respectively. $(x^L_{Hand}(t), y^L_{Hand}(t))$ and $(x^R_{Hand}(t), y^R_{Hand}(t))$ denote the coordinates of "Left Hand" and "Right Hand" respectively. For example, we can summarize the relationships between the behaviors and the positions $\boldsymbol{p}^{WB}(t)$ of some parts detected by OpenPose as follows;

- Writing the content on a whiteboard: $x_{Neck}(t) \neq 0$, $x^L_{Eye}(t) = 0$, $x^R_{Eye}(t) = 0$.
- Explanation to "learning" students by speech: $\{x^L_{Eye}(t) \neq 0$ and $x^R_{Eye}(t) \neq 0\}$, $\{x^L_{Hand}(t) \neq 0$ and $x^R_{Hand}(t) \neq 0\}$.
- Explanation to "learning" students with a whiteboard: $\{x^L_{Eye}(t) \neq 0$ or $x^R_{Eye}(t) \neq 0\}$, $\{x^L_{Hand}(t) \neq 0$ or $x^R_{Hand}(t) \neq 0\}$.

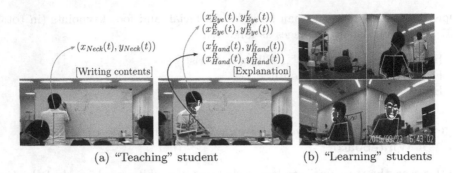

(a) "Teaching" student   (b) "Learning" students

Fig. 2. Positions of some body parts and non-verbal behaviors of "teaching/learning" students in the case of using a whiteboard.

2.4 Detection of Non-verbal Behaviors in the Case of Not Using a Whiteboard

In this case, the "teaching" and "learning" students sitting around a table have the following behaviors; (i) taking notes, (ii) explanation to "learning" students, and (iii) listening to the explanation as shown in Fig. 3. Furthermore, Fig. 3(a) and (b) shows the number of "teaching/learning" students. We can evaluate the number of "teaching/learning" students as the activity for the cooperative learning. Therefore, in this case, we use some body parts "Neck", "Eye", and "Finger" for the detection of each behavior as follows; (i) taking notes, (ii) explanation to "learning" students, and (iii) listening to the explanation. Similarly, we define the positions $p_i^{Table}(t)$ of some body parts for non-verbal behaviors of "teaching" and "learning" students sitting around a table as follows;

$$p_i^{Table}(t) = (x_{Neck,i}(t), y_{Neck,i}(t), x_{Eye,i}^L(t), y_{Eye,i}^L(t), x_{Eye,i}^R(t), y_{Eye,i}^R(t),$$
$$x_{Hand,i}^L(t), y_{Hand,i}^L(t), x_{Hand,i}^R(t), y_{Hand,i}^R(t))^T, \qquad (2)$$

where i denotes the student number. For example, we can summarize the relationships between the behaviors of "learning/teaching" students and the positions $p_i^{Table}(t)$ of some body parts detected by OpenPose as follows;

- Taking notes: $x_{Neck,i}(t) \neq 0$, $x_{Eye,i}^L(t) = x_{Eye,i}^R(t) = 0$, $\{x_{Hand,i}^L(t) \neq 0$ or $x_{Hand,i}^R(t) \neq 0\}$,
- Looking at a whiteboard: $x_{Neck,i}(t) \neq 0$, $\{x_{Eye,i}^L(t) \neq 0$ or $x_{Eye,i}^R(t) \neq 0\}$, $|y_{Eye,i}^R(t) - y_{Eye,i}^L(t)| > 0$,
- Speaking, listening and and/or other students: $x_{Neck,i}(t) \neq 0$, $\{x_{Eye,i}^L(t) \neq 0$ or $x_{Eye,i}^R(t) \neq 0\}$, $|y_{Eye,i}^R(t) - y_{Eye,i}^L(t)| > 0$.

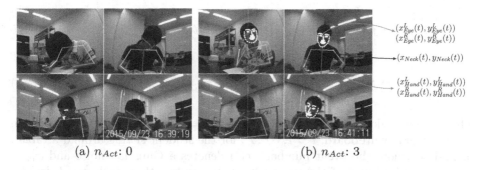

(a) n_{Act}: 0   (b) n_{Act}: 3

Fig. 3. Positions of some body parts and non-verbal behaviors of "teaching/learning" students in the case of not using a whiteboard (n_{Act} denotes the number of students looking at other students).

3 Modeling of Non-verbal Behaviors of Students

3.1 Modeling of Non-verbal Behaviors of Students Based on Neural Networks

In the cooperative learning, the non-verbal behaviors of students have strong relations with the understandings and interests for the given contents and the explanation by "teaching" students. Therefore, we have to discuss the interactions between the non-verbal behaviors of all students. In this section, we discuss a modeling method for the interaction among students.

First, we can convert the positions $\boldsymbol{p}^{WB}(t) = (p_m^{WB}(t))$ and $\boldsymbol{p}_i^{Table}(t) = (p_{m,i}^{Table}(t))$ of some body parts represented by the coordinate into the features $\boldsymbol{x}_m(t) = \{x_{m,i}(t)\} = \{x_m^{WB}(t), x_{m,1}^{Table}(t), \cdots, x_{m,P}^{Table}(t)\}$ represented by the binary for the m-th event (e.g: Whether there is each behavior?) as follows;

$$x_m^{WB}(t) = \begin{cases} 1 & p_m^{WB}(t) \neq 0, \\ 0 & \text{Otherwise.} \end{cases} \qquad x_{m,i}^{Table}(t) = \begin{cases} 1 & p_{m,i}^{Table}(t) \neq 0, \\ 0 & \text{Otherwise.} \end{cases}$$

where $i(= 1, 2, \cdots, P)$ and $m(= 1, 2, \cdots, M)$ denote the student number and the event number respectively.

Next, non-verbal behaviors of "teaching/learning" students have relationships with each other in the cooperative learning. Therefore, we evaluate the strength of the interactions between behaviors of "teaching/learning" students by using the models with the time-delay. We introduce the following non-linear time-series model for the features $\boldsymbol{x}_m(t) = \{x_{m,i}(t)\}$ represented by the binary for the event (e.g., Whether eyes were detected?) for "teaching/learning" students. Concretely, this model can predict the m-th feature of the i-th student by the past features $x_{n,k}(t - \ell)$ of all students.

$$x_{m,i}(t) = f\left(\sum_{j=1}^{J} \alpha_{m,i,j} h_{m,j}(t-\ell)\right) + e(t),$$

$$= f\left(\sum_{j=1}^{J} \alpha_{m,i,j} f\left(\sum_{n=1}^{N}\sum_{k=0}^{P}\sum_{\ell=1}^{L} w_{n,j,k,\ell} x_{n,k}(t-\ell)\right)\right) + e(t), \qquad (3)$$

where i and k denote the student number ($i = 0$: for the student standing in the front of a whiteboard, $i = 1, \cdots, P$: for the student sitting around a table). m and n denote the event numbers. $e(t)$ denotes a Gaussian noise and $\alpha_{m,i,j}$ denotes the influence of the non-verbal behavior by other students. J denotes the number of hidden units and $h_{m,j}(t-\ell)$ denotes the output of the hidden unit. Moreover, $w_{n,j,k,\ell}$ denotes the time-correlation for the non-verbal behavior of the k-th student. The weights $\alpha_{m,i,j}$ and $w_{n,j,k,\ell}$ are initialized by the random number. $f(\cdot)$ denotes the sigmoid function $f(x) = \tanh x$.

Furthermore, the non-linear time-series model defined by Eq. 3 can be represented by the neural network [8] model shown in Fig. 4. The learning object for a neural network model shown in Fig. 4 is to minimize the following error function.

$$E = \sum_{t=1}^{T} E_t = \sum_{t=1}^{T}\sum_{m=1}^{M}\sum_{i=0}^{P}(x_{m,i}(t) - \hat{x}_{m,i}(t))^2, \qquad (4)$$

where T denotes the length for the modeling section and $\hat{x}_{m,i}(t)$ denotes the prediction value for the feature $x_{m,i}(t)$ for the m-th event of the i-th student. Here, we use the forgetting learning algorithm [9] for the purpose of the clarifying of the internal representations of neural networks by the elimination of unnecessary weights.

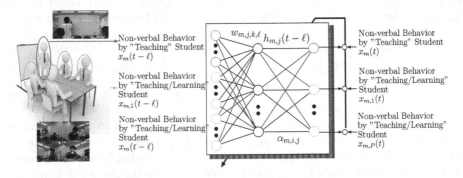

Fig. 4. Neural network model for Eq. 3.

3.2 Evaluation of the Interaction Based on the Differential Coefficient

We represented the interaction between the behaviors of "teaching/learning" students in Eq. 3. In this equation, the weights $\{\alpha_{m,i,j}\}$ and $\{w_{m,j,k,\ell}\}$ play important roles on the interaction. Here, we evaluate that the change of the output $x_{m,k}(t)$ (e.g., Whether eyes were detected?) in the output units by the input $x_{m,i}(t - \ell)$ in the input units with the time-delay ℓ as follows;

$$\frac{\partial x_{m,k}(t)}{\partial x_{m,i}(t - \ell)} = x'_k(t) \sum_{j=1}^{J} \alpha_{m,i,j} w_{m,j,k,\ell} h'_{m,j}(t - \ell), \tag{5}$$

where $'$ denotes the differential operator. Here, we assume that $x'_k(t) \approx 0$ under the condition which the error function E becomes small.

Here, we define the index $\Delta_{k,i}$ which can evaluate the change of the output $x_k(t)$ (e.g., Whether eyes were detected?) in the output units by the input $x_i(t-\ell)$ in the input units with the time-delay ℓ.

$$\Delta_{k,i} = \frac{1}{TJLM} \sum_{m=1}^{M} \sum_{t=1}^{T} \sum_{j=1}^{J} \sum_{\ell=1}^{L} \left(\alpha_{m,i,j} w_{m,j,k,\ell} h'_{m,j}(t - \ell)\right)^2. \tag{6}$$

4   Experimental Results

4.1   Outline of Experiments

We had the two video lectures concerning on the derivation of the formula for two trigonometric functions (law of sines and law of cosines). Four "teaching" and "learning" students are undergraduates. Moreover, we recorded movies for "learning" students sitting around a table by "Meeting Recorder" (Kingjim Co. Ltd., 640 × 480 [pixel], 30 [fps]) which is equipped with four cameras and an omni directional microphone. Moreover, we recorded movies for "teaching" students standing in the front of a whiteboard by "MacBook Air" (Apple Co. Ltd., 1280 × 720 [pixel], 30 [fps]). The procedure of this experiment is as follows;

1. before-test (about 10 [min]),
2. taking video lectures and taking notes (about 10 [min]),
3. **cooperative learning using a whiteboard (about 10 [min])**,
4. after-test (about 10 [min]).

Table 1 shows scores of before- and after-test and evaluation of notes taken by students for given video lectures. Such scores for tests and notes are evaluated by the three authors. From this table, we can see that Student-A and B have higher scores. The test scores by Student-A, B, and C are improved through the cooperative learning in Lecture-1 and Lecture-2. However, the score of after-test of Student-D is lower ($1.67 \rightarrow 4.00$) than that of before-test in Lecture-2.

Table 1. Scores (1:best, 4:worst) of before/after tests and evaluation of notes.

Student	Lecture-1		Lecture-2	
	Test (Before/After)	Note	Test (Before/After)	Note
A	1.33/1.33	1.67	2.00/1.67	1.33
B	3.67/1.00	2.67	4.00/1.00	1.67
C	3.67/2.00	3.00	3.33/2.67	1.33
D	3.33/3.33	2.33	1.67/4.00	2.33
Ave.	3.00/1.92	2.42	2.75/2.34	1.67

4.2 Features for Behaviors of "Teaching/Learning" Students

Fig. 5(a) shows the behaviors (Writing/Explaining) and the features $x(t)$ for body parts "Neck", "Eyes" and "Hands" of "teaching" students in Lecture-1. In Fig. 5(a), student-A moves to a whiteboard at 350 [sec]. If $x_{Eye}^{L/R}(t) = 0$ and $x_{Hand}^{L/R}(t) \neq 0$, then this "teaching" student is writing the content in a whiteboard. If $x_{Eye}^{L/R}(t) \neq 0$ and $x_{Hand}^{L/R}(t) \neq 0$, then this "teaching" student is explaining to "learning" students sitting around a table.

On the other hand, Fig. 5(b) shows the behaviors (Taking Notes/Looking at other students) and the features $x_B(t)$ for the "learning" student (Student-B) in Lecture-1. In Fig. 5(b), the features change according to the non-verbal behaviors of Student-B ("learning" student). If $x_{Neck,B}(t) \neq 0$, the student is sitting around a table. If $x_{Eye,B}^{L/R}(t) \neq 0$, then the student is looking at other students. If $x_{Eye,B}^{L/R}(t) = 0$ and $x_{Hand,B}^{L/R}(t) \neq 0$, then the student is taking notes.

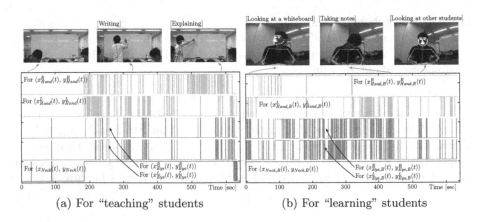

(a) For "teaching" students   (b) For "learning" students

Fig. 5. Behaviors and features of "teaching/learning" students (Lecture-1).

4.3   Modeling Results of the Non-verbal Behaviors of Students

We used the non-linear time-series model defined by Eq. 3. This model can be represented by the neural network model shown in Fig. 4. Here, we use the following parameters for the size of neural networks;

- the number of students: $P = 4$, the length for the modeling: $L = 10$ [sec],
- the number of body parts: $M = 5$ (Neck, LR-Eyes, LR-Hands),
- the numbers of input, hidden and output units: $L \times M \times (P+1)$, $J = 10$ and $M \times (P+1)$ (Here, $P+1$ includes the standing student).

Table 2 shows the index $\Delta_{k,i}$ (Influence of the i-th student on the k-th student). Here, "0" denotes the standing student and "A", "B", "C" and "D" denote the sitting student. In Lecture-1, $\Delta_{k,0}$ (0: 2.017, A: 2.349, B: 0.000, C: 0.000, D: 0.000) in the case of $i = 0$ means that Student-0 is influenced by oneself and Student-A. Moreover, Student-A and Student-B are influenced by Student-C ($\Delta_{C,A} = 3.943$ and $\Delta_{C,B} = 8.144$). Furthermore, Student-C and Student-D are influenced by the behavior of oneself ($\Delta_{C,C} = 13.850$ and $\Delta_{D,D} = 84.053$). Similarly, we can discuss the interactions among "teaching/learning" students In Lecture-2.

Table 2. $\Delta_{k,i}$: Influence of the i-th student on the k-th student.

(a) Lecture-1						(b) Lecture-2				
$i \backslash k$	0	A	B	C	D	$i \backslash k$	0	A	B	C	D
0	2.017	2.076	3.590	1.451	2.883	0	2.629	1.128	2.240	3.908	3.763
A	2.349	1.841	1.916	1.513	1.331	A	2.888	0.012	0.010	4.445	1.412
B	0.000	1.125	0.801	3.944	0.104	B	0.000	1.181	3.209	1.023	2.830
C	0.000	3.943	8.144	13.850	0.560	C	1.400	2.493	3.528	0.675	2.260
D	0.000	3.427	4.256	7.664	84.053	D	0.000	2.381	7.937	4.009	3.332

In Fig. 6 shows the sum $X_i(t) = \sum_m x_{m,i}(t)$ of the features $x_m(t) = \{x_{m,i}(t)\}$ for the m-th event defined in Sect. 3.1. Here, i denotes the student number ($i = 0$: standing student, $i = $ A, B, C, D: sitting students). When the sum $X_i(t)$ becomes large, it means that many body parts of Student-i are recorded by the camera. On the other hand, when the sum $X_i(t)$ becomes small, it means that the movement of the student is small. In Fig. 6(a), Student-A is standing at a whiteboard at 180 [sec] and the sum $X_C(t)$ changes according to the non-verbal behavior. Moreover, $X_C(t)$ and $X_D(t)$ of Student-C and Student-D are comparatively large and they are no influenced by the behavior of standing student (Student-0). Similarly, $\Delta_{C,C}$ and $\Delta_{C,C}$ of Student-C and Student-D in Table 2(a) becomes large. It is shown that the index $\Delta_{k,i}$ has a relation with the sum $X_i(t)$. In Fig. 6(b), Student-A becomes "teaching" student in the sections of [240–405] and [450–470] and Student-C becomes "teaching" student in the sections of [20–238] and [430–450]. Furthermore, the sum of features of Student-B changes at 240 [sec]. It is shown that "learning" Student-B is given the different influences by Student-A and Student-C as the standing "teaching" students.

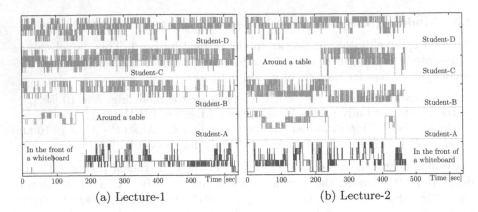

(a) Lecture-1   (b) Lecture-2

Fig. 6. $X_i(t) = \sum_m x_{m,i}(t)$ of features of the i-th students.

5 Conclusions

In this paper, we have discussed the modeling for the interactions between non-verbal behaviors of "teaching/learning" students in a cooperative learning environment. First, we have used the positions of eyes, face and hands detected by OpenPose [7]. Next, we have proposed a modeling method for the interactions of non-verbal behaviors of students based on neural networks. Furthermore, we have proposed the index $\Delta_{k,i}$ for representing "interactions" based on the internal representations of neural networks. From experimental results, we have shown that the index $\Delta_{k,i}$ has give a strong influence on the modeling of the non-verbal behaviors of students. As future work, we would like to discuss carefully the followings; (i) the application to other cases, the usage of various behaviors of students, (ii) the relationships among the modeling results, the progress of the cooperative learning, and the understandings of students.

Acknowledgments. This work was supported by JSPS KAKENHI Grant Numbers 19K12261 and 19K03095. The authors would like to thank for the valuable and inspire comments of the reviewers.

References

1. Sugie, S.: An invitation to cooperative learning. Nakanishiya (2011)
2. Johnson, D.W., Johnson, R.T.: Circles of Learning: Cooperation in the Classroom. Interaction Book Co., Edina (1993)
3. Otsuka, K., Araki, S., Ishizuka, K., Fujimoto, M., Heinrich, M., Yamato, J.: A realtime multimodal system for analyzing group meetings by combining face pose tracking and speaker diarization. In: Proceedings of ICMI, pp. 257–264 (2008)
4. Shinnishi, M., Kasuya, Y., Inamoto, H.: Wi-Wi-Meter: a prototype system of evaluating meeting by measuring of activity. IEICE Technical report. HCS2014-63, pp. 19–24 (2014)

5. Martinez-Maldonado, R., Yacef, K., Kay, J.: TSCL: a conceptual model to inform understanding of collaborative learning processes at interactive tabletops. Int. J. Hum.-Comput. Stud. **83**, 62–82 (2015)
6. Watanabe, E., Ozeki, T., Kohama, T.: Analysis of non-verbal behaviors by students in cooperative learning. In: Yoshino, T., Chen, G.-D., Zurita, G., Yuizono, T., Inoue, T., Baloian, N. (eds.) CollabTech 2016. CCIS, vol. 647, pp. 203–211. Springer, Singapore (2016). https://doi.org/10.1007/978-981-10-2618-8_16
7. Cao, Z., Simon, S., Wei, S., Sheikh, Y.: Realtime multi-person 2D pose estimation using part affinity fields. https://arxiv.org/abs/1611.08050. Accessed 12 Dec 2018
8. Rumelhart, D.E., McClelland, J.L.: The PDP Research Group: Parallel Distributed Processing. MIT Press, Cambridge (1986)
9. Ishikawa, M.: Structural learning with forgetting. Neural Netw. **9**(3), 509–521 (1996)
10. Watanabe, E., Ozeki, T., Kohama, T.: Analysis of interactions between lecturer and students. In: Proceedings of the 8th International Conference on Learning Analytics and Knowledge, 5 pages (2018)

Implementing a Serious Game to Improve Communication and Social Skills for Children with Autism

Mamoun Nawahdah[1]([✉])[iD] and Wafa'a Ihmouda[2]

[1] Faculty of Engineering and Technology, Birzeit University, Birzeit, Palestine
mnawahdah@birzeit.edu
[2] Birzeit University, Birzeit, Palestine
wafaaihmouda@gmail.com
https://www.birzeit.edu/

Abstract. In this research, we have developed a serious game app to help children with autism to overcome their social and communication problems. This game is implemented based on PECS system. The developed game is an educational game with educational target by containing educational roles based on PECS and other attractive factors. The educational roles are given in a form of visual scanning, matching, ability to distinguish, build a complete sentence based on functional communication skills, ask and comments. The preliminary experiment results revealed a positive impact in promoting children with autism motor skills and their interactive functionality.

Keywords: Computer supported collaborative learning (CSCL) · Serious games · Autism

1 Introduction

Usually, a person who has good communication and social skills can effectively express his ideas and feeling to others through his gestures, and can easily interact well with others by facial expressions or verbal communication. However, Having communication and social skills in the autism world is different and definitely must be converted to other skills; such as realizing the relation between objects, body control (when to start and when to stop), understanding surrounding context cues, basic language concepts, memorization, following instructions, having good eye contact, and turn talking (listening skills) [1]. Limitations in communication and social skills for children with autism consider the main reason for not accepting them in the public in many countries. In term of intervention for children with autism, the more motivations in learning, the more positive effects they will get.

In this research, we employed the intervention system Picture Exchange Communication System (PECS)[1] to implement our serious game. Our game

---

[1] https://pecsusa.com/pecs/.

© Springer Nature Switzerland AG 2019
H. Nakanishi et al. (Eds.): CRIWG+CollabTech 2019, LNCS 11677, pp. 202–211, 2019.
https://doi.org/10.1007/978-3-030-28011-6_14

is integrated with the elements of serious game, which play an important role in attracting and motivating the children. Understanding the autism requirements and the suggestions from the participants and the valuable improvement from the therapists and speech language pathologist were considered an important contribution in delivering our game. The educational components which need to be delivered in the game is gradually embedded in order to introduce attractive environment for encouraging the participants to keep on playing and take benefits.

Despite the inability to demonstrate the effect of our game on improving communication and social skills in real life for children with autism. The game was successfully stimulated the functional communication skills on request, ask, reject that the participants have not appeared in their life at all. Moreover, the game levels targeted the collaboration skills encouraged the participants to show social behaviors during the game.

2   Literature Review

2.1   Autism

Autism Spectrum Disorder (ASD) is a neurodevelopmental and mental disorder, which effects on development and function of the brain. Usually, ASD symptoms appear on the child before the age of three [2]. People with ASD show different symptoms that vary widely. Nevertheless, the most common symptoms are:

- Weakness in communication and social interactions
- Language latency
- Unusual behaviors and delays in cognition
- Sensory processing disorder.

2.2   PECS Approach

PECS is developed in 1994 as one of augmentative and alternative communication (AAC) [3] strategies for solving language deficits of children with autism. AAC strategies allow individuals with autism to communicate through using different strategies such as (communication books, speech generating devices, sign language, picture symbols and gestures) [4]. PECS technique has a notably developed with six phases:

- Phase 1: learning to request for exchanging the picture with preferred object. This phase depends on physical prompt (pick-up, reach and release).
- Phase 2: increasing the exchange distance between the child and therapist and change the environment and therapist.
- Phase 3: Child is learned to distinguish between different pictures and learn to match the picture with preferred object.
- Phase 4: The child learns to build a sentence strip in order to obtain what he wants.
- Phase 5 and Phase 6: Expand the instruction to include helping, commenting and asking questions.

2.3   Serious Game

Using game thinking in learning is a way to get rid of boring and frustration feeling of students in classroom. In general, Kapp [5] states that game depends on emotional reaction from the player to obtain outcome by building a mechanism of interactivity, constrains and feedback supporting with realistic elements or casting to fulfill game's goals. Projecting game principles in learning or training environment dubbed as "Serious Game" or "Gamification" [6].

2.4   Using Serious Game for Individuals with Autism

Serious game has shown a positive impact to empower autistic children compared with other disability categories. Bartolome and Zapirain [7] evaluated the impacts of using serious games to develop communication and interaction skills of two control groups (children with ASD and neurotypical development). Three objectives were identified in that research; knowing the strength points of autistic children to develop a game, that applies to rehabilitate their abilities, evaluating the interaction between autistic children with others through the incorporation environment by using caregiver and distinguishing between autistic children and neurotypical development based on cognitive behavior. The result showed that the reaction time of autistic children is slightly over the neurotypical development group.

Autism serious game can be applied in different sectors. For example, Bosseler et al. found a positive impact of using serious game to teach autistic children new vocabulary by using computer virtual character dubbed as "Baldi" [8]. In meeting environment, Strickland et al. worked with adolescent with autism by using "SecondLife" virtual reality application to simulate employment interview to practice autistic teenagers, whereas people with autism unlikely to obtain jobs because of impairment in social interaction [9]. In traveling, Mazurek and Engelhardt developed "Route Mate" a serious game is designed to promote traveling independently for individuals with intellectual disability [10]. In social life, Fernandes designed a Virtual character for helping autistic children to recognize others feeling [11]. They found effective role of context in improving the reaction of autistic children with games.

Serious game can be used as an assistive tool for people with autism, whereas games can lead to addict. Fernandes et al. mention of addiction problem of using video game for both individuals with ASD and individual with ADHD [12]. Autistic children are losing interaction with others, so they stick on tablet devices.

3   Game and Experimental Design

3.1   Game Design

This section describes the structure of the implemented serious game to be used to support social and communication skills of children with autism. Individuals with autism took part in different sessions (fifteen sub-levels). The level of difficulty proportionally increases with the game level; the first thirteen sub-levels played as individual to gradually develop their communication and social skills, where the last two sub-levels is considered as a collaboration game between two players aiming to improve the social skills. The following game elements were employed in our game:

Fig. 1. The first level of game that covers the first level of PECS.

- Storytelling Coherent: We employed Storytelling in different levels. For instance, in Fig. 1, the girl wants to pass the bridge. Unfortunately, the bridge is broken and the girl will still move to pass the bridge. If the girl wants to survive and does not fall down, the player must help her to rebuild the bridge by matching a series of hint objects to the objects in the top of screen.
- Goal: The goals of this game is to promote learning around both communication and social skills. Therefore, storytelling should support this and it is important to keep the leaner through flow channel. We employed the principle goals in the game as follow:
  - Levels that practice the first, second and third phases of PECS: the main goal in these levels is to achieve differentiation and recognition skills.
  - Levels that practice the fourth phase of PECS: the main goal of these levels is to make the learner be able to communicate with others and build a complete sentence.
  - Levels that practice the fifth and sixth phases of PECS: The main goal here is to accomplish the progress in communication by giving comments and request a help.

- Levels of cooperative phase: The main goal here is to be more social, whereas the previous levels are lack of social activities, do partnership and have friends.
- Feedback: factors such as sounds and animation is essential in creating an interactive environment, which motivate the children with autism and give them more sense of control.
- Time: in this game three types of time techniques where used:
  - In the levels that practice the first two phases of PECS: embedded time is used, where it means the value of time to express how much the child's response was fast to do the correct action.
  - In the levels that practice the phase four of PECS: mapping time is used, where it means link the time with something logical, to give an impression to do the quick required action before the time runs out. In this game, we used a burnt rope.
  - In cooperative levels PECS, which practice the phase 5 and 6 of PECS: we used a timer. Figure 2 represents the structure of cooperative game.
- Rewards: the player will be reward by collecting coins, souls and gemstones.
- Instructional methods: pictures and written cues can help children with autism to learn. Sometimes oral cues is not enough to deliver a correct message, whereas some of them have problem in understanding language. Instructional methods must take in consideration diversity among children with autism, their abilities and their needs change over time.
- Behavior rules: the following rules are used in cooperative levels:
  - Two tablet devices are used.
  - Two player should contribute to finish the game.
  - Cooperative game aims to increase the interactive social skills of children with autism which is represented by simple interactive dialog, understand the others, logic prediction.
- Functional rules: these rules was covered by PECS concepts and phases.

3.2 Participants and Environment Selection

Participants: The participants in the preliminary experiment were selected based on the therapist notes and the experimental activities that we did in two autism centers. We picked up a small sample group consists of four participants taking in considerations the following aspects:

- Age.
- Gender.
- Diversity of participants' abilities (strong, weak).
- Have a communication problem.
- Have a social problem.
- He/She can use a tablet device.
- Does not use PECS before.

Fig. 2. Cooperative game.

Environment: The following is a list of the issues we considered for the individual game environment in the first four levels:

– The experiment was conducted in a classroom that equipped with table, chair, and tablet.
– Removed any distraction factors that maybe confuse and reducing the attention of the child.
– Removed any other applications exist on the tablet.
– Only the player, therapist and experimenter attended in the classroom.
– The therapist role was to help the child to react to changes and to guide him if he asked.
– The experimenter role was to deal with any technical issues and take notes.
– The following is the extra issues we considered for the cooperative game environment in the last two levels:
– Conducted the game on classroom that equipped with one table, two chairs, and two tablets.
– Only the two players, PECS game environment, therapist, and experimenter attended in the classroom.

3.3 Data Collection

The four participants took part in the preliminary experiment and the data observed and collected throughout different sessions, while the majority of data was digitally collected directly from the game itself and posted automatically to the server database. The notes and observations were recorded by the camera and manually by both the experimenter and therapist. The following is the collected variables related to individual levels:

- Response time: this is the required time that the player needs to start doing an activity (moving the objects, moving the actors) after he/she sees an evidence guiding the player to start.
- Language skills parameters. Table 1 presents the assessment parameters of language.
- Stay focused and engagement time.
- Behavior functioning: these are the motor skills; such as asking for help or other interesting behavior that appear during the game.
- Ease of learning.

Table 1. Assessment of language skill parameters.

	Skill	Pretest	During the game	Posttest
1	Request-edibles			
2	Request-toys			
3	Request-activities			
4	Request-help/assistance			
5	Request/ item based on its characteristics			
6	Reject-item			
7	Reject-activity			
8	Request-item for task			
9	Affirm/accept			
10	Comment-on activities			

In the other hand, the following is the collected variables related to the cooperative levels:

- Look to the partner.
- Talk to help the partner.
- Talk to correct the partner.
- Talk to encourage the partner.
- Complain verbally.
- Comment.
- Smile.
- Laugh.
- Using gestures.

In Table 1, the Pretest of functional communication skill values were filled after we interview the therapists to evaluate the player ability in creating complete sentences based on ten language skill parameters. The third column during the game were filled during the game and present the ability of the player to pass the game levels. Post-test was filled after the experiment and it used the real

PECS cards to present the ability of the child on forming a complete sentence based on the phases 4, 5, and 6 of PECS.

We used a camera to record non predefined parameters to be analyzed along be-side observational parameters. Table 2 illustrate observational variables of individual levels. The final stage of the data collection, after the experiment procedure was per-formed a questionnaire was given to the therapists. The questionnaire goal was to measure how much the game facilitates the developing communication skills for children with autism by preparing a list of questions given to the therapists who have attended the testing sessions and other therapists who have tried the game and have a good experience on dealing with children with autism and their abilities. We distributed twenty questionnaires with ten questions to the specialists and caregivers in two centers to investigate the ability of the game on motivating children with autism by developing their social and communication skills, to what extent their feedback is close enough for our data results for long-term as well as short-term in the daily life of autistic children.

Table 2. Level1 & level2 Observation parameters of individual level.

Measured parameters	Variables
Laughing	Stay focused and love the game.
Ask for help from therapists to complete a level	Can interact with others to ask for Helping.
Engagement time	Time that the child want to keep on and play the other levels.
Correctly using UI	Pause button and effects of embedded time.
Instructional methods	Pictures and written cues can help autistic children to learn.

4 Preliminary Results

We used three ways of collecting results to evaluate the effectiveness of developed game. The preliminary results are summarized as bellow:

Observational Results: These results are used to observe the social behaviors that the participants have showed during the game, these results are collected on individual and cooperative levels. The observational results indicate that the developed game have been successfully stimulated some behaviors that children in normal situations have not showed before, such as exchange eye contact, ask for help, talk with a partner, etc. In addition, using the serious game technology encourages children to join in activities and increase their attention. Related to cooperative levels nine intentions of communication were observed to indicate showing of socially responsible behaviors between two players.

Collected Results: These data results posted directly to server database for further analyzing process, we collected these results in the first four levels of the game (individual game stage) to measure the response time, number of no response, wrong triggers and reloading of level and playing duration values. In addition, these results give indication of the participant's enjoying. The collected results showed a positive impact for our game in promoting autistic children motor skills, their interactive functionality. Pretest and post-test results showed a significant difference in the language skills of children before and after the game, which proved the effectiveness of the game in improving the language skills in requesting, rejecting, etc.

Questionnaire Results are collected to investigate the ability of the game on motivating children with autism be developing their social and communication skills, to what extent their feedback is close enough for our data results for long-term as well as short-term in the daily life of children with autism. Out of the specialists answers to the questionnaire about if the child really has enjoyed the game, the majority of them confirmed the ability of the game in enjoying children with autism and attracting them, which support our observations and collected data about the motivational variables. In addition, the questionnaire results indicate the ability of the game to develop both social and communication skills.

Despite the inability to demonstrate the effect of the game on improving communication and social skills in real life for children with autism. The game is successfully stimulated the functional communication skills on request, ask, reject that the participants have not appeared in their life at all. Moreover, the questionnaire results show the ability of the game to improve communication and social skills of children with autism in their daily life and on long term period, whereas when we asked specialists of autism "The effectiveness of the game in helping children with autism in their daily life" 60% answered on average were 30% answered a lot.

5   Conclusion

In this research, we developed a serious game for children with autism to help them in developing their communication and social skills. The game developed based on the official intervention system "PECS" to be the core of the game with the integration with the elements of serious game, which play an important role in attracting and motivating the children. In one hand, the employed serious game elements such as feedback and ability to choose the game's character added attractive factors to the participant to play the game. In the other hand, the educational roles were given in a form of visual scanning, matching, ability to distinguish, build a complete sentence based on functional communication skills, ask, and comments. In addition to that, the educational components, which needed to be delivered in the game, is gradually embedded in order to introduce attractive environment for encouraging the participants to keep on playing and take benefits.

References

1. Delaney, T.: 101 Games and Activities for Children with Autism, Asperger's, and Sensory Processing Disorders. McGraw-Hill, New York (2009)
2. Ecker, C., Bookheimer, S., Murphy, D.: Neuroimaging in autism spectrum disorder: brain structure and function across the lifespan. Lancet Neurol. 14(11), 1121–1134 (2015)
3. Georgiades, S.: Measurement and Classification of the Heterogeneous Autism Phenotype (2013)
4. Travers, J., Tincani, M., Thompson, J., Simpson, R.: Picture exchange communication system and facilitated communication: contrasting an evidence-based practice with a discredited method. In: Instructional Practices With and Without Empirical Validity, pp. 85–110 (2016)
5. Kapp, K.: The Gamification of Learning and Instruction. Wiley, San Francisco (2012)
6. Ibáñez, M., Di-Serio, A., Delgado-Kloos, C.: Gamification for engaging computer science students in learning activities: a case study. IEEE Trans. Learn. Technol. 7(3), 291–301 (2014)
7. Aresti-Bartolome, N., Garcia-Zapirain, B.: Cognitive rehabilitation system for children with autism spectrum disorder using serious games: a pilot study. Bio Med. Mater. Eng. 26(s1), S811–S824 (2015)
8. Bosseler, A., Massaro, D.: Development and evaluation of a computer-animated tutor for vocabulary and language learning in children with autism. J. Autism Dev. Disord. 33(6), 653–672 (2003)
9. Strickland, D., Coles, C., Southern, L.: JobTIPS: a transition to employment program for individuals with autism spectrum disorders. J. Autism Dev. Disord. 43(10), 2472–2483 (2013)
10. Brown, D., McHugh, D., Standen, P., Evett, L., Shopland, N., Battersby, S.: Designing location-based learning experiences for people with intellectual disabilities and additional sensory impairments. Comput. Educ. 56(1), 11–20 (2011)
11. Mazurek, M., Engelhardt, C.: Video game use in boys with autism spectrum disorder, ADHD, or typical development. Pediatrics 132(2), 260–266 (2013)
12. Fernandes, T., Alves, S., Miranda, J., Queirós, C., Orvalho, V.: LIFEisGAME: a facial character animation system to help recognize facial expressions. In: Cruz-Cunha, M.M., Varajão, J., Powell, P., Martinho, R. (eds.) CENTERIS 2011. CCIS, vol. 221, pp. 423–432. Springer, Heidelberg (2011). https://doi.org/10.1007/978-3-642-24352-3_44

DiAna-AD: Dialog Analysis for Adjusting Duration During Face-to-Face Collaborative Discussion

Naruaki Ishikawa[✉], Taishi Okazawa, and Hironori Egi

Graduate School of Informatics and Engineering,
The University of Electro-Communications, 1-5-1 Chofugaoka, Chofu,
Tokyo 182-8585, Japan
{ishikawa-egilab,hiro.egi}@uec.ac.jp

Abstract. This research proposes a DiAna-AD (dialog analysis for adjusting duration) system that adjusts the duration time of discussions based on the discussion situations. Participants may be dissatisfied with excessive or insufficient fixed time of discussion. The proposed system is intended to terminate the discussions at the appropriate time. The situations of the discussions are estimated only from nonlinguistic acoustic features collected by wearable devices. The criteria of termination by the system are obtained from the analysis of an experiment of satisfaction. The analysis result revealed that the subjective satisfaction of the participants is reduced by the desire to shorten the duration time of the discussion. An algorithm to terminate discussions is implemented via the proposed system. Furthermore, an experiment with the system is conducted to evaluate the effectiveness of the system for improving participants' satisfaction in a discussion. The result of the experiment with the system is compared with that of the experiment on satisfaction, and there are no significant differences between the results. On the other hand, from the result of the interview, the proposed DiAna-AD system is found to be effective in shortening the duration time of inactive discussions.

Keywords: Face-to-face discussion · Improvement of satisfaction ·
Adjusting duration · Dialog analysis

1 Introduction

In this paper, we design a DiAna-AD (dialog analysis for adjusting duration) system that adjusts the length of discussions in face-to-face environments.

A discussion is considered one of the essential activities by which decisions are made and opinions shared. It can be face-to-face, online, or text-based. Moreover, with advances in technology, online discussions can be performed in real-time using multimedia [1]. This paper aims to improve the discussion skills of participants. Both direct and indirect methods are considered to be effective in improving participants' discussion skills. The direct method possesses artificial processes of discussion to affect the improvement of participants' skills directly. On the other hand, in the indirect method, participants must improve their discussion skills by repeatedly participating in

© Springer Nature Switzerland AG 2019
H. Nakanishi et al. (Eds.): CRIWG+CollabTech 2019, LNCS 11677, pp. 212–221, 2019.
https://doi.org/10.1007/978-3-030-28011-6_15

ordinary conversations. Furthermore, in this method, the participants are required to be willing to improve their discussion skills. The approach of this research is based on the indirect method. Besides, participants' satisfaction with a discussion is critical to enabling them to maintain a willingness to discuss. Therefore, in this paper, we propose a system that improves participants' satisfaction with discussions.

In face-to-face discussions, the duration of discussions is determined in advance based on the experiences of the teachers; however, this fixed duration may be excessive or insufficient. With a short time of discussion, it is difficult for participants to discuss adequately; on the other hand, they feel bored when the assigned discussion time is excessively much. Thus, assigning an appropriate duration of discussions may improve participants' satisfaction.

2 Related Work

Research aimed at improving the conditions of discussion have been previously carried out. One such example is a study [2] on enabling feedback from the teacher to students after a discussion was conducted. In the study, the authors utilized a rubric to clarify evaluation items. In [3], enrolling in Massive Open Online Courses was considered a means to acquire discussion skills. In the research, students share ideas using a discussion forum that is an asynchronous text-based discussion environment. It is notable that these researches aim to improve not the discussion skills but the condition of discussion.

Research on a non-speech section of pair conversation was conducted in [4], and it was found that non-speech sections are not suitable for those who feel weakness in their ability to talk. Furthermore, it was recommended that at the time of the non-speech section, discussions should be by topic presentation. There is a conventional approach to eliminating inactive discussion. However, methods for changing topics do not apply to a discussion with a fixed topic.

Furthermore, in [5], the authors aim to emphasize and maintain the relevance of face-to-face communication. By utilizing a touch-shake device to enable physical contact, they achieved high-quality communication. The device uses light and sound in response to physical contact. In this paper, we aim to improve the quality of discussion with a different approach.

3 Adjusting Duration During Face-to-Face Discussion

3.1 Dialog Analysis Based on Nonlinguistic Acoustic Information

Communication comprises transfer of verbal and non-verbal information. Verbal information refers to the understanding of the meaning of an utterance. In [6], verbal information was employed to create a corpus from transcribed dialogs and to analyze emotions. Non-verbal information includes facial expression and gaze, voice height, tone of voice, and gestures. In [7], the authors utilized non-verbal information to investigate gaze patterns using an eye tracker. From verbal information, it is possible to analyze the contents of the discussions. However, this analysis is manually performed by human observations. On the other hand, it is possible to analyze the attitude of participants and the intention of an utterance from non-verbal information. However, several types of non-verbal information require equipment specially prepared for collecting the information. In [8], a system that detects dialog breakdown in chat dialog from nonlinguistic acoustic information is proposed. However, the DiAna-AD system presented in this paper uses nonlinguistic acoustic information collected by wearable devices for analyzing discussions.

3.2   Nonlinguistic Acoustic Features Used in DiAna-AD System

In this subsection, we introduce the following features to estimate the situation of a discussion: time percentage of an utterance, percentage of silent time, and coefficient of speech overlap. These values are calculated from only nonlinguistic acoustic information per unit time.

Time Percentage of Utterance. This value is the utterance time of a participant per unit time, and it is calculated for each participant in a group discussion. The value is given in the range from 0% to 100%. The degree of participation of each participant in the group discussion is obtained by checking the transition of this value.

Percentage of Silent Time. This value is the time that nobody speaks per unit time, and it is calculated for a group. The value is given in the ranges from 0% to 100%. The degree of stagnation of the group in the discussion is obtained by checking the transition of this value.

Coefficient of Speech Overlap. This value is the sum of the total time percentage of the utterance of all the participants in a group and the percentage of silent time of the group on discussion, and it is calculated for a group. Besides, this value is given in the range from 1 to the number of participants in the group. Furthermore, if there is no overlap of speech, the coefficient of speech overlap is 1. The degree of activeness of the group on the discussion is known by checking the transition of this value.

3.3   Architecture of DiAna-AD System

The DiAna-AD system consists of wearable devices and an aggregation server.

The wearable devices are Raspberry Pi 3B+ attached to a unidirectional USB microphone which collects participants' utterances. The aggregation server is a laptop that controls the wearable devices and calculates nonlinguistic acoustic features from collected data in real-time. The DiAna-AD system decides the end of the discussion based on the features discussed in Subsect. 3.2. An end notification is sent by a notification device which is made up of Raspberry Pi 3B+ and a speaker. The wearable devices, the aggregation server, and the notification device are connected using Wi-Fi, while data is sent via UDP connection.

The data flow of DiAna-AD system is as follows: first, each of the participants wears the headset of the wearable device. When the discussion begins, the wearable devices start sending data to the aggregation server. During the discussion, only the volume values are extracted from the voice input of the unidirectional microphones.

The server associates the received values of IP addresses, the volume values, and the timestamps. Then, the utterances of each participant are determined with the associated data.

The features are calculated every 20 s. Moreover, the percentage of silent time and the coefficient of speech overlap are used to decide the end of the discussion. The termination of the discussion is notified by the system when it continues for more than one minute that the percentage of silent time exceeds 40% and the coefficient of speech overlap becomes less than 1.07. These thresholds are examined in the experiment to improve discussion satisfaction. Figure 1 shows the diagram of DiAna-AD system while Fig. 2 shows the dataflow of the system.

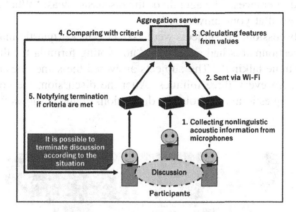

Fig. 1. Diagram of DiAna-AD system

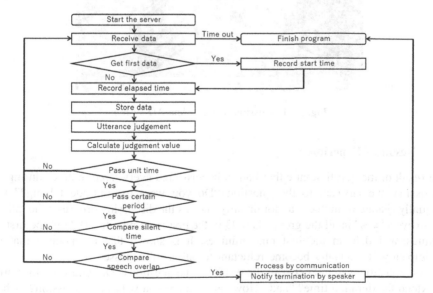

Fig. 2. Dataflow of DiAna-AD system

4 Experiment of Satisfaction

4.1 Procedure of Experiment

In this research, we conducted an experiment to validate the appropriateness of the criteria of termination by the DiAna-AD system. To this end, we investigated the relationship between the duration of discussions and the personal satisfaction of participants.

The subjects of the experiment were fifteen students from a science and engineering university. Five groups of three students were formed. The task of the experiment was a discussion for ten minutes. During the discussion, the subjects wore the wearable devices to record utterances. The agenda of the discussion was: "What is the point you want to be improved at your university?"

During the discussion, the subjects were asked to answer questionnaires every three minutes. The questionnaires had a "yes" or "no" voting formula for the question "Do you want to continue talking?" The subjects answered the same question using ballot boxes for each item every three minutes. After the discussion, we conducted a subjective evaluation questionnaire about the discussion. Figure 3 shows the setting of the experiment.

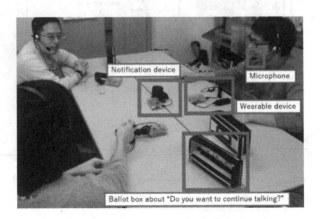

Fig. 3. Discussion using DiAna-AD system

4.2 Result of Experiment

The result of the questionnaire that had to be answered every three minutes during the discussion, the answers to the question "Do you want to continue talking?" will gradually change from "yes" to dominantly "no" as the discussion progress; the ratio of the answers "yes" in all the groups is 0.93 in the first three minutes, 0.73 in the first six minutes, and 0.40 in the first nine minutes. It is shown that a tendency that the participant will gradually become reluctant to talk as time passes.

A correlation is found between the results of the questions "Did you want to shorten or extend the duration time?" and "How satisfied are you with the discussion?" which are items of the questionnaire after the discussion (r = 0.79, p < 0.001). It was found that the duration of discussions influences the satisfaction of participants.

Also, a correlation was found between the result of the question "How satisfied are you with the discussion?" and the coefficient of speech overlap (r = 0.65, p < 0.01).

4.3 Criteria for Termination

Experimental results of participants' satisfaction with a discussion revealed a strong tendency of decrease in speech motivation within the first six to nine minutes of the discussion. In the first nine minutes' vote, it was only in one group that all the subjects answered "yes" to the question "Do you want to continue talking?" Thus, the group did not have to shorten the assigned duration as the discussion was active.

We analyzed the percentage of silent time and the coefficient of speech overlap from the first six to nine minutes of the other four groups. Based on the analysis result, 40% is decided as the criteria of the percentage of silent time for termination because the deviation value of the groups is 40. The ratio of 1.07 is decided as the criteria of the coefficient of speech overlap because the median value of the groups is 1.07. The rising of the percentage of silent time indicates strong stagnation of discussions, while a decline in the coefficient of speech overlap indicates strong inactivity of the discussion group. Therefore, as the criteria for termination, the percentage of silent time exceeding 40% and the coefficient of speech overlap less than 1.07 are adopted.

The rule to notify termination is as follows: once a discussion meets both the criteria and the condition lasts one minute, a termination notification is sent.

5 An Experiment on DiAna-AD System

5.1 Procedure of Experiment

In this subsection, we conducted an experiment with the DiAna-AD system to evaluate the effectiveness of the system to improve participants' satisfaction with a discussion.

The subjects of the experiment were fifteen students of the science and engineering university mentioned earlier; however, this set of students were different from those used in the experiment on satisfaction. We formed five groups of three subjects each. Two sessions of discussion were conducted as the task of the experiment. The duration of the discussion varies; a minimum of seven minutes and maximum 13 min. We asked the subjects to remove any time-measuring devices in their possession such as watches and smartphones. During the discussion, the subjects wore the wearable devices to record utterances. The topic of the first discussion is "What is the point you want improved at your university?" and that of the second discussion is "How do you involve children in learning programming?"

The DiAna-AD system is applied to both the first and second discussions. Additionally, the groups are notified about termination from the system respectively based on the criteria of termination. The subjects are required to wrap up the ongoing discussion once an end notification is indicated by the notification device.

We set time limitations to shorten or extend the duration of discussions. Even if the group is inactive from the beginning of the discussion, a certain time should be spent for the discussion to occur successfully. On the other hand, even if the discussion is continuously active, it must be wrapped up in a certain time.

After both discussions, we carried out a subjective evaluation questionnaire about the discussion. The questions in the subjective evaluation were the same as asked in the experiment of satisfaction.

Furthermore, we showed the subjects the duration times of each discussion after they answered the questionnaire of the second discussion. The mechanism of adjusting the time according to the activity of discussion by the system was also shown to the subjects. Finally, a questionnaire and an interview on the evaluation of the DiAna-AD system was answered by the subjects.

5.2　Result of the Experiment

We designated the five groups as G1 to G5. Table 1 shows the duration time of the discussions using the DiAna-AD system.

Table 1. The duration time of the discussions

Group	First [min: sec]	Second [min: sec]
G1	13:00	13:00
G2	13:00	13:00
G3	13:00	13:00
G4	13:00	13:00
G5	7:00	7:40

The system detected that the discussions of G1 to G4 were active and adjusted the duration time of discussions to the maximum. Table 2 shows the answers to the question "Do you want to shorten or extend the discussion time?"; it verifies that the adjustment was appropriate. The scores in the table are as follows: 1 means "want to shorten strongly," 2 means "want to shorten," 3 means "moderate," 4 means "want to extend," and 5 means "want to extend strongly." Each answer is the result collected from three subjects in each group.

Table 2. The answer to the question "Do you want to shorten or extend the discussion time?"

Group	First	Second
G1	3, 4, 4	2, 3, 2
G2	1, 3, 3	2, 3, 3
G3	2, 2, 2	3, 3, 3
G4	1, 4, 2	2, 4, 3
G5	3, 2, 4	2, 3, 4

12 out of the 30 answers are "want to shorten" the discussion where the duration time was adjusted by the DiAna-AD system. 12 answers are "moderate," and six answers are "want to extend". Although the discussions are already extended, the feeling of the subjects differed in extending or shortening the duration time of the active discussions.

Tables 3 and 4 show the number of times that the termination criteria were met every 20 s during the discussion. It indicates that the end notification was made when the value in the brackets is three or more between seven minutes and 13 min. In this experiment, all the groups met the criteria multiple times, but the values are less than three. Several groups met the continuing criteria of three times in less than seven minutes; however, the discussion kept going.

Table 3. Classification of the end notification in the first discussion.

Group	[min: sec (number of judgments)]
G1	0:40(2), 3:00(1), 5:00(1), 11:20(1), 13:00(1)
G2	0.20(1), 6:20(3), 7:00(1), 9:00(1)
G3	6:20(1), 9:20(1)
G4	5:20(2), 6:40(1), 8:20(1), 9:20(1), 10:20(1), 12:20(1)
G5	1:00(3), 2:00(2), 3:00(2), 4:40(2), 7:00(4)

Table 4. Classification of the end notification in the second discussion.

Group	[min: sec (number of judgments)]
G1	4:20(2), 6:40(3), 11:20(1), 12:40(1)
G2	0.40(2), 3:20(1), 7:40(1), 11:40(1)
G3	1:00(1), 2:00(1), 3:40(1)
G4	0:40(2), 1:20(1), 7:00(1), 7:40(1), 8:20(1), 12:40(1)
G5	1:00(3), 2:00(2), 4:20(7), 6:00(3), 7:40(3)

Table 5 shows the voting results of the first discussion on the question "Do you want to continue talking?" It indicates that the willingness to speak decreased in the vote of the first nine minutes. However, it also revealed that the willingness was recovered in the vote of the first 12 min in several groups.

In the questionnaire on the evaluation of the DiAna-AD system, the question "Are you satisfied with the system's decision?" was asked. The scores in the question are as follows: 1 means "not satisfied," 2 means "partly not satisfied," 3 means "moderate," 4 means "partly satisfied," and 5 means "satisfied." The average score of the question is 4.27, and the standard deviation is 0.85. 13 out of 15 subjects answered "satisfied" to the decision by the DiAna-AD system. One subject answered "not satisfied." However, it was found that the subjects in general accepted the decision criteria of the system.

Table 5. The answers to the question "Do you want to continue talking?" in the first discussion ("Yes"/"No")

Group	3 min	6 min	9 min	12 min
G1	3/0	3/0	3/0	2/1
G2	3/0	3/0	2/1	2/1
G3	3/0	0/3	0/3	2/1
G4	3/0	2/1	1/2	2/1
G5	3/0	2/1	N/A	N/A

5.3 Discussion

This research aimed at improving participants' satisfaction in a discussion by adjusting the duration time of the discussion. Therefore, in the experiment of the proposed system, we set the same agenda of the experiment on satisfaction to the first discussion. The degree of satisfaction with a discussion was asked from 0% to 100% in 10% increments. Regarding the experiment on satisfaction, the average degree of satisfaction was 70%, and the standard deviation is 21%. On the other hand, for the experiment of system, the average was 65.3% and the standard deviation was 15.9%.

In addition, the average score for the question "Do you want to shorten or extend the discussion time?" in the experiment on satisfaction was 3.20 and the standard deviation was 1.05. Additionally, the average score in the experiment of the system was 2.67 and the standard deviation was 1.01. A correlation was found between the degree of satisfaction in a discussion and the answer to the question "Do you want to shorten or extend the discussion time?" of the first discussion in the experiment of the system ($r = 0.61$, $p < 0.05$).

From the result of the interview, it can be inferred that it is painful to keep participating in an inactive discussion. Hence, it is considered necessary to reduce the duration time of inactive discussions. On the other hand, there is a widespread opinion that "it was not good that the discussion time was excessively extended" by the subject who answered "not satisfied" to the decision of the system. Moreover, it is crucial to consider the degree of extended duration time of active discussions.

6 Conclusion and Future Work

In this research, we designed a DiAna-AD system that adjusts the duration time of discussions in face-to-face environments. The system aims to increase participants' satisfaction in a discussion by adjusting the duration time based on the discussion. The system utilizes the nonlinguistic acoustic information obtained from participants. We investigated the influence of the system on the participants. The experimental result of the proposed system revealed that there are no significant differences in the satisfaction of the participants. However, there is an effective adjustment of the duration time of inactive discussions.

In future work, we intend to review the degree to which duration time needs to be adjusted in active discussion. Finally, we shall also attempt to contribute to increasing participants' motivation to repeat discussions to improve discussion skills.

Acknowledgements. This work has been partly supported by the Grants-in-Aid for Scientific Research (No. JP17H02001, JP19K03175 and JP19H01710) by MEXT (Ministry of Education, Culture, Sports, Science and Technology) in Japan.

References

1. Xiao, X., Shi, Y., Zhang, N.: ErmdClime: enabling real-time multimedia discussion for collaborative learning in mobile environment. In: 2006 IEEE International Conference on Multimedia and Expo, pp. 2093–2096. IEEE (2006)
2. Omori, Y., Ito, K., Nishida, S., Kihira, T.: Study on supporting group discussions by improving discussion skills with ex post evaluation. In: 2006 IEEE International Conference on Systems, Man and Cybernetics, vol. 3, pp. 2191–2196. IEEE (2006)
3. Ayer, N., Sukhathankar, H., Deshmukh, U., Sahasrabudhe, S.: Impact of learner-centric discussion forums on learner engagement in skill development MOOC. In: 2018 IEEE Tenth International Conference on Technology for Education (T4E), pp. 69–72. IEEE (2018)
4. Nishihara, Y., Yoshimatsu, K., Yamanishi, R., Miyake, S.: Topic switching system for unfamiliar couples in face-to-face conversations. In: 2017 6th IIAI International Congress on Advanced Applied Informatics (IIAI-AAI), pp. 319–323. IEEE (2017)
5. Yamaguchi, Y., Yanagi, H., Takegawa, Y.: Touch-shake: design and implementation of a physical contact support device for face-to-face communication. In: 2013 IEEE 2nd Global Conference on Consumer Electronics (GCCE), pp. 170–174. IEEE (2013)
6. Ondas, S., Mackova, L., Hladek, D.: Emotion analysis in DiaCoSk dialog corpus. In: 2016 7th IEEE International Conference on Cognitive Infocommunications (CogInfoCom), pp. 151–156. IEEE (2016)
7. Raidt, S., Bailly, G., Elisei, F.: Gaze patterns during face-to-face interaction. In: 2007 IEEE/WIC/ACM International Conferences on Web Intelligence and Intelligent Agent Technology – Workshops, pp. 338–341. IEEE (2007)
8. Abe, M., Tsunakawa, T., Nishida, M., Nishimura, M.: Dialogue breakdown detection based on nonlinguistic acoustic information. In: 2018 IEEE 7th Global Conference on Consumer Electronics (GCCE), pp. 689–690. IEEE (2018)

Group Dynamics in Gameful Collaborative Innovation Processes

Sarah-Kristin Thiel[1]([✉]), Jeanette Falk Olesen[2], Kim Halskov[2],
and Ida Larsen-Ledet[1]

[1] Department of Computer Science, Aarhus University, Aarhus, Denmark
{thiel,ida.ll}@cs.au.dk
[2] Centre for Digital Creativity, Aarhus University, Aarhus, Denmark
jfo@cc.au.dk, halskov@cavi.au.dk

Abstract. Creativity is widely recognized as a valuable trait. The aim of this research is to explore the usefulness of incorporating elements of both game and play into creativity methods, so called design games or gameful ideation methods. This paper presents findings from a study in which a Gameful Idea Generation (GIG) was conducted. GIG is a collaborative creativity method that draws on concepts from design games and hackathons. We focus on intra-group dynamics in order to gain insights on how gamefulness influences collaborative creative processes. We analyse performance in relation to the level and nature of collaboration displayed during group-based ideation. Our insights provide relevant pointers for the design of future collaborative creativity enhancing technologies.

Keywords: Creativity methods · Gamefulness · Collaboration · Ideation · Design games · Group dynamics · Divergent thinking

1 Introduction

Over the last decade, research has introduced a plethora of creativity methods to support idea generation and facilitate innovation processes at large. With studies having suggested that gamefulness can promote creativity (e.g. [12]), concepts known from games have lately been introduced into creativity methods coining so called design games [1,10]. This paper investigates how collaboration unfolds in a creative design process and how a gameful framing affect the nature of collaboration (i.e. intra-group dynamics) and the outcomes of the ideation process (i.e. quality of ideas).

We do so by drawing on data collected during a one day event with high school students in which we conducted a *Gameful Idea Generation* (introduced in [19]). Based on gathered insights on how participants worked together in the collaborative creative process, we hope to provide pointers that can be used to inform the design of technologies to support collaborative creativity. Our insights can furthermore contribute to research on hackathons, which are usually not

© Springer Nature Switzerland AG 2019
H. Nakanishi et al. (Eds.): CRIWG+CollabTech 2019, LNCS 11677, pp. 222–231, 2019.
https://doi.org/10.1007/978-3-030-28011-6_16

designed to support learners [7], even when used in educational settings. Structuring hackathons via methods such as *Gameful Idea Generations* has potential in this perspective.

2   Background

This work focuses on collaborative ideation processes that take place in a setting where novel and meaningful solutions for a given problem are generated, prioritized and demonstrated (e.g. business meeting). With the term collaborative, we refer to a setting where two or more persons work together in a joint effort.

2.1   Card-Based Gameful Creativity Methods

The use of tangible cards is a well established approach to stimulate divergent thinking as well as guide design processes (e.g. [9,15]). During ideation, cards have been found to foster divergent thinking by triggering ideas that go beyond the present context allowing to creatively interpret possibilities [11].

For the context of this work, we are interested in those creativity methods that adopt principles known from games. Rationales for incorporating gamefulness into creative processes include that playing is said to stimulate creativity by facilitating the cognitive (i.e. skill domain) and affective (i.e. eliciting positive emotions) dimensions of creative processes. Furthermore, being based on a set of rules, games follow systematic structures (e.g. sequences of interaction) that help generate a creative flow [13]. We posit that such a gameful (rule) structure might foster creativity [13,22]. Competition creates a tension that becomes a driving force [15], which can facilitate idea generation processes. Through balancing intrinsic pleasure (i.e. fun) and the level of difficulty (i.e. challenges), games achieve a state of flow that helps retain motivation throughout a game (or process) [4] and may also promote collaborative thinking [8,14].

2.2   Collaborative Innovation

Within studies of collaboration, common themes are conversation analysis and hand-over/turn-taking through artifacts. Understanding the interaction between employed artifacts (e.g. technology, cards) and collaboration at a minute-to-minute level are a key requirement for designing future techniques and technologies that support efficient and effective work processes that lead to valuable and usable outcomes.

Being social situations, collaborative innovation processes entail a number of social challenges, especially if groups and their members are co-located and brainstorming is done verbally, in which case participants do not have the shelter of anonymity. The most documented challenges are production blocking (only one idea can be suggested at a time; [6]), evaluation apprehension (being concerned about how others perceive one's ideas; [3]), social loafing (tendency to let others do the work; [18]). These challenges motivate a range of other research that investigates the role of collaboration, group size and group composition on creative output. An initial question here is often whether group-based (and thus collaborative) ideation produces more/less creative outcomes than individual ideation [14,21]. Whether groups can in fact achieve a higher level of creativity depends both on how creative outcomes are measured [2] and on how group members work together and is hence tied to the nature of the collaboration.

3   Methodology: Gameful Idea Generation

Gameful Idea Generation (GIG) is a creativity method that implements concepts from card-based innovation workshops and design games. As such, the method employs gamefulness on various levels, both for structuring the method and during the actual ideation. The method consists of three distinct phases: a *Teaser*, where the problem to be addressed by participants is introduced; *Gamebidea*, a gameful method to facilitate ideation; and *Prototyping*, where participants can manifest their ideas into something tangible. Both Gamebidea and the Prototyping are group-based, where about 2–3 people work together. The method of GIG is described in more detail here [19]. Gamebidea represents the phase where the actual brainstorming takes place. This phase is further broken down in three steps: *Invent, Pitch* and *Auction*. These three steps are repeated about 2–3 times depending on available time (see Fig. 1).

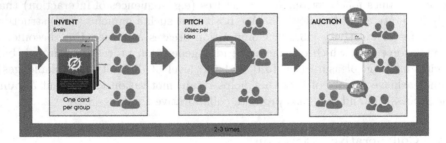

Fig. 1. Illustration of Gamebidea (based on material of the original *Game of Things*).

During the **Invent** step, individual groups have five minutes to generate as many ideas as possible addressing the given problem. Inspiration cards, which each describe one game mechanic (based on Marczewski's list [16]) and are randomly drawn by groups, guide this brainstorming but are also required to be incorporated in the generated ideas. Examples for such game mechanics are "Exploration", "(Experience) Points" and "Unlockable Content". The latter is described as: "Add to the feeling of self expression and value, by offering unlockable or rare content for free spirits to make use of." During the ATU GIG (see next section), this mechanic was for example incorporated in an idea addressing plastic waste where the more non-plastic articles one buys the more discount one gets on one's purchase. After the Invent step, all groups come together for the **Pitch** step. Here each group presents all of their ideas in an elevator pitch format (60 s per idea). In the subsequent **Auction** step, each group can bid for individual ideas using game money (GM). This bidding and the resulting end prize determine the value (i.e. perceived quality) of an idea. The buying group gives the money to the inventing group and receives the idea which they can use in the Prototyping phase to inspire their solution. Ideas that no group bid for are discarded.

Inspired by hackathon formats, we hypothesize that including a **prototyping** phase in the workshop encourages grounding the ideas into something tangible and orient the idea generation towards production and presentation, rather than generating abstract ideas only. In this phase, groups have one and a half hours to build a prototype which illustrates one or multiple of their own or acquired ideas and using different analogue materials, such as paper, pens, sticky notes, cardboard, pipe cleaners, and modelling wax.

4   Case Study

In order to explore group dynamics and behavior as well as the effect of using game mechanics as inspiration cards, we facilitated a GIG in the context of a workshop with high-school students. The event was targeted at students from the local "Academy of Talented Youth" (ATU). The problem which the students worked on was finding ways to reduce plastic waste and was introduced by showing a short video illustrating issues related to plastic waste.

Participants received no compensation for their participation (apart from lunch and refreshments provided during the event). The event lasted approximately 7 h (including a one hour lunch break) and attracted 11 high school students (7f, 4m; mean (M) age = 17.5) resulting in four pairs (group A–D) and one group of three students (group E).

In total, 41 ideas were generated during three iterations of Gamebidea. The idea that was sold for the highest bid was worth 6,000 GM and was bought by group D. About a third of the ideas (35%) sold for the minimum bid of 1,000 GM and about 13% sold for 4,000 GM.

Data Collection. Since GIGs are high-paced events that follow a tight schedule, we assessed stress levels and mental workload during the creative process. Accordingly, after the second and third round of Gamebidea as well as after the prototyping phase, participants filled in a questionnaire consisting of two scales, the DSSQ [17] to assess participants' stress level (based on task engagement, distress and worry) and the NASA TLX to assess mental workload.

To assess the level of collaboration that groups and individual participants engaged in during the ideation phase, namely Gamebidea, we draw on group-based video recordings of the Invent steps and the prototyping phase. With *level*, we refer to for how long and to what extent participants worked together during ideation (e.g. turn-taking). For this activity dimension, we coded sequences where individual participants documented ideas (i.e. wrote on idea templates) or talked (i.e. speaker shifts). Turn-taking therefore describes the division of the interaction between participants, and their dominance in each. For dominance, we defined a threshold of 60%, meaning in order for one participant to be considered as dominating a particular measure (e.g. talk) he or she had to be active in that way at least 60% of the total time both participants engaged in that activity. Codings of the activity dimension are neither mutually exclusive within nor across each other. This means that a participant could be both documenting an idea and talking at the same time.

4.1   Results

Results of our quantitative data analysis regarding intra-group dynamics during the GIG are grouped into three categories: performance (i.e. creative outcomes; quality of ideas), collaboration, and experience of individual participants.

Performance. For evaluating performance in GIG, we consider game money (GM) *earned* per group, and number of ideas *sold* per group in addition to number of ideas *generated.*

Of the 41 ideas that were generated during the Gamebidea phase, the groups came up with 13 ideas in the first iteration (round one, R1), 18 in round two (R2), and 10 in round three (R3). Four ideas that were generated during Invent phases ended up not being presented by the respective groups in the Pitch phase, which meant that they were not offered in the Auction. Of the remaining 37, six ideas were discarded, meaning that no group bid for them (one in R1, three in R2 and two in R3). The average number of ideas generated was 2.7 per group per round, and 8.2 in total per round. Except for one group, all groups produced a slightly larger number of ideas in R2 (M: 3.6) than in R1 (M: 2.6). Group E can be seen as an outlier since they generated 5.3 ideas per round (R1: 6, R2: 7; R3: 3). In the third and last round, the number of generated ideas went down to the level of R1 (avg. 2.0) and for the case of group E even lower than that.

Based on the value ideas sold for, the auction mechanic can be used to rate and prioritize novel and meaningful ideas. This value surely depends on the number of groups involved as well as the time the idea entered the auction (i.e. remaining game money of individual groups to spend on ideas). Despite these factors, we argue that the value of individual ideas provides a valid indication of a group's performance. On average, during the three rounds of Gamebidea, groups earned 13,600 GM. There was a stark contrast in the value of ideas between individual rounds. Ideas sold in R3 were the most expensive selling for on average 3,000 GM. Ideas sold for considerably less money in R1 (M: 2,111 GM) and were the cheapest in R2 (M: 1,666 GM).

The group which earned the most is clearly group E with 28,000 GM, whereas the least was earned by group A (5,000 GM; see Table 1). The number of ideas sold in the three rounds is fairly consistent, with 9 ideas being auctioned off in both R1 and R2 and 6 ideas sold in R3. There is a discrepancy between the number of ideas being generated (e.g. R1: 13) and number of ideas being sold (e.g. R1: 9). The remaining ideas were either discarded (e.g. R1: 1) or never presented (e.g. R1: 3). This discrepancy is particularly high for R2, where only 50% of generated ideas were sold (three ideas were discarded). As another concrete measure for group performance, we propose the average value for how much individual groups sold their ideas in relation to how many ideas got discarded. According to this measurement group C performed best and group D showed the poorest performance.

Table 1. Overview of group's performance during the Gamebidea phase of the ATU GIG. *Talk & Write* in min. **Performance** = *GM earned/(Ideas sold + Ideas discarded)*.

Group	Ideas		GM		Talk			Write		
	Sold	Discarded	Earned	Performance	R1	R2	R3	R1	R2	R3
A	2	1	5,000	1666.67	4.04	2.83	2.60	2.45	5.20	1.90
B	6	0	13,000	2166.67	2.97	1.67	1.80	6.33	7.33	4.67
C	5	0	16,000	3200.00	3.95	2.15	2.75	1.67	2.92	2.43
D	4	2	6,000	1000.00	2.35	1.27	1.78	2.72	3.05	1.32
E	6	3	28,000	3111.11	2.95	1.97	2.45	3.30	10.25	6.43

Collaboration. There is a clear difference in the amount of talk over the rounds. While in R1 individual groups on average talked for about 3.25 min (49% of round duration), they talked half as much in R2 (1.97 min; 32%). In R3, participants again spent some more time discussing ideas (2.23 min; 40%). The difference in time spent talking between groups is not significant.

Taking a closer look at the percentage of time spent talking during idea generation provides an indication to the level of collaboration within individual groups. Since we base our evaluation on quantitative measures only but did not transcribe actual conversation, we cannot be sure that all talk was in fact task-related. We term brainstormings where group members spent more than 50% of the time talking *conversational brainstorming*, this occurred twice in R1 (group A & C) and once in R3 (group A).

Whereas amount of talk clearly declined over rounds, the amount of time spent writing saw a peak in R2 (i.e. least writing activity in R3, most in R2, medium in R1). When looking at writing, one needs to keep in mind that the duration can actually be longer than the total brainstorming duration, since both participants could be writing at the same time. Since there are large differences in the time spent noting down ideas both across rounds as well as for individual groups, providing average numbers would not provide a clear picture of the situation. Overall, summing all rounds, group E spent the most time to document ideas (19.98 min), followed by group B (18.33 min). Group C & D spent the least time documenting ideas (7.02 min; 7.09 min). Representative for these great differences, the time spent noting down ideas in the second round increased by more than 300% for group E (R1: 3.30 min, R2: 10.28 min).

Seeing that the number of generated ideas can have an impact on the time spent documenting those, we further looked at the relationship of time spent writing and number of generated ideas. Except for group A, who spent 2.45 min documenting one idea in R1, all groups on average spent about 0.64 min of writing per idea. R3 sees a slight increase, with 0.82 min per idea.

Regarding dominance in talk, for the majority of groups the share in talking was about equal. In six cases, one participant dominated by speaking more than 60% of the time either of them talked. Group C is a special case in this respect, as in all three rounds the same participant dominated the talk. The share of talk stands in contrast to the share in writing. In 10 out of 15 cases, one participant took the lead in noting down ideas on the idea templates. In five of these cases, the other participant never wrote a line. This is the case for all three rounds for group C, where one participant (the one not dominating talk) was responsible for documenting ideas.

Individual Experience. As a third factor to be considered for evaluating innovation processes, we assessed participants' experience on two dimensions, stress level and mental workload. Task engagement during R2 was rather high (M: 18.36, standard deviation (SD): 1.36; max 20). Whereas individual participants indicated rather similar task engagements for R2, task engagement for both R3 and during prototyping (P) varied a lot (R3 M: 15.09, SD: 4.30; P M: 14.82, SD: 4.35). This contrast also applies within groups. Difference in task engagement within groups was especially high during prototyping (A: 7, D: 10, E: 9). With the exception of two participants, task engagement slightly declined from R2 to R3 (M: 15.09). Although showing a slight overall decrease during prototyping, engagement remained considerably high.

The second stress dimension assesses distress regarding tension and participants' confidence in their (task-relevant) abilities. Across R2 (M: 10.36, SD: 3.29; max. 20), R3 (M: 10.45; SD: 2.91) and prototyping (M: 8.64; SD: 2.69) distress was mediocre, meaning that they neither felt distressed about having to perform well nor were they indifferent about their success in the given task. Distress in R2 varied quite a bit (min: 4; max: 16).

Worry, the third stress dimension, assesses to what extent people are worried about the impression they are making towards others (i.e. self-focus). Worry was rated mediocre during R2 (M: 11.55, SD: 3.27; max. 20), R3 (M: 9.82, SD: 2.52) and prototyping (M: 10.64, SD: 2.69) and varied the most during R2. Within groups, worry was rather similar across all steps for groups B, C and E, but varied quite a bit for groups A (avg. diff. 7.00) and D (avg. diff. 6.33).

To the question as to how successful they thought their groups were, individual participants responded with rather low ratings in all rounds (R2: 7.09; R3: 8.55; P: 7.94; max. 20). Group C (M: 13.5) & D (M: 10.75) seemed mildly satisfied with their performance. Despite this low satisfaction regarding own performance, participants indicated low to very low frustration during R2 (M: 6.27), R3 (M: 3.27) and prototyping (M: 3.73). Mental demand averaged on a moderate level with slightly decreasing over rounds (R2 M: 12.00; R3 M: 10.73; P M: 9.91). Apart from group B in R3, all groups were equally (dis-)satisfied with their performance during R2 and R3.

5   Discussion

Departing from previous work on differences between individual and group-based brainstorming which suggest a higher performance for individual brainstorming, it might be inferred that participants in group E worked individually. Yet from their amount of talk, it becomes clear that they did collaborate. In particular for round two and three this collaboration served more the purpose of receiving feedback on (individual) ideas instead of developing ideas together and hence had a support function. This observation applies to the majority of the groups during round two and round three.

Based on the example of group A, which came second to last according to our proposed performance measure, it can be posited that conversational brainstorming (i.e. extensively discussing ideas) does not necessarily result in a high performance during creative processes. Moreover, the group that talked the least over all rounds (group D) showed the lowest performance.

Participants in group C showed a clear division of work between talking and documenting. Along with the decline in talk and increase in writing is the development that previously less active participants became more active in the latter round, making participation within groups more balanced than in the first round. One explanation for this might be that after having witnessed that others welcome innovative, "funny" ideas, individual participants felt a desire to be recognized for good ideas (i.e. gain status; [5]).

Money spent and money earned directly influence each other since earned money is used to purchase more ideas in the Auction of the subsequent round. It is further determined by the strategy of the respective group; (a) ending up with as much money as possible or (b) collecting the most valuable (and thus "best") ideas. The fact that not all generated ideas were sold during the respective rounds indicates that participants actually did select ideas, hence moving on from divergent thinking to convergent thinking. Further, the varying prizes can be interpreted as a result of various degrees of interests and hence perceived value in a respective idea. The value can thus be used to prioritize and even estimate the perceived quality of the ideas. During the second round this selection was especially prevalent (e.g. three discarded ideas in R2). This selective behavior might also be due to groups wanting to save some game money for the last round.

Those groups (B & E) that indicated on average a high task engagement during R2 and R3 performed rather well according to the purchase value of their ideas. Group A & D, which indicated a mediocre task engagement performed worst, which indicates a relationship between task engagement and performance during creative processes.

Reflecting on the low satisfaction in contrast to the rather high task engagement, it might be posited that participants' critical self-evaluation motivated them to keep up their efforts. While we cannot be certain about this, we speculate that the inter-group competition contributed to this motivation. Group E showed a clear discrepancy between satisfaction with own performance (M: 1.67) and actual performance (placed 2nd). Group C, however, seemed to be both aware of and satisfied with (M: 13.5) their good performance (1st).

Our findings indicate that during gameful collaborative ideation processes, groups show various forms of collaboration (potentially oriented on their game strategy) and adapt these over time. Selection and development of ideas can be supported by gameful means, demonstrated here by exchanging (= buying) other groups' ideas. In addition to drawing on collaborative aspects, support for critical self-evaluation may push for improved quality of the work (as studied e.g. in connection with collaborative writing [20]). With support from further empirical work we hope to be able to provide a clear set of design guidelines for gameful collaborative technologies.

6 Conclusion

This paper has presented insights from a gameful creativity method, named Gameful Idea Generations. The analysis concentrated on intra-group collaboration and evaluation of the creative process. As part of the analysis, we proposed a method to assess the performance of a group in relation to the quality of ideas produced.

Being aware that this study was conducted in a rather special context (different from a hackathon) with a small and homogeneous user group, we plan on running more Gameful Idea Generations while varying user demographics (e.g. elderly, design students) and study designs such as including control groups in order to investigate the effect of certain game mechanics. To that end, we also plan to explore both cross-cultural and cross-generational influences on promoting creativity through gamefulness.

References

1. Brandt, E., Messeter, J.: Facilitating collaboration through design games. In: Proceedings of PDC 2004, pp. 121–131. ACM (2004)
2. Chung, W.J.: Effective ideation method for collective creativity. In: Chung, W.J., Shin, C.S. (eds.) AHFE 2018. AISC, vol. 790, pp. 153–161. Springer, Cham (2019). https://doi.org/10.1007/978-3-319-94601-6_17
3. Connolly, T., Jessup, L.M., Valacich, J.S.: Effects of anonymity and evaluative tone on idea generation in computer-mediated groups. Manag. Sci. 36(6), 689–703 (1990)
4. Csikszentmihalyi, M.: Flow: The Psychology of Optimal Experience: Finding Flow. Harper Perennial, New York (1990)
5. Dennis, A.R., Reinicke, B.A.: Beta versus HVS and the acceptance of electronic brainstorming technology. MIS Q. 28(1), 1–20 (2004)

6. Diehl, M., Stroebe, W.: Productivity loss in brainstorming groups: toward the solution of a riddle. J. Pers. Soc. Psychol. **53**(3), 497 (1987)
7. Easterday, M.W., Gerber, E.M., Rees Lewis, D.G.: Social innovation networks: a new approach to social design education and impact. Des. Issues **34**(2), 64–76 (2018)
8. Gandolfi, E.: You have got a (different) friend in me: asymmetrical roles in gaming as potential ambassadors of computational and cooperative thinking. E-Learn. Digit. Media **15**(3), 128–145 (2018). https://doi.org/10.1177/2042753018757757
9. Halskov, K., Dalsgård, P.: Inspiration card workshops. In: Proceedings of the 6th Conference on Designing Interactive Systems, pp. 2–11. ACM (2006)
10. Hornecker, E.: Creative idea exploration within the structure of a guiding framework: the card brainstorming game. In: Proceedings of TEI 2010, pp. 101–108. ACM (2010)
11. Hornecker, E., Buur, J.: Getting a grip on tangible interaction: a framework on physical space and social interaction. In: Proceedings of the SIGCHI Conference on Human Factors in Computing Systems, pp. 437–446. ACM (2006). https://doi.org/10.1145/1124772.1124838
12. Jackson, L.A., Witt, E.A., Games, A.I., Fitzgerald, H.E., Von Eye, A., Zhao, Y.: Information technology use and creativity: findings from the children and technology project. Comput. Hum. Behav. **28**(2), 370–376 (2012). https://doi.org/10.1016/j.chb.2011.10.006
13. Kultima, A.: The organic nature of game ideation: game ideas arise from solitude and mature by bouncing. In: Proceedings of The International Academic Conference on the Future of Game Design and Technology, pp. 33–39. ACM (2010)
14. Lee, H., et al.: Cooperation begins: encouraging critical thinking skills through cooperative reciprocity using a mobile learning game. Comput. Educ. **97**, 97–115 (2016)
15. Lucero, A., Arrasvuori, J.: PLEX Cards: a source of inspiration when designing for playfulness. In: Proceedings of the 3rd International Conference on Fun and Games, pp. 28–37. ACM (2010)
16. Marczewski, M.: New downloadable version of the gamification inspiration cards on sale. https://www.gamified.uk/2018/11/02/new-downloadable-version-of-the-gamification-inspiration-cards-on-sale/
17. Matthews, G., Szalma, J.L., Panganiban, A.R., Neubauer, C., Warm, J.S.: Profiling task stress with the dundee stress state questionnaire. Psychol. Stress **1**, 49–91 (2013)
18. Paulus, P.B., Dzindolet, M.T.: Social influence processes in group brainstorming. J. Pers. Soc. Psychol. **64**(4), 575 (1993)
19. Thiel, S.K., Falk-Olesen, J., Halskov, K.: Gameful idea generations (2019, Under Review)
20. Türkay, S., Seaton, D., Ang, A.M.: Itero: a revision history analytics tool for exploring writing behavior and reflection. In: Extended Abstracts of the 2018 Conference on Human Factors in Computing Systems, CHI EA 2018, pp. LBW052:1–LBW052:6. ACM, New York, April 2018. https://doi.org/10.1145/3170427.3188474
21. Voiskounsky, A.E., Yermolova, T.D., Yagolkovskiy, S.R., Khromova, V.M.: Creativity in online gaming: individual and dyadic performance in minecraft. Psychol. Russ. **10**(4), 40 (2017)
22. Williams, T.M., Fleming, J.W.: Methodological study of the relationship between associative fluency and intelligence. Dev. Psychol. **1**(2), 155–162 (1969)

Discovering Latent Country Words: A Step Towards Cross-Cultural Emotional Communication

Heeryon Cho[1]([⊠])(iD) and Toru Ishida[2]

[1] College of Computer Science, Kookmin University, Seoul 02707, South Korea
heeryon@kookmin.ac.kr
[2] School of Creative Science and Engineering, Waseda University,
Tokyo 1698555, Japan
toru.ishida@aoni.waseda.jp

Abstract. Knowing what concepts are substantial to each country can be helpful in enhancing emotional communication between two countries. As a concrete example of identifying substantial country concepts, we focus on a task of finding latent country words from cross-cultural texts of two countries. We do this by combining word embedding and tensor decomposition: common words that appear in both countries' texts are selected; their country specific word embeddings are learned; a three-way tensor consisting of word factor, word embedding factor, and country factor are constructed; and CANDECOMP/PARAFAC decomposition is performed on the three-way tensor while fixing the country factor values of the decomposed result. We tested our method on a motivating example of finding latent country words from J-pop lyrics from Japan and K-pop lyrics from South Korea. We found that J-pop lyrics words feature nature related motifs such as 'petal', 'cloud', 'universe', 'star', and 'sky', whereas K-pop lyrics words highlight human body related motifs such as 'style', 'shirt', 'head', 'foot', and 'skin'.

Keywords: Cross-cultural text analysis · Tensor decomposition · Word embedding

1 Introduction

Let us suppose that two countries' representatives are trying to resolve a common issue through bilateral discussion, and the discussion is being recorded in the form of meeting minutes. Later, based on the meeting minutes, we want to identify a list of words that are used more substantially by each country's representatives. How can we do this?

This research was supported by the National Research Foundation of South Korea (NRF) grant funded by the South Korean government (NRF-2017R1A2B4011015). This research was partially supported by a Grant-in-Aid for Scientific Research (A) (17H00759, 2017–2020) from Japan Society for the Promotion of Science (JSPS).

H. Nakanishi et al. (Eds.): CRIWG+CollabTech 2019, LNCS 11677, pp. 232–241, 2019.
https://doi.org/10.1007/978-3-030-28011-6_17

One way to find such latent country words is to build a three-way tensor consisting of a list of common, frequent words used by the two countries' representatives in the first dimension (i.e., word factor), the word embedding values of each country's words in the second dimension (i.e., word embedding factor), and the degree of country aspect in the third dimension (i.e., country factor). Since the word embedding representation learns the hidden relationships between words, country-wise speech texts can learn country specific relationship between words. We then perform tensor decomposition on the country-wise word embedding data, while adjusting the country factor values, to find substantial words used by each country's representatives.

Advances in three-way component analysis techniques have realized the summarization of all information in a large three-way data set [1]. Three-way data refer to data that can be arranged in a three-dimensional array, i.e., three-way tensor. Recently, tensor factorization and decomposition has become an important tool for data mining since they can explicitly take into account the multi-way structure of the data that would otherwise be lost when analyzing the data by matrix factorization approaches [2]. CANDECOMP (canonical decomposition)/PARAFAC (parallel factors) [3,4] decomposition (hereafter referred to as CP decomposition) is a popular tensor decomposition method that decomposes a tensor as a sum of rank-one tensors [5]. In this study, we apply CP decomposition on the aforementioned three-way tensor while deliberately fixing the country factor values of the decomposed result in order to identify latent country words.

2   Discovering Latent Country Words

To describe our method concretely, we present a motivating example of finding latent lyrics words from J-pop and K-pop lyrics texts. We aim to discover latent country motifs from J-pop/K-pop lyrics by learning country specific word embeddings and applying CP decomposition on the two countries' lyrics word embedding tensor. Figure 1 displays the overview of discovering latent J-pop and K-pop lyrics words. The overall process includes lyrics data collection and tokenization, J-pop/K-pop lyrics word mapping (i.e., language unification) and filtering, country specific word embedding learning, and tensor decomposition.

2.1   Data Gathering and Tokenization

Ten years (2008–2017) worth of yearly top 100 ranking J-pop and K-pop hit song lyrics were gathered as target data. For J-pop lyrics, a total of 1,142 lyrics were crawled from a major Japanese music ranking portal, *Oricon Chart*, and two lyrics search engines, *Uta-Net* and *J-Lyric.net*.[1] For K-pop lyrics, a total of 1,000 lyrics were crawled from a major South Korean music ranking portal, *Melon Chart*.[2] There were more J-pop lyrics than K-pop lyrics since the *Oricon Chart* allowed multiple tied rankings. The two countries' lyrics were then tokenized

---

[1] https://www.oricon.co.jp/, http://www.uta-net.com, http://j-lyric.net/.
[2] https://www.melon.com/.

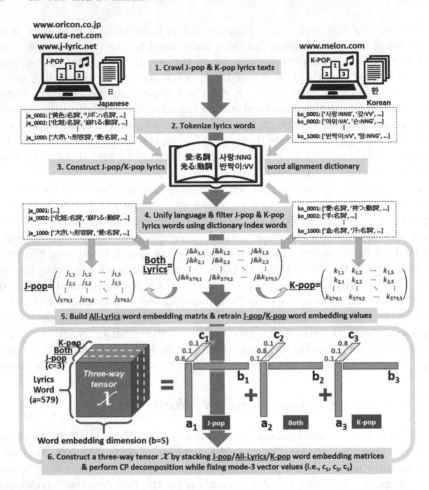

Fig. 1. Overall process of discovering latent J-pop/K-pop lyrics words through word embedding learning and CP decomposition.

using Japanese/Korean morphological analyzers. Nouns, verbs, and adjectives were selected as the unit of analyses. Table 1 summarizes the statistics of the gathered data. We see that the J-pop lyrics' vocabulary size is more than twice that of K-pop's as evidenced by the total number of unique words.

Table 1. J-pop/K-pop lyrics data statistics.

Gathered years: 2008–2017	J-pop	K-pop
Total number of lyrics	1,142	1,000
Avg. number of words per lyric	110	77
Total words (total unique)	125,205 (13,086)	77,092 (5,797)

2.2 J-Pop/K-Pop Lyrics Word Mapping and Filtering

Once the nouns, verbs, and adjectives were obtained from the J-pop/K-pop lyrics data, the similar meaning J-pop lyrics words were manually mapped to K-pop lyrics words to build a J-pop/K-pop lyrics word alignment dictionary. This dictionary was used later for unifying the J-pop/K-pop lyrics data into a single language. Table 2 displays three sample entries of the J-pop/K-pop lyrics word alignment dictionary. Approximate English translation is given as reference in the first column. Note that the parts of speech were not distinguished in this dictionary; rather, words with similar concepts were grouped using a '|' delimiter to constitute a single dictionary word (e.g., "get_angry:verb|anger:noun").

Table 2. Sample entry of J-pop/K-pop lyrics word alignment dictionary.

English translation	J-pop lyrics word	K-pop lyrics word
heart:noun	心:名詞|こころ:名詞|ココロ:名詞	마음:NNG|맘:NNG
get_angry:verb|anger:noun	怒る:動詞|怒り:名詞|···	화내:VV|분노:NNG|···
voice:noun	声:名詞	목소리:NNG

The J-pop/K-pop lyrics word alignment dictionary was constructed as follows. Presented with a list of unique J-pop and K-pop lyrics words and frequency counts, a bilingual Korean with more than ten years' experience of living in Japan first grouped the similar meaning words for each country, and then mapped the grouped words across the two countries. Then, a professional Korean-Japanese translator with twenty years of translation expertise reviewed and corrected the alignment dictionary and further expanded the dictionary. The dictionary building process continued until a sizable dictionary was constructed. From this dictionary, the dictionary words with both countries' frequency counts that were less than six were discarded. As a result, a J-pop/K-pop lyrics word alignment dictionary with 579 J-pop/K-pop lyrics word mappings was constructed. Note that when the delimiter was removed from the grouped dictionary words, the number of atomic J-pop and K-pop lyrics words were 1,065 and 870 respectively.

Using this alignment dictionary, J-pop/K-pop lyrics texts were filtered to contain only the grouped dictionary words. Then, the filtered K-pop lyrics words were converted to J-pop lyrics words by referring to the dictionary mapping. As a result, a list of filtered Japanese grouped dictionary words were obtained for both the J-pop and K-pop lyrics data. For some lyrics, there were no matching dictionary words, and hence, those lyrics were discarded. Consequently, a total of 1,134 and 986 J-pop and K-pop lyrics data were used for constructing the country specific word embeddings.

Table 3 summarizes the statistics of the filtered J-pop/K-pop lyrics word data and the J-pop/K-pop lyrics word alignment dictionary. The overall dictionary coverage was calculated by dividing the number of total filtered words by the total number of words given in Table 1. Even with the limited number of dictionary atomic words, i.e., 1,065 and 870, which constitutes approximately 8% and 15% of unique J-pop and K-pop words respectively (these percentages were calculated by dividing the number of dictionary atomic words by the total unique words in Table 1), the filtered words covered a close to half (48.8%) and three-quarters (74%) of the J-pop and K-pop lyrics data respectively. This indicates that the alignment dictionary covers many of the frequently used words in each country's lyrics. Table 4 lists the top-20 most frequently appearing dictionary noun words in the filtered J-pop/K-pop data. English translation of each word is also given. Although we have grouped the words into similar concepts regardless of the parts of speech, hereafter we select the most representative parts of speech word when presenting our results.

Table 3. Filtered data & dictionary statistics.

	J-pop	K-pop
Total filtered lyrics	1,134	986
Total filtered words	61,094	57,049
Total grouped dictionary words	579	579
Total atomic dictionary words	1,065	870
Overall dictionary coverage	48.8%	74.0%

Table 4. Top-20 total frequent J-pop & K-pop lyrics nouns.

Rank	J-pop lyrics nouns			K-pop lyrics nouns		
	English	Japanese	Korean	English	Japanese	Korean
1	love	愛	사랑	love	愛	사랑
2	now	今	지금	words	言葉	말
3	everyone	みんな	모두	day	日	날
4	heart	心	마음	heart	心	마음
5	dream	夢	꿈	moment	時	때
6	moment	時	때	person	人	사람
7	hand	手	손	inside	中	속
8	inside	中	속	night	夜	밤
9	front	前	앞	eyes	目	눈
10	eyes	目	눈	chest	胸	가슴
11	world	世界	세상	final	最後	마지막
12	day	日	날	tears	涙	눈물
13	person	人	사람	thought	想い	생각
14	future	未来	미래	time	時間	시간
15	sky	空	하늘	front	前	앞
16	chest	胸	가슴	world	世界	세상
17	as is	まま	이대로	one day	一日	하루
18	tomorrow	明日	내일	top	上	위
19	tears	涙	눈물	happiness	幸せ	행복
20	thing	事	일	[at one's] side	そば	곁

Tables 5 and 6 list the top-10 most frequent verbs and adjectives appearing in the filtered J-pop/K-pop lyrics data. We see that many of the same words are used frequently in both countries' lyrics (marked in *italics*), e.g., *'love'*, *'heart'*, *'look'*, *'know'*, *'good'* and *'sad'*.

Table 5. Top-10 most frequent J-pop & K-pop lyrics verbs.

Rank	J-pop lyrics verbs			K-pop lyrics verbs		
	English	Japanese	Korean	English	Japanese	Korean
1	*go*	行く	가다	*look*	見る	보다
2	*look*	見る	보다	*know*	知る	알다
3	*know*	知る	알다	*laugh*	笑う	웃다
4	give	くれる	주다	forget	忘れる	잊다
5	meet	会う	만나다	*live*	生きる	살다
6	come	来る	오다	grasp	掴む	잡다
7	*laugh*	笑う	웃다	*go*	行く	가다
8	change	変わる	변하다	leave	離れる	떠나다
9	believe	信じる	믿다	cry	泣く	울다
10	*live*	生きる	살다	take	取る	들다

Table 6. Top-10 most frequent J-pop & K-pop lyrics adjectives.

Rank	J-pop lyrics adjectives			K-pop lyrics adjectives		
	English	Japanese	Korean	English	Japanese	Korean
1	*good*	いい	좋다	*absent*	無い	없다
2	*sad*	悲しい	슬프다	*good*	いい	좋다
3	*far*	遠い	멀다	*painful*	痛い	아프다
4	*painful*	痛い	아프다	many	多い	많다
5	*absent*	無い	없다	*far*	遠い	멀다
6	scared	怖い	두렵다	*sad*	悲しい	슬프다
7	joyful	楽しい	즐겁다	tough	つらい	힘들다
8	kind	優しい	착하다	small	小さい	작다
9	lonely	寂しい	외롭다	late	遅い	늦다
10	hot	熱い	뜨겁다	deep	深い	깊다

2.3 Word Embedding Learning

Using the filtered lyrics word data, the J-pop/K-pop lyrics' country specific word embedding values were learned using the Word2Vec algorithm [7]. Word embedding maps each word to a vector of real numbers. Traditionally, to represent a word in a document, each word occupied one dimension of the document vector; consequently, a vocabulary of ten thousand words required ten thousand dimension vector. Word embedding introduced a way to express each word using a continuous vector space with much lower dimension of few hundreds.

It is known to capture the context of a word such as semantic and syntactic similarity, and the relation with other words. However, to learn useful embeddings, abundant data are needed. Due to the limited amount of the lyrics data, we first learned the initial word embedding values using both the J-pop and K-pop data, and then updated the initial embedding values by separately using the K-pop and J-pop data to build country specific J-pop/K-pop lyrics word embeddings following the work in [6].

With regard to the word embedding dimension size, we tested different dimension size of 5, 10, and 100. Due to the limited amount of data, we found that 5 was the most adequate among the three, and hence set the size of the embedding dimension to 5. Once the J-pop and K-pop lyrics word embedding values were learned, three 579×5 sized Word2Vec matrices, one for J-pop, one for both J-pop and K-pop (i.e., the initial word embedding values), and one for K-pop, having different embedding weights were created. The three Word2Vec matrices were then stacked back to back to create a three-way tensor of size $579 \times 5 \times 3$, which contained the J-pop, Both, and K-pop lyrics word embedding values (see Fig. 1 bottom).

2.4   Performing CP Decomposition

CP decomposition was performed on this three-way tensor using the alternating least squares algorithm to approximately decompose the tensor into a sum of three components of rank-one tensors (Fig. 1 bottom). Although the number of components in CP decomposition are determined by gradually increasing the component size after evaluating the fit of each optimal solution, this approach did not apply to our example task since we formulated a CP decomposition with a predetermined component size of three which matched J-pop, Both, and K-pop. This formulation allowed us to obtain the rank-one vectors (i.e., a_1, a_2, and a_3 in Fig. 1) that corresponded to the dictionary lyrics words reflecting the J-pop, Both, and K-pop lyrics words. To obtain the latent J-pop/K-pop lyrics words, the values of the mode-3 vectors (i.e., the vectors c_1, c_2, and c_3 in Fig. 1 bottom), which represent the country aspect, were adjusted to emphasize the J-pop, Both, and K-pop aspect. We set the mode-3 vector values as [[0.8, 0.1, 0.1], [0.1, 0.8, 0.1], [0.1, 0.1, 0.8]], and proceeded with the CP decomposition.

3   Results and Analyses

Table 7 lists the top-20 latent J-pop/K-pop lyrics noun words discovered using the proposed method. These latent country words were obtained by sorting the a_1 and a_3 rank-one vector values (Fig. 1 bottom) along with the corresponding lyrics words, and selecting the top-20 or bottom-20 lyrics noun words with the larger absolute top-most or bottom-most element value (i.e., the first and the 579th elements' absolute values were compared). We see in Table 7 an underlying theme in the latent J-pop/K-pop lyrics noun words.

Table 7. Top-20 latent J-pop & K-pop lyrics nouns.

Rank	J-pop lyrics nouns			K-pop lyrics nouns		
	English	**Japanese**	**Korean**	**English**	**Japanese**	**Korean**
1	petal	花びら	꽃잎	style	スタイル	스타일
2	*blood*	血	피	brother	兄ちゃん	오빠
3	cherry blossom	桜	벚꽃	bell	ベル	벨
4	light	光	빛	charm	魅力	매력
5	darkness	闇	어둠	shirt	シャツ	셔츠
6	quietness	静か	고요	impossibility	無理	무리
7	cloud	雲	구름	head	頭	머리
8	universe	宇宙	우주	toe	つま先	발끝
9	night sky	夜空	밤하늘	danger	危険	위험
10	winter	冬	겨울	taste	味	맛
11	color	色	색깔	clothes	服	옷
12	fire	火	불	woman	女	여자
13	star	星	별	sweat	汗	땀
14	wave	波	파도	money	お金	돈
15	sky	空	하늘	foot	足	발
16	needle	針	바늘	top	上	위
17	spring breeze	春風	봄바람	skin	肌	피부
18	spark	火花	불꽃	body	身	몸
19	rain	雨	비	*blood*	血	피
20	bottom	下	아래	music	音楽	음악

We see in Table 7 that nature related motifs such as 'petal', 'cherry blossom', 'light', 'darkness', 'cloud', 'universe', 'night sky', 'fire', 'star', 'wave', 'sky', 'spring breeze', and 'rain' are present in J-pop lyrics words while human related motifs such as 'style', 'brother', 'charm', 'shirt', 'head', 'toe', 'clothes', 'women', 'sweat', 'foot', 'skin', 'body', and *'blood'* are present in K-pop lyrics words. *'Blood'* is a common noun word listed in both countries.

Tables 8 and 9 list the top-10 latent J-pop/K-pop verbs and adjectives. Three verbs, *'fly'*, *'dance'*, and *'melt'*, appear in both countries. When we exclude these verbs, we are left with nature related verbs for J-pop (e.g., '[leaves] fall', '[rain] fall', 'glitter', 'shine' and 'blow') and human related verbs for K-pop (e.g., 'wave', 'steal', 'fit', 'suit', 'wear', 'take off', and 'run'). In the case of adjectives, J-pop adjectives focus on color/vision related expressions (e.g., 'white', 'stark white', 'red', 'blue', 'beautiful', and 'bright') while K-pop adjectives focus on human perception based expressions (e.g., 'cumbersome', 'delicious', 'stylish', 'pretty', 'hot', 'light', *'cold'*, and 'shy'). *'High'* and *'cold'* are common adjectives.

For reference, the top-20 latent words that encompass both J-pop and K-pop lyrics (i.e., 'Both' a_2 vector in Fig. 1) regardless of the parts of speech are 'top', 'bottom', 'cherry blossom', '[leaves] fall', 'mirror', 'spring breeze', 'flower', 'half', 'hi/bye', 'leaf', '[tell a] lie', 'distance', 'style', 'shine', 'red', 'die', 'words', 'summer', 'love', and 'sorry'.

Table 8. Top-10 latent J-pop & K-pop lyrics verbs.

Rank	J-pop lyrics verbs			K-pop lyrics verbs		
	English	Japanese	Korean	English	Japanese	Korean
1	[leaves] fall	散る	흩날리다	wave	振る	흔들다
2	*fly*	飛ぶ	날다	steal	盗む	훔치다
3	[rain] fall	降る	내리다	*dance*	踊る	춤추다
4	glitter	光る	반짝이다	fit	合う	맞다
5	shine	照らす	비추다	[it] suit[-s you]	似合う	어울리
6	*dance*	踊る	춤추다	wear	着る	입다
7	echo	響く	울리다	take off [clothes]	脱ぐ	벗다
8	penetrate	突き抜く	뚫다	*melt*	溶ける	녹다
9	blow	吹く	불다	run	走る	뛰다
10	*melt*	溶ける	녹다	*fly*	飛ぶ	날다

Table 9. Top-10 latent J-pop & K-pop lyrics adjectives.

Rank	J-pop lyrics adjectives			K-pop lyrics adjectives		
	English	Japanese	Korean	English	Japanese	Korean
1	white	白い	하얗다	*high*	高い	높다
2	*high*	高い	높다	cumbersome	面倒い	귀찮다
3	stark white	真っ白い	새하얗다	large	大きい	크다
4	red	赤い	붉다	delicious	美味しい	맛있다
5	blue	青い	파랗다	stylish	かっこいい	멋있다
6	deep	深い	깊다	pretty	かわいい	예쁘다
7	beautiful	美しい	아름답다	hot	熱い	뜨겁다
8	spacious	広い	넓다	light	軽い	가볍다
9	bright	眩しい	눈부시다	*cold*	寒い	춥다
10	*cold*	寒い	춥다	shy	恥ずかしい	부끄럽다

4   Discussion and Conclusion

How can knowing the top-n latent country words help cross-cultural communication? Recall that the proposed method learns the hidden relationships between the words in each country's text in the form of word embeddings, and combining the two countries' word embeddings and performing partially fixed CP decomposition while adjusting the degree of country aspect enables the discovery of the substantial words hidden within each country's text. Such elicitation of the latent country words can aid in understanding the subtle differences underlying the two countries' texts. Revisiting the bilateral meeting minutes example presented at the outset of this paper, by using the proposed method, we could learn the hidden emphasis placed by each country's representatives on the common issue through analyzing the latent country words. We have demonstrated the potential of the proposed approach through the example task of finding latent J-pop/K-pop lyrics words; we discovered that the hidden motifs present in J-pop and K-pop lyrics texts were 'nature' and 'human'.

As the method analyzes the frequent and common words shared by the two countries' texts, the method can be viewed as finding each country's *dominant* concepts from a set of shared concepts; this is very different from finding *distinct* concepts that do not overlap across two countries. Moreover, the proposed method is unsupervised; both the word embedding learning and CP decomposition do not require any labeled training data (we assume that the country information can be automatically collected with the country texts). As long as there exists two countries' texts, the proposed method can be applied. However, the construction of reliable country-specific word embeddings is the key to finding meaningful latent country words, and thus a sufficient amount of two countries' texts is required for successful analysis.

Recent advances in information technology have enabled the easy collection of cross-cultural texts. Nowadays, there are abundant cross-cultural texts generated by two countries' participants that cover a common subject; examples range from two countries' bilateral meeting minutes to movie reviews written by two countries' audiences. We believe the method proposed in this paper can provide a viable data-driven approach to highlighting the hidden emphasis placed on a common subject discussed by the two countries' participants, and in turn aid in understanding the hidden differences underlying the two countries.

Acknowledgments. We thank the anonymous reviewers for many constructive comments. A heartwarming thanks to Yangjean Cho for revising and expanding the J-pop/K-pop lyrics word alignment dictionary.

References

1. Kiers, H.-A.-L., Van Mechelen, I.: Three-way component analysis: principles and illustrative application. Psychol. Methods **6**(1), 84–110 (2001)
2. Mørup, M.: Applications of tensor (multiway array) factorizations and decompositions in data mining. WIREs Data Min. Knowl. Discov. **1**(1), 24–40 (2011)
3. Carroll, J.-D., Chang, J.-J.: Analysis of individual differences in multidimensional scaling via an N-way generalization of 'Eckart-Young' decomposition. Psychometrika **35**, 283–319 (1970)
4. Harshman, R.-A.: Foundations of the PARAFAC procedure: models and conditions for an "explanatory" multi-modal factor analysis. UCLA Working Papers in Phonetics, vol. 16, pp. 1–84 (1970)
5. Kolda, T.-G., Bader, B.-W.: Tensor decompositions and applications. SIAM Rev. **51**, 455–500 (2009)
6. Cho, H., Yoon, S.-M.: Issues in visualizing intercultural dialogue using Word2Vec and t-SNE. In: Proceedings of 2017 International Conference on Culture & Computing, Kyoto, Japan, pp. 149–150 (2017)
7. Mikolov, T., Sutskever, I., Chen, K., Corrado, G., Dean, J.: Distributed representations of words and phrases and their compositionality. In: Proceedings of the 26th International Conference on Neural Information Processing Systems, Nevada, USA, pp. 3111–3119 (2013)

Evaluation of a Campus Navigation Application Using an AR Character Guide

Yamato Kuwahara[1(✉)], Hung-ya Tsai[2], Yuya Ieiri[1], and Reiko Hishiyama[1]

[1] Graduate School of Creative Science and Engineering, Waseda University,
3-4-1, Okubo, Shinjuku-ku, Tokyo 169-8555, Japan
kuwayama08@akane.waseda.jp, ieyuharu@ruri.waseda.jp, reiko@waseda.jp
[2] Osense Technology Co., Ltd.,
8F., No. 325, Sec. 4, Zhongxiao E. Road, Da'an District, Taipei City, Taiwan
hungyatsai@osensetech.com

Abstract. In recent years, many studies have been conducted to realize easy route navigation for pedestrians using augmented reality (AR). Many of these studies use methods where the direction or sign is indicated using AR. However, only a few have focused on using AR for route navigation to follow. Our research aims to realize easy route navigation using an AR character agent. We develop a navigation application wherein the user follows an AR character agent. We evaluate it from the behavior of the user. For that purpose, we conduct an experiment at a university festival using the navigation application. We then analyze the experimental data and questionnaire responses. The results show that route navigation by the AR character agent makes route identification easy. However, problems involving many participants feeling uneasy or being lost are encountered. Problems in accuracy caused by errors in the positional information are also observed. In future, a method to indicate directions more accurately must be considered.

Keywords: A context-aware AR navigation system ·
Human–agent interaction · Human wayfinding performance ·
Interactive behavior

1 Introduction

In recent years, many studies have been conducted to realize easy route navigation for pedestrians using augmented reality (AR). Yokoi et al. [1] developed a system wherein a user can intuitively understand the direction of the destination by displaying the landmark using AR. However, many previous studies displayed direction and signs using AR, and only a few focused on the route navigation following using AR. Therefore, this study aimed to realize easy route navigation using an AR character agent. We focus herein on the efficiency of route navigation by an AR character agent. We then make a hypothesis that the route is

© Springer Nature Switzerland AG 2019
H. Nakanishi et al. (Eds.): CRIWG+CollabTech 2019, LNCS 11677, pp. 242–250, 2019.
https://doi.org/10.1007/978-3-030-28011-6_18

easily detected, which gives the user a sense of security. In addition, we establish a hypothesis that the navigation by AR character agent can accurately guide the user to the destination. We verify these hypotheses using the experimental results. The remainder of this paper is structured as follows: Sect. 2 discusses several previous studies; Sect. 3 provides the hypotheses; Sect. 4 presents the developed application and describes the experiment; Sect. 5 discusses the analysis of the results of the questionnaire and log data; and Sect. 6 provides the conclusions and the future works.

2   Related Work

Many studies using AR for pedestrian navigation were conducted. Hervas et al. [2] evaluated a useful system for people with cognitive impairment by combining AR and text. Chang et al. [3] proposed a system for guiding historic buildings. Chu et al. [4] indicated that navigation using AR was superior to that using a map in terms of time and accuracy. As mentioned earlier, using AR for pedestrian navigation is effective.

However, Dunser [5] showed that users encountered more problems with using the AR view alone for navigation compared to using the AR and the map in combination. In addition, Pankrats et al. [6] showed that AR navigation may lose accuracy because of an error in the positional information. Therefore, research on pedestrian navigation using AR must be conducted.

Some studies have also focused on the user experience of navigation using AR. Sekhavat et al. [7] showed that in location- and marker-based AR, the former user experience without the task of reading markers was better than the latter. Mulloni et al. [8] focused on where and how users use AR. They showed that they often use AR at corners of streets in navigation applications. Campbell et al. [9] showed that navigation by a character enabled faster navigation along a shorter route than that by an arrow. We focus herein on the human behavior of navigation, in which the user only follows the guide.

3   Hypotheses

The user was assumed to be able to easily understand the route by following the AR character agent. Moreover, the user was assumed to not feel uneasy or lost. We made the following two hypotheses from the factors mentioned earlier:

Hypothesis 1: The navigation by the AR character agent is easy for the user to understand.
Hypothesis 2: The navigation by the AR character agent provides a sense of security to the user.

Moreover, this guide seems to be able to correctly lead the user to the destination. The following are defined herein as correct navigation:

- Walking on the right route

– Not going right or left on a straight road
– Not turning back the way they came.

We judge the guide to be incorrect when an action does not meet the above-mentioned criteria. We then establish Hypothesis 3.

Hypothesis 3: The navigation by the AR character agent is accurate.

4   Method

We developed a navigation application, called "BearNavi," to guide the user around the Waseda University campus. In this application, the university's bear mascot character guides the user. Using this application, we held an event called the "BearNavi Tour" at Waseda University on November 3 and 4, 2018, with 16 participants. Two of them were familiar with the campus, but the others didn't know the campus. Therefore, the application functioned as a navigation system. Furthermore, we followed them and observed their behavior. We then analyzed the experimental data and the questionnaire and evaluated the guide. Finally, we verified Hypothesis 1 and Hypothesis 2 from the results of the questionnaire and Hypothesis 3 from the log data results.

The user repeated the following actions in this application:

1. Reading the QR code of the poster
2. Moving to the destination following the guiding AR character
3. Finding the "Bear Coin," which can be tapped to reveal a quiz
4. Answering the quiz.

First, the user starts the tour by reading the QR codes of the posters on the wall. The character then appears on the screen and starts walking in front of the user. The character stops at a certain interval and waits for the user to catch up. When the user comes closer enough, the character starts walking again. The character repeats these actions until the user reaches the destination. A "Bear Coin" is displayed when the user reaches the destination. The user then attempts a quiz that appears when they tap the "Bear Coin." This application is for introducing the campus to people coming to the university for the first time, so the quizzes are about campus facilities and the university. The user can move to the next destination, regardless of the quiz correctness. The user repeats this flow thrice and finally reaches the goal point. Figure 1 shows a screen shot of each of these steps as example.

For this application, we used an indoor space computerization AI system [10] that obtains location information based on a video recorded with a smart terminal. Therefore, the user can be guided indoors and outdoors, and the user behavior in various places, such as the stairs and in narrow passages, can be evaluated. Figure 2 shows the route guided by the "BearNavi Tour." The segment in gray shows a buildings and in white shows a passage. We created a route on the Waseda University campus, where the user leaves the start point, passes two

(a) Screen shot of reading the QR code   (b) Screen shot of navigation

(c) Screen shot of finding the "Bear Coin"   (d) Screen shot of attempting the quiz

Fig. 1. Screen example of "BearNavi"

checkpoints, and reaches the goal point. We call the route from the start point to checkpoint A route 1, from checkpoint A to checkpoint B route 2, and from checkpoint B to the goal point route 3. The "Bear Coin" and a quiz were placed at each point. Posters were also set up.

The experimental flow is as follows:

1. Explanation
   First, the participants downloaded the application, and it was explained to them.
2. Main experiment
   The participants walked the route using the application.
3. Questionnaire
   Finally, the participants answered the questionnaire about this application.

5   Results and Discussion

5.1   Questionnaire

We asked the participants to answer the questionnaire on the route navigation of this application after the experiment. First, the participants answered the

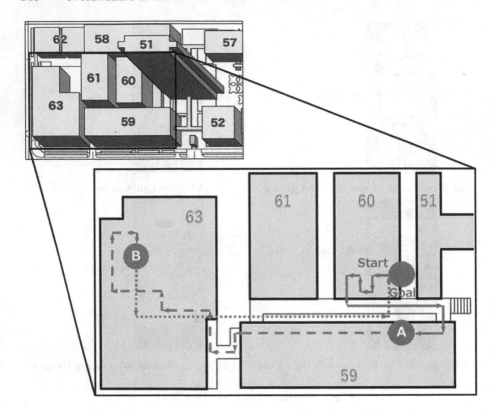

Fig. 2. Route guided by the "BearNavi Tour" [11]

following question in six levels: "Was navigation by the character easy to follow?"
Table 1 shows the choices and the number of people who answered.

Approximately 70% of the participants (i.e., 11 of 16 participants) answered
either "I think so," "I think so somewhat," or "I think so if anything." The
most common reason was "I just follow the character" (i.e., 7 of 11 participants
selected this reason). Therefore, the navigation method of following the character
tended to easily assist users. In contrast, the participants who did not think it
was easy to follow the route answered, "Because the direction was difficult to
understand" or "the character sometimes went to a place that is not on the
path."

Next, the participants answered in six levels to the following question: "Were
you feeling uneasy if you were walking the right path?" Table 2 shows the choices
and the number of people who answered. More than 80% of the participants
answered either "I was," "I was somewhat," or "I was if anything" (i.e., 13 of
16 participants). This result implies that some situations made the user feel
uneasy. The most common reason for this uneasiness was "since the character
sometimes went to a position outside the path, there could be errors in the positional information." Ten out of 13 participants expressed this reason, which can

Table 1. Answer of the first question (N = 16)

Choice	Number of people
I think so	4 (25% of the total)
I think so somewhat	5 (31.3% of the total)
I think so if anything	2 (12.5% of the total)
I don't think so if anything	2 (12.5% of the total)
I don't think so somewhat	2 (12.5% of the total)
I don't think so	1 (6.3% of the total)

be attributed to the fact that the positional information cannot be correctly measured, and an error frequently occurs in the positional information. Particularly on route 2, the character passed through a non-aisle area, and the situation where the user stopped moving forward and started over again occurred many times. This problem seemed to have influenced the questionnaire results.

Table 2. Answer of the second question (N = 16)

Choice	Number of people
I was	4 (25% of the total)
I was somewhat	7 (43..8% of the total)
I was if anything	2 (12.5% of the total)
I wasn't if anything	0 (0% of the total)
I wasn't somewhat	2 (12.5% of the total)
I wasn't	1 (6.3% of the total)

Finally, the participants answered on six levels to the question "Did you lose your way?" Table 3 shows the choices and the number of people who answered. More than 80% of the participants answered either "I did," "I did somewhat," or "I did if anything" (i.e., 13 of 16 participants). This result indicates that a situation occurred, in which the user loses direction. This also seemed to be caused by the error of the positional information.

The questionnaire results indicated that navigation using this application tended to be considered easier; however, many participants felt uneasy or lost.

5.2   Human Behavior Analysis

We obtained as log data the coordinate data every 3 s from the point where the QR code was read. We made the movement locus of the participants from the coordinate data and clarified the user behavior while using the application. This movement locus showed three actions that did not meet the conditions of

Table 3. Answer of the third question (N = 16)

Choice	Number of people
I did	4 (25% of the total)
I did somewhat	7 (43.8% of the total)
I did if anything	2 (12.5% of the total)
I didn't if anything	2 (12.5% of the total)
I didn't somewhat	0 (0% of the total)
I didn't	1 (6.3% of the total)

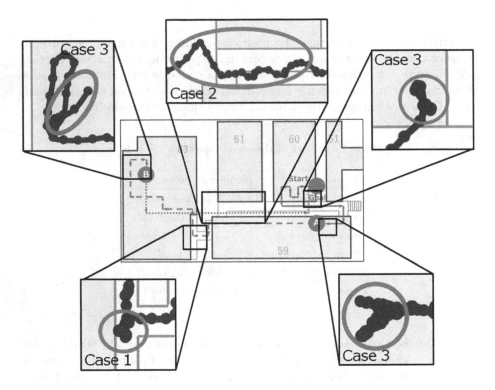

Fig. 3. Movement locus of subjects

the correct guide defined in Sect. 3 (i.e., "Going in the opposite direction to the real direction," "Going right or left on a straight road," and "Turning back the way"). "Going in the opposite direction to the real direction" and "Going right or left on a straight road" were counted as 1 for cases where the user acted for over 9 s. "Turning back the way" was counted as 1 for cases where the user acted twice or more in the same straight line. Figure 3 shows movement locus of subjects.

Case 1. Five of 16 participants exhibited the behavior of "Going in the opposite direction to the real direction" at the same point on Route 2. At the point encircled in the figure, the subject went to the left when it should go to the right. This behavior arose from the problem that the character moved in reverse because of an error in the positional information.

Case 2. Seven of 16 participants exhibited the behavior of "Going right or left on a straight road." Six participants exhibited this behavior at the point encircled. The cause of this behavior was thought to be the character going right or left on a straight road because of an error in the positional information. Many stores opened in this street on the day of the event, and many people were here. The user needed to go ahead by avoiding people. This seemed to also have influenced this behavior.

Case 3. The behavior of "Turning back the way" was the most common among the three, and 11 participants exhibited this behavior. As shown in the figure, this behavior was frequently observed near checkpoints A, B, and the goal point, and seemed to be an action wherein the participants searched for "Bear Coins" and quiz tips. "Bear Coins" and quiz tips are found as soon as the user follows the character. However, such behavior seemed to be observed because the participants were not correctly guided to the destination.

5.3 Discussion of Hypotheses

The questionnaire results showed that the navigation of this application tended to easily catch the route. Nevertheless, the user felt uneasy and lost direction. In addition, three actions of the user considered to be abnormal were seen. Therefore, the navigation of this application lacked accuracy. These results supported one of the three presented hypotheses. Each hypothesis is discussed below.

Hypothesis 1 (i.e., "The navigation by the AR character agent is easy for the user to understand.") was supported. The questionnaire results showed that the users tended to easily understand the routes. Hypothesis 2 (i.e., "The navigation by the AR character agent provides a sense of security to the user.") was not supported. The questionnaire results showed a situation in which the user felt uneasy. Hypothesis 3 (i.e., "The navigation by the AR character agent is accurate.") was not supported. The log data results indicated that the navigation of this application was not accurate.

6 Conclusion and Future Work

This study focused on the efficiency of route navigation following an AR character agent. We assumed that the navigation leads to an easy understanding of the route, provides a sense of security, and guides correctly. We evaluated the guide by conducting an experiment using the navigation application. Consequently, users thought that the navigation using the AR character agent easily helps finding and following the route. Therefore, this paper's contribution is the realization of an easy route navigation.

However, some situations made the user feel uneasy and lost. The navigation of this application also lacked accuracy. As mentioned earlier, some problems were encountered. The implementation of experiments with a larger number of participants, comparative experiments with other navigation systems, and analysis of the interaction between the user and AR in more detail will be future tasks. In particular, comparison with other navigation methods is necessary to clarify the effect of AR character.

References

1. Yokoi, K., Yabuki, N., Fukuda, T., Michikawa, T., Motamedi, A.: Way-finding assistance system for underground facilities using augmented reality. In: Proceedings of Indoor–Outdoor Seamless Modelling, Mapping and Navigation, International Archives of the Photogrammetry Remote Sensing and Spatial Information Sciences, vol. 44, no. W5, pp. 37–41 (2015)
2. Hervas, R., Bravo, J., Fontecha, J.: An assistive navigation system based on augmented reality and context awareness for people with mild cognitive impairments. IEEE J. Biomed. Health Inform. 18(1), 368–374 (2014)
3. Chang, Y.L., Hou, H.T., Pan, C.Y., Sung, Y.T., Chang, K.E.: Apply an augmented reality in a mobile guidance to increase sense of place for heritage places. Educ. Technol. Soc. 18(2), 166–178 (2015)
4. Chu, C.H., Wang, S.L., Tseng, B.C.: Mobile navigation service with augmented reality. IEEJ Trans. Electr. Electron. Eng. 12, S95–S103 (2017)
5. Dunser, A., Billinghurst, M., Wen, J., Lehtinen, V., Nurminen, A.: Exploring the use of handheld AR for outdoor navigation. Comput. Graph. UK 36(8), 1084–1095 (2012)
6. Pankratz, F., Dippon, A., Coskun, T., Klinker, G.: User awareness of tracking uncertainties in AR navigation scenarios. In: Proceedings of 12th IEEE and ACM International Symposium on Mixed and Augmented Reality – Arts, Media, and Humanities, ISMAR-AMH 2013, pp. 285–286 (2013)
7. Sekhavat, Y.A., Parsons, J.: The effect of tracking technique on the quality of user experience for augmented reality mobile navigation. Multimed. Tools Appl. 77(10), 11635–11668 (2018)
8. Mulloni, A., Seichter, D., Schmalstieg, D.: User experiences with augmented reality aided navigation on phones. In: Proceedings of 10th IEEE International Symposium on Mixed and Augmented Reality, Basel, 26–29 October 2011
9. Campbell, A.G., Stafford, J.W., Holz, T., O'Hare, G.M.P.: Why, when and how to use augmented reality agents (AuRAs). Virtual Reality 18(2), 139–159 (2014)
10. Thai, T.H., Chang, C.H., Chen, S.W.: Vision based indoor positioning for intelligent buildings. In: Proceedings of 2nd International Conference on Intelligent Green Building and Smart Grid (IGBSG), pp. 50–53 (2016)
11. Faculty of Science and Engineering, Waseda University. https://www.waseda.jp/fsci/en/. Accessed 15 June 2019

An Automated Structural Approach to Support Theatrical Performances by Introducing Gesture Recognition to a Cuing System

Kosuke Sasaki[1], Anne-Catherine Luther[2], Tomoo Inoue[1(✉)], and Wolfram Luther[3]

[1] University of Tsukuba, Tsukuba, Japan
{ksasaki,inoue}@slis.tsukuba.ac.jp
[2] RWTH Aachen, Aachen, Germany
anne.luther@rwth-aachen.de
[3] University of Duisburg-Essen, Duisburg, Germany
luther@inf.uni-due.de

Abstract. In this article, we explain how to process and interpret stage directions in order to support actors' performances. To this end, we specify the function of coverbal gesture and movement as an additional statement by an actor. We introduce a classification of communicative gestures by individuals and groups based on a description with typical body triangles and their sensor-detectable vertices moving in time. We claim that with the help of a speech and gesture recognition system, the occurrence of semantic isotopies to characterize a scene with speech and accompanying metaphoric gestures described in the stage directions can be detected and encoded in a feature vector. As a proof of concept, we highlight the ritual theater play *Orphée d'Afrique*, which was written as a second part of a homonymous chant novel and presents an implementation of a gesture- and voice-detection cuing system.

Keywords: Performance · Stage directions · Encoding standard · Body gesture and speech recognition system · Body gesture model · Cuing system

1 Introduction

A theater play is a cooperative task in which actors express themselves through text, gestures, sound and movements based on stage directions and a story, usually in the form of a script. They are assisted by prompters and technical staff responsible for actors' performances, set design, lighting, sound and music during rehearsals and performances. Some of these tasks have been taken over by technical installations and systems in research [13]. Takatsu et al. [15] proposed a system that detected speech and movement to support an actor's performance within an interacting group. The authors described the rehearsal cuing system architecture and developed a study to show that

© Springer Nature Switzerland AG 2019
H. Nakanishi et al. (Eds.): CRIWG+CollabTech 2019, LNCS 11677, pp. 251–261, 2019.
https://doi.org/10.1007/978-3-030-28011-6_19

the system helped actors by cuing the flow of events to each actor individually. An evaluation indicated the system might enhance actors' theatrical performance practice.

Ronfard [12] developed a complete workflow to publish recorded video data and the corresponding metadata from performances and related rehearsals online as Open Data. Recent improvements in ultrasound imaging enabling new opportunities for hand pose detection using wearable devices were reported in McIntosh [11]. Jessop [7] created and evaluated the Gestural Media Framework for gestural control of media in rehearsal and performance recognizing continuous gesture and translating Laban Effort Notation into the realm of technological gesture analysis. In [14], the authors propose "Digital-Script", a kind of stage directions that "focus on actor's performance factors, standing position, head direction and timing of actions." An implemented "theatrical practice support system detects user's standing position and head direction. In the virtual space, a virtual actor is shown as he performs along with Digital-Script information".

A crucial prerequisite for this is, in addition to suitable recognition hardware and software, to develop schemas for the standardized encoding of plays, orchestral scores, stage directions and scripts in order to be able to assess the participants' performance. For the encoding of drama and records of parliamentary debates, the element <stage> (for stage directions) was adopted in P5 Guidelines for Electronic Text Encoding and Interchange (TEI) [9, 16], and a formal transcription system for conversational gestures is described in [17].

According to Eco [2], *isotopy*, a concept first introduced by Greimas [5], has become "an umbrella term, a rather general notion that can allow for various more specific ones defining different textual phenomena"—even a gesture with a textual metaphorical interpretation. The recurrent occurrence of certain (clas)semes and subordinated lexemes in the text can be recognized and summarized as discursive isotopies together with their accompanying gestures described in the stage directions. Combining related discursive isotopies into a narrative strategy represents a reliable computer-based method for describing and quantifying literary constructs of interest.

To describe gestures, we adopt an approach followed by the authors in [8] providing a formal semantic analysis of coverbal iconic and deictic gestures with three important features based on the observation that speech and gesture together form a 'single thought'. First, the content of language and gesture are represented jointly in the same logical reasoning. Second, rhetorical relations connect the content of coverbal gesture and synchronous speech. Third, language and gesture are interpreted jointly within an integrated architecture for linking the form and meaning of utterances. Linguistic models can be applied to nonlinguistic objects in a metaphorical interpretation, but they supplement the nonlinguistic objects rather than replacing them, as the authors argue. Trippel [17] proposes the formal transcription system CoGesT, a machine processable computational model for annotating a subset of conversational gestures. Source and target location; trajectory described in terms of direction, type of movement, shape of the body part, and change in body shape during the movement; and modifiers for speed and size are composed to create a gesture feature vector; a BNF-grammar for the CoGesT system is offered in [4].

As examples of gesture types and their semantic content, the authors mention iconic, metaphoric, deictic and emblematic gestures. *Iconic*, word-like gestures clarify the spatial and dynamic features of a concrete concept/object; the notion *metaphoric* refers to gestures that depict the content of an abstract idea through a physical action; *deictic* refers to pointing to a physically present or absent referent; *emblematic* gestures conform culturally and are universally understood by a community.

Section 2 deals with stage directions and proposes a classification of intended gestures and movements with emphasis on communicative gestures. Section 3 is devoted to gesture and body movement modeling based on relevant triangles, their trajectories and constraints combined with scene context in order to construct a feature state vector for motion description. In Sect. 4, M.-J. Hourantier's version of a ritual theater play *Orphée d'Afrique* [6] is presented as a use case. Section 5 describes a cuing system for an automated structural approach to its implementation and function. Finally, Sect. 6 offers conclusions and discusses further work.

2 Intentional Gestures and Movements Classification

The scope and frequency of stage or production directions vary according to the history of the theatre from quasi-nonexistence to taking an important place in the contemporary theatre [18]. Whereas in the dialogue the characters are speaking, in the didascalia the author himself directs, assigns positions to actors, has them speak or participate in a conversation and describes their gestures and actions. As Gallèpe [3] states, "Almost all of the didascalic indications concern bodily presence and its manifestations"; some describe the various locations. The didascalic mode is the most easily identifiable. First of all, it includes the stage directions formally inserted in multiple parts of the text and provides details about the body and its role in communication. The naming of the body in remarks made by the actors themselves is a second internal instruction mode [18]. The third mode is an implicit one: the body and its actions must be inferred from what the characters say or even from the tension existing between an intention and the content of the directions for obvious reasons of place and feasibility. Many didascalia are devoted to the indications concerning the personal façade of interacting characters. It seems preferable to focus exclusively on the didascalia dealing with notations of the gestures and positions of the bodies in the interactions: *Textual gestures* concern the phonation of the oral text of the interaction, *protextual gestures* partially overlap pantomimic figurative or quasi-linguistic gestures, *coverbal gestures* constitute the nonverbal context of replicas, they correspond to the accompanying register, and *contextual gestures* denote activities that are not directly communicative but center on another action in relation to a concrete situation.

The method used by Gallèpe is as follows: he undertakes a methodical analysis of the didascalia of a number of German and French plays of various genres and periods constituting a basic corpus. For each of these 13 pieces, the first hundred replicas were considered. In 171 stage directions, the body is explicitly mentioned; in 77 it is only involved. The other didascalia relate to the various locations. They are classified according to four criteria: *unintentional gestures; gestures without intention of communication; intentional gestures of communication; undecidable.* The assignment of the gestures to a role is clearly described in the vast majority of cases. The corporal signifiers allowing translation within the gestures vary and are left open to interpretation. The different registers with occurrences found in the didascalia are as follows:

mimic (26), paraverbal utterance (23), gaze (19), static (7) and dynamic (29) posture, kinesics (20) (undifferentiated, hands, head, arm, torso, lower limbs), and proxemics (88). In this study, we decided to focus on the last four categories: static and dynamic posture, kinesics, and proxemics.

Greimas [5] differentiates between practical, mythical and communicative gestures. He mentions two lists covering behaviors such as (a) walking, running, sleeping, standing upright, etc. and (b) taking, giving, holding, pulling, pushing, etc. These two lists suggest the possibility of a very small inventory of simple and sufficiently general physical activities at the same time comparable to the very limited number of phonemes accounting for the totality of known articulations of natural languages. This sheds light on the parallelism between the gestural phenomena and the sememes covered by the verbs. In semantics, *sememe* is a bundle of minimal semantic strokes (called *semes*) whose formal correspondent is the lexeme.

According to an inventory of simple natural behaviors, it seems possible to reduce the gestural substance to figures in the visual plane and thus allow the division of this gestural text into minimal units whose combinatorial composition produces gestural statements and gestural speech itself. Unlike Greimas, Cosnier [1] emphasizes the absence of linear segmentation and the combinatorics of elementary units: gestures given their three-dimensional deployment can associate, combine, and condense. For this reason, we limit ourselves to a limited sample of gesture examined in Sect. 5.

3   Gesture and Body Movement Modeling

Recognizing the gestures and movements of a group of actors requires a few preliminary considerations and preparations, including their formal description and software. The process is as follows: Identify actors performing there, and record the positions. This makes it possible to judge whether each actor stays in a specific position correctly in each scene. Actors' body parts are also recorded so that their movements can be recognized by a machine-readable computational model that measures geometrical figures. It translates the stage directions into a machine-processable form (classifies the gestures in accompanying, replacing, explaining text), resulting in a script. With respect to a theater rehearsal, the script tags elements such as typical actors' constellations (i.e., how the scenes have been blocked) and their speech, gestures and movements based on the TEI P5. Formal description of body gestures is essential to recognizing actors' movements. The procedure is illustrated below.

- Place a depth camera in front of a stage to detect the vertices of the actors' body.
- A spatiotemporal description of an actor's movement as a sequence of body gestures is produced using involved triangles T_k. Also, a trajectory t can be constructed using an individual's (p) positions and directions, start/source position s and endpoint/target position e on a surface, and timespan. Each position is described in an xyz coordinate system, each actor's endpoint position is checked to ensure he or she is in the correct position at the end of each scene.
- Spatial relations and constraints C rely on topological, directional, proximal or distance features and connectivity containment using contiguity predicates.

A depth camera is used to detect the vertices of each actor's head, neck, shoulders, elbows, hands, torso, femur balls, knees, and feet. Also, triangles constructed with vertices on the head, arms and legs, upper body, lower body, whole body, and three edges are measured to determine the normal vector pointing away from the body (cf. Table 1). Body gestures are modeled by moving the limbs and recording trajectories (cf. Table 2). For example, encounters between persons and communication can be described as distances of the corresponding body parts and directions of the triangles T_1, T_4, T_5, T_6, T_7, e.g., extending arms, a handshake or a hug. Using the triangles and their normal vectors, trajectories $t_k(v_a)$, $t_k(v_b)$, $t_k(v_c)$, distances $d(v_{k1}, v_{k2})$ and gesture vectors f can be computed.

Table 1. Examples of body movements and their descriptions using 24 vertices v_k, 16 triangles T_k, and normal vectors nv_k pointing outside (os). In the current version, T_2, T_3, T_{13} and T_{14} cannot be acquired with the system, but they can be relevant to individual movements, depending on the camera positions.

T	Body part	Vertex a	Vertex b	Vertex c	ab × ac = nv
1_{fb}	Front/Back (F/B) Body	Front/occiput	Right (R) forefoot/heel	Left (L) forefoot/heel	Forward/Backward
2	Head1	Chin	L cheekbone	R cheekbone	Forward
3	Head2	Occiput	Right ear	Left ear	Up
4	Head3	Nose	Right shoulder	Left shoulder	Forward
5	Upper body	Abdomen/navel	Left shoulder	Right shoulder	Forward
6	Right arm	Right shoulder	Right elbow	Right palm	To the right os
7	Left arm	Left shoulder	Left palm	Left elbow	To the left os
8	Right leg	Right femur b.	Right heel	Right patella	To the right os
9	Left leg	Left femur ball	Left patella	Left heel	To the left os
10	Lower body1	Abdomen/navel	Right forefoot	Left forefoot	Forward
11	Lower body2	Abdomen/navel	Right patella	Left patella	Forward/up
12	Lower body B	Pelvis	Right heel	Left heel	Backward
13	Left lower leg	Left patella	Left forefoot	Left heel	To the left os
14	R lower leg	Right patella	Right heel	Right forefoot	To the right os
15	Action hands	Nose	Right palm	Left palm	Forward

The advantage of using gesture modeling with triangles, vertices, and their normal vectors is that triangles always lie in a plane described by *Hesse normal form* $nv_x(x - v_{ax}) + nv_y(y - v_{ay}) + nv_z(z - v_{az}) = 0$. If one assumes the standard case of a plane stage, then it can be equipped with an orthogonal three-dimensional coordinate system (x, y, z). The actors move on the floor $z = 0$ following flat curves, and many constraints can be checked concerning distances or the position of a point with respect to a plane, circle or polygon by inserting the point coordinates into curve or surface equations.

Table 2. Examples of body movements and their descriptions: a non-exhaustive list.

Textual/graphic description in 3-dim. space	Triangle $_pT_k$ v_a,v_b,v_c, nv Persons p,q	Trajectories t $_pt$ (v.) $s_v \rightarrow e_v$, d(p,q), d(v_i,v_j)	Constraints C $C_j(_pt(_pT_k)$, $cond_j)$ $C_j(_pt(_pT_{k1})$, $_qt(_qT_{k2})$, $cond_j)$
↑→←↑ [a] 2, 2n persons	$_pT_1$ $(_pT_5)$ $_qT_1$ $(_qT_5)$	Decreasing distances, opposite directions $_{p,q}$nv	Feet on the ground, triangles ⊥ to the plane of motion
Handshake 2, 2n persons	$_1T_6$, $_2T_6$	Hand distances decrease	Walking upright, feet on the ground
Go upright to a certain place e	T_1	Decreasing distance to the goal d(v_b,e)	Feet in the plane, triangles ⊥ to the plane of motion
Hold an object in both hands	T_6, T_7	Same distance between both palms v_b, v_c	Hands are holding a musical instrument
Climb the seven steps reach attic, look to the sky	T_1, T_2 (T_4)	Repetitive distances between forefeet v_b, v_c direction of $NV(T_2)$ ↗	Starting point s, eight changing positions of left and right forefoot; end point e on attic
Spinning in a ○ in the xy-plane	T_1	Subsequent positions	Point in circle $nv_x/\sqrt{nv_x^2 + nv_y^2}$ passes through $[-1, 1]$
Lie/roll on the bed 1, 2 persons	T_1, T_5, (T_6, T_7); T_5	Static horizontal position e = s; nv in yz-plane	Vertices of the triangles in/near the plane

[a]Two persons p, q walk upright, following trajectories $_pt$, $_qt$ to meet each other, the normal vectors $_pnv_1$, $_qnv_1$ of the front body triangles $_pT_1$, $_qT_1$ are directed nearly parallel to the ground (z = 0) and opposite, the distance between the triangles (smaller than $\min_{1 \le i,j \le 3} d(_pv_i, _qv_j)$) falls below a certain limit.

4　Gestures in Ritual Theater Play: A Use Case

The purpose of the second author's dissertation [10], *Werewere Liking: Ritual and Writing: The Postcolonial Subject and Its Discursive and Narrative Strategies*, is to examine Liking's five chant novels: *A la rencontre de…* (1980), *Orphée Dafric* (1981), *Elle sera de Jaspe et de Corail* (1983), *L'Amour-cent-vies* (1988) and *La mémoire amputée* (2004) from the angle of common research topics. In the novel *Orphée Dafric*, Orpheus goes through a series of exams and meditations—an individual initiation enriched with positive achievements—and including abstract images that he tries to render concrete and effective in accomplishing an archetypal rebirth.

The object of the research is to find coherence and differences between the five novels and to establish the paradigm of human development from a person who is alienated, ill, searching, and decadent to one who is responsible, engaged, and harmonious—a member of a new mankind, in five different variations: the binary, archetypal, prophesized, liminal and transgenerational accomplishment of human character development. Semantic isotopies and narrative strategies are made visible in the process of a character's metamorphosis during the phases of denunciation, perspective development and synthesis. Systematic analyses of 10 preselected isotopy groups based on the semantic breakdown of the ambiguities in the corresponding 34 lexemes enable the various developments of the main characters to be described and located at a higher level and distinguishable narrative strategies to be identified. (Clas) semes and subordinated lexemes are found by means of an encyclopedic definition; automatically searched related citations are listed in a table, then contextualized, actualized or virtualized in relation to both main and minor characters. A similarity measure was developed which determines differences in how the main characters evolve [10, p. 435]. After an initial exemplary analysis of the play *Orphée d'Afrique* [6], it turns out that in addition to the genre-related differences to the novels, content and structural peculiarities also occur that require an adaptation of the chosen method and selected isotopies. While, as in the novel the characters are in an initial state of unconsciousness, impotence, deprivation and isolation, other elements of initiation and development become decisive in the play. Formulated definitions, such as of the term initiation, need to be adapted, figure constellations and their dynamics must be rewritten.

As an extension, this approach analyzes the speech and movements of the actors in parallel using a recognition system to synchronize text isotopies and typical coverbal or mythical gestures: Stretch out, lie down, sit down, get up, take a few steps, climb stairs, stay motionless, leave or enter the scene, kneel down, bring something to the audience, take/hold something in hands, make several forms with the hands, perform ritual actions like baptism or passing within a circle or polygon (cf. Table 3).

Table 3. Actors, isotopies, accompanying movements, and gesture type.

LE NDINGA	(Chanting his sentence with the mvet*, goes to Orpheus.) * stringed musical instrument	Coverbal
ORPHEUS Engaged, responsible: active, positioned, fighting	With help from the tam-tam, O. looks for a rhythm that inspires him. A flute is born	(Pro)textual
ORPHEUS Searching (cherchant): deprivation, paralysis, wish, quest	Spinning in circles, looking for an object; An object circulated among the spectators will be the symbol of Orpheus's quest	Contextual Extra-communicatory
ORPHEUS Sick (malade): cause, symptom, cured	Lies down, turns on the bed	Contextual
ORPHEUS Decadent: decline, absurdity, perversion, restart	He climbs "seven steps" and reaches the attic, stops and is looking up at the sky	Contextual Mythical
ORPHEUS Initiated: transformed, firm, conscious, harmonious, healthy	Traverse several compartments of a circle; Should be assigned to the new isotopy "challenge"	Contextual Mythical

The system localizes people, one near or above the other, alone or in pairs, at the top or in the middle of a group and detects which of these patterns are in sync with text isotopies. Clear scripts and stated directions illustrating dialogues or concerning the gestures or movements of the actors, formally described and tagged, support the premise that this computerized approach could be successfully implemented.

5 System Design and Implementation

This section briefly explains how the cuing system has been designed, implemented and enhanced with gesture recognition.

5.1 Stage Directions

First, a standardized digital version of the play's stage directions is made with the actors, with their accurately dimensioned body triangles in a basic position with respect to a standard rectangular flat stage. Then, actors' gestures, movements, and actions are listed in a common timeline with accompanying text and instructions in the detailed standardized XML format.

5.2 Recognition of Actors' Gestures

Actors' gestures can be recognized as described in the following examples taken from Table 3.

For stair climbing, "Climb the seven steps to reach the attic, look at the sky", the start and end points of the trajectory and the midpoint between the foot markers of triangle T_1 occur along a straight line. The z-coordinate is controlled with regard to uniform increments from 0.5 to 6.5 times the height of the step. Finally, the direction of the normal vector of the head triangle T_2 now points diagonally above.

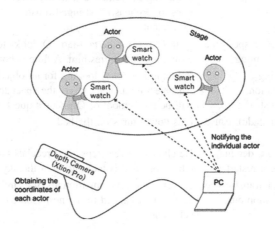

Fig. 1. The cuing system.

For "Spinning in a circle", the trajectory of the feet vertices of T_1 stays in the circle and $nv_x/\sqrt{nv_x^2 + nv_y^2}$, the cosine of the x- and y-coordinate of the normal vector nv in the plane, varies from 1 over -1 back to 1. For "Lies down and turns on the bed", take the upper body triangle T_5 and the cosine of the y and z coordinates of the normal vector nv in the yz-plane. Normal vectors are calculated by the system.

5.3 Implementation

The system has been implemented according to the design. It uses Xtion PRO as a depth sensor and OpenNI to obtain the three-dimensional coordinates of each vertex. It calculates the normal vectors in the Sect. 3 to recognize actors' gestures. Each actor wears a smartwatch, and the server notifies the individual actor when he/she should start speaking or acting (Fig. 1).

```xml
<?xml version="1.0" encoding="UTF-8"?>
<body>
 <head>Passing an Item</head>
 <sp n="0">
  <pos>-1287.4366,240.55136,3361.6633,1194.0463,266.115,3434.0425</pos>
  <speaker>Actor A</speaker>
  <move pref="stand" type="onStage"/>
  <p>I give you a present.</p>
 </sp>
 <sp n="1">
  <pos>-437.1841,228.42166,3336.9055,379.03928,232.34496,3465.1372</pos>
  <speaker>Actor B</speaker>
  <move pref="approach(A,B)" type="onStage"/>
 ....
```

Fig. 2. An example XML script.

An XML script file is stored in advance that includes encoded text and the position coordinates indicating where actors should stay in each scene (Fig. 2). In a play, it measures any positional gap between the coordinates in the script and the actors' actual positions. It also compares gestures with those in the script.

(a) The system detects that actors' positions are converging by investigating the two normal vectors nv directed against each other (Table 2 "↑ →← ↑").
(b) The system detects that the distance between the actors' right hands is decreasing (Fig. 3).

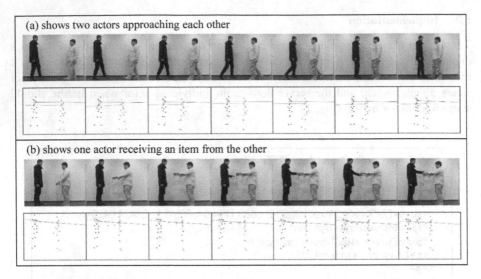

Fig. 3. In each set of images, upper images show the actors captured by RGB camera and lower images show the body vertices, triangles T$_5$, and normal vectors nv. The time axis runs from left to right.

The system also detects whether an actor is speaking or not to track the script automatically. Only the volume of their voices is used to avoid any influence from inaccuracy of speech recognition.

6   Conclusions and Further Work

With the help of a speech- and gesture-recognition system for cuing actors' utterances and gestures, we have shown that body gestures detailed in stage directions can be recognized and brought into a machine processable form. By combining semantic isotopies from an actor's speech and his body gestures, an individual story is generated that can largely be diversified by actors' spontaneous interactions.

However, a lot of practical work remains to be done to enhance the system. It should be extended to include full speech recognition, to detect and classify improvised actions and to deal with larger scale plays. With such a system, a database of collected descriptors of body gestures from a number of plays already recorded in the literature can be built, which is a prerequisite for investing in the implementation of a scene editor and player. Also, several open questions remain: How can the simultaneous actions of audiences be modeled? How should instructions concerning rhythm and facial expressions or behavioral gestures be described? What is the best way to describe complex actions like creating harmony or fighting effectively?

In addition, a research team of literacy, media and computer science experts could undertake an analysis of multimodal interactions in theater plays, including musical performances and dance, based on patterns from primitives of a multimodal gesture and sound language. There is a reasonable presumption that semantic isotopy analysis can be most profitably extended to various kinds of theater with a mixture of language, intonation, gesture and dance for a better description and understanding of multimodal utterances.

References

1. Cosnier, J., Vaysse, J.: Semiotics of communicative gestures. New Semiot. Acts **52**, 7–28 (1997)
2. Eco, U.: Two problems in textual interpretation. Poet. Today **2**(1a), 145–161 (1980). Roman Jakobson: Language and Poetry
3. Gallèpe, Th.: Joindre le corps à la parole: Quelle place pour le corps dans les textes de théâtre? Université Michel de Montaigne, Bordeaux, Cahier du C.I.E.L. Paris (1998–1999)
4. Gibbon, D., Gut, U., Hell, B., Looks, K., Thies, A., Trippel, Th.: A computational model of arm gestures in conversation. In: Proceedings of Eurospeech, Geneva, pp. 813–816 (2003)
5. Greimas, A.J.: Sens, Semiotic Essays. Seuil, Paris (1970)
6. Hourantier, M.-J.(Manuma ma Njock): Orphée d'Afrique: théâtre-rituel d'initiation, Paris, L'Harmattan (1981). Together with Liking W.: Orphée Dafric, chant novel
7. Jessop, E.A.: A gestural media framework: tools for expressive gesture recognition and mapping in rehearsal and performance. B.A., Amherst College (2008)
8. Lascarides, A., Stone, M.: A Formal semantic analysis of gesture. J. Semant. **26**(4), 393–449 (2009)
9. Lüngen, H., Sperberg-McQueen, C.M.: A TEI P5 document grammar for the IDS text model. J. Text Encoding Initiat. **3** (2012). http://journals.openedition.org/jtei/508
10. Luther, A.C.: Werewere Liking – Ritual und Schreiben: A Critical Debate in Africa and Latin America. Peter Lang (2017). (in German)
11. McIntosh, J., Marzo, A., Fraser, M., Phillips, C.: EchoFlex: hand gesture recognition using ultrasound imaging. In: Proceedings of CHI 2017, CHI Conference on Human Factors in Computing Systems, pp. 1923–1934. ACM, New York (2017)
12. Ronfard, R., Encelle, B., Sauret, N., Champin, P.-A., Steiner, Th., et al.: Capturing and indexing rehearsals: the design and usage of a digital archive of performing arts. In: Digital Heritage, Grenade, Spain, September 2015, pp. 533–540. IEEE (2015)
13. Sasaki, K., Inoue, T.: Coordinating real-time serial cooperative work by cuing the order in the case of theatrical performance practice. Mob. Inf. Syst. **2019** (2019). Article ID 4545917, 10 pages
14. Shimada, M., Takano, T., Shigeno, H., Okada, K.: Supporting theatrical performance practice by collaborating real and virtual space. In: Yoshino, T., Chen, G.-D., Zurita, G., Yuizono, T., Inoue, T., Baloian, N. (eds.) CollabTech 2016. CCIS, vol. 647, pp. 17–30. Springer, Singapore (2016). https://doi.org/10.1007/978-981-10-2618-8_2
15. Takatsu, R., Katayama, N., Inoue, T., Shigeno, H., Okada, K.: A wearable action cueing system for theatrical performance practice. In: Yoshino, T., Chen, G.-D., Zurita, G., Yuizono, T., Inoue, T., Baloian, N. (eds.) CollabTech 2016. CCIS, vol. 647, pp. 130–145. Springer, Singapore (2016). https://doi.org/10.1007/978-981-10-2618-8_11
16. TEI P 5 Release, TEI P5: Guidelines for Electronic Text Encoding and Interchange. http://www.tei-c.org/guidelines/p5/
17. Trippel, Th., et al.: CoGesT: a formal transcription system for conversational gesture. In: Proceedings of IRES, pp. 2215–2218 (2004)
18. Ubersfeld, A.: Lire le théâtre I, Belin Lettres Sup. (1996). 240p. English version Reading theatre. Toronto Press (1999)

Proposal of Emphasized Pseudo Expression for Improving the Recognition of the Presence and Contribution of Remote Participants in Cooperative Work

Yuta Akematsu$^{(\boxtimes)}$ and Takashi Yoshino

Graduate School of System Engineering, Wakayama University,
Sakaedani 930, Wakayama, Japan
akematsu.yuta@g.wakayama-u.jp, yoshino@sys.wakayama-u.ac.jp
http://www.wakayama-u.ac.jp/en/

Abstract. In cooperative work environments, many people gather at the same location and a few people join from remote locations. When the remote participants execute a task, other participants (in the shared space) rarely acknowledge their participation in the work. In this study, we propose a pseudo expression which shows the remote person's collaborative operation (object's motion) to the other participants in the shared space. In our experiment, we evaluated whether the participant in the shared space can recognize it. The experiment yields the two results: (1) The emphasized pseudo expression can help the recognition of remote participants. (2) The count of the operations performed by remote participants is not recognized by members in the shared space without the use of the emphasized pseudo expression.

Keywords: Supporting communication · Cooperative work ·
Remote meeting · Sense of existence

1 Introduction

At present, cooperative work occurs on face to face and remote bases. Cooperative work can be said to be of three types (Fig. 1) - "face to face type", "remote type", and "mixed type". The "face to face type" is the case in which all participants gather at the same location. Here, all participants' operation can be seen clearly and therefore, there is no problem with their acknowledgement. The "remote type" is the case in which all participants are in different locations. Here too, all participants' operations are acknowledged. The "mixed type" is the case in which some participants work from remote environments. Contribution acknowledgement is a problem in this case because members in the shared space are rarely aware whether remote participants have contributed to the work. For example, when the remote participants move an object on a sharing screen, it appears at the new location to the participants in the shared space. Because of

© Springer Nature Switzerland AG 2019
H. Nakanishi et al. (Eds.): CRIWG+CollabTech 2019, LNCS 11677, pp. 262–271, 2019.
https://doi.org/10.1007/978-3-030-28011-6_20

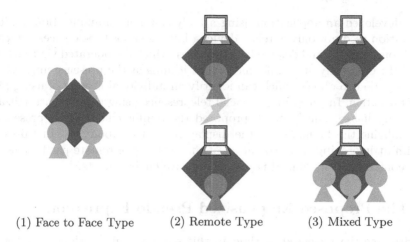

(1) Face to Face Type   (2) Remote Type   (3) Mixed Type

Fig. 1. Different categories of a cooperative work

this difference of the recognition, it is a possible that they will be left behind in work or communication that occurs during work on the remote type, especially the mixed type. In this study, we propose an emphasized pseudo expression that shows the remote participants' contributions (moving objects) to those in the shared space. This expression uses a symbol to represent the individuals who perform operations when they perform operations; thus enhancing the pseudo expression. In this paper, we aim at solving the problem they will be left behind in work or communication, by improving the presence and acknowledgement of remote participants and their contributions, respectively, by using the emphasized pseudo expression when they operate.

2   Related Work

Higuchi et al. showed that the visualization of the job instructor's gaze position in remote collaborative work helps improve the work support efficiency and decreases the number of failures [1]. Yamamoto et al. showed the improvement in the efficiency of remote work by presenting body motion using a head mount display [2]. In this study, it is different in that it supports each person's work and not work instruction.

In a study on the recognition of collaborative work by remote participants, Suzuki et al. developed a communication support system using robots [3]. Doucette et al. used the user's own arms in various ways to improve presence [4], Suzuki et al. investigated whether the user's task execution could be improved with the presence of a physicalized agent in the form of a silhouette [5]. In a communication system, body area networks[1] is a focus [6,7] and Varga

---

[1] It is a wireless network constructed by connecting small terminals located on the surface, inside and in the vicinity of the body by wireless communication.

et al. developed an application using a body channel communication [8]. Their application used not only wireless devices, but also floor type devices, which are placed on the floor, and deferred type devices, which are operated via touch with hands. In this study, it is different in that it aims at the presence improvement using the pseudo object which can identify an individual instead of using physical information. In the study on social telepresence using partial materialization of a body image, Onishi et al. proposed the reinforcement of telepresence by materializing the boundary of the display part of the body [9]. In this study, we aim at improving the recognition of the presence of remote participants and their contribution in "mixed type" cooperative environments.

3   The Proposed Emphasized Pseudo Expression

We describe the proposed method in this section. This method assumes that there is collaborative work when there are participants sharing the same space and also remote participants. Moreover, in supporting cooperative works, there are some systems with using card type information [10,11], then it is assumed that participants use a card (displayed on the screen) on which information is written to present their opinions as a task. In this method, when the remote site sides are collaborating with the shared space side, it uses to delay by the expression that can distinguish who operated. As a tool that distinguish who operated, we can give USE-together[2], remote collaborative tool, has remote collaborator's cursors have his/her name around the arrow icon. However, in this case, we display the face of the operator.

This expression displays as follows.

(1) Click on the card to be moved on the remote device.
(2) Determine the destination of the card and click on the remote device.
(3) The device ID, the card to be moved, and the information of the required destination is sent to the device on the shared space side.
(4) The use the information received by the device on the shared space side is as such: the object to be represented is placed on the moved card, and the object is moved linearly to the required destination.

The card operated by the remote participant cannot be manipulated until the state overwriting, the highlighting pseudo expression, is finished functioning. Moreover, when an operation is performed on the shared space side, the pseudo expression does not occur on the remote sides, even when the state is overwritten in the operation on the remote side. Figure 2 shows the state on the shared space side being overwritten after remote side operation. In Fig. 2, the figure on the left shows how the operator moves the card in the direction of the arrow from the upper right, and the figure on the right shows the pseudo expression on all devices other than that of the operator after the operation. It shows how the card moves in a straight line.

---

[2] https://www.use-together.com (confirmed on June 13, 2019).

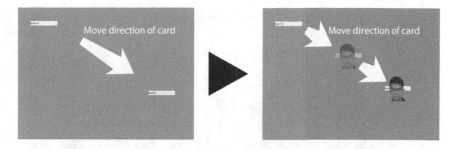

Fig. 2. Use of the proposed emphasized pseudo expression

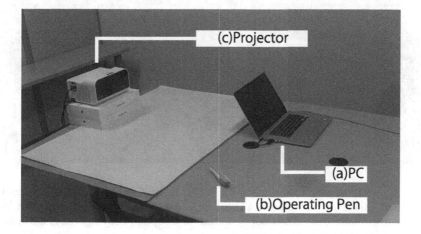

Fig. 3. Experiment construction in the shared space

4   Experiment

We evaluated the performance of the proposed expression method. Figure 3 shows the experimental construction in the shared space. In this experimental setup in the shared space, the screen of the PC (Fig. 3-(a)) was projected by a projector (Fig. 3-(c)), and a dedicated pen (Fig. 3-(b)) was used the operation. The subjects of this experiment divided 20 cards, which had proverbs[3] written on them and which were produced by the system with and without emphasized pseudo expression. Figure 4 shows the screen displaying the work to be carried out. In this work, a participant moves pairs of cards that seem to have the same meaning to the same colored areas. The time allotted for this work was 10 min, but if the work did not finish within 10 min, it was stopped. However, all groups finished the work in 10 min. Additionally, before the actual work, in order to get familiar with the operation of the pen on the shared space side, they worked on dividing 20 cards with numbers from 1 to 20 into the same pair at the end of

---

[3] Select from https://proverb-encyclopedia.com/primary-school/ (confirmed on September 23, 2018).

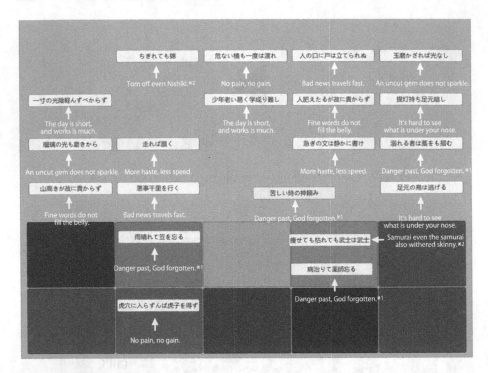

Fig. 4. A screen of work on the experiment. *1: In English, two pairs of sayings have the same meaning, but in Japanese, the proverbs mean are different phrasing. *2: When an existing English saying could not be found for a Japanese saying, the English saying was directly translated from Japanese.

the digit. Here, numbers 0 to 9 were written in the move destination areas, and the number written in the area and the digit on the card were to be matched. In this experiment, three persons in the shared space and one person working remotely were assumed to be of the same sex, and the experiment on the shared space side was performed with 12 persons in total, with four groups of three persons. In consideration of the order effect, two groups worked from the side with emphasized pseudo expression first, and the remaining two groups worked from the section without emphasized pseudo expression. After the work, questionnaires were given to the participants in the shared space. The number of people operating with the pen (Fig. 3-(b)) was not changed on the shared space side. Figure 5 shows the experiment in each position. Figure 5(1) is a scene of the remote space. The participant used a PC in the experiment. Figure 5(2) is a scene of the shared space. The participants did the work looking at the screen projected from the projector, and the participant in the front in the figure used the operating pen.

(1) Remote Space   (2) Shared Space

Fig. 5. Scenes of the experiment

5   Experimental Results and Discussion

5.1   Recognizing Task Participation in Remote Participants

Table 1 shows the results of the questionnaire on the recognition of participation in the activity by remote participants. In the 5-step evaluation of the Likert scale, for the question "I felt that the remote person participated in the work", those using emphasized pseudo expression all answered "strongly agree" or "agree" and the median and the mode were 4. Those participating without the emphasized pseudo expression comprised of 2 people answering "strongly agree", 8 people answered "agree", 2 people answered "neither agree nor disagree", and the median and the mode were 4. In the free-form description, people who used the emphasized pseudo expression had the opinions that "The face appeared when the card moved and it was easy to understand", "I knew who moved the card"; the emphasized pseudo expression for those who did not use it had the opinion that "I knew it was operated on because it moved quickly, but I had no sense of presence." From the results of the experiment, it was shown that the emphasized pseudo expression has the potential to help the recognition of remote participants, but there was no significant difference in recognition from the case of non-expression.

5.2   Recognizing the Number of Card Movements

We discuss the results in terms of the difference in how much the shared space side recognizes the contribution of the remote participant, depending on the presence or absence of the emphasized pseudo expression for each group. In the questionnaire, we asked whether there was an expression or not, whether they noticed the operation of a remote participant, and if they did not notice it, we counted the number as 0.

Figure 6(a) shows the difference between using emphasized pseudo expression and the average is -1.67 times (SD $= 0.47$), and the difference without emphasized pseudo expression is -4.67 times (SD $= 0.47$) on average. In both cases, the participants in the shared space were aware that the remote person operated the card, but the difference in the average value in this group was due to

Table 1. Questionnaire on recognition of participation in work by remote participants (5-step evaluation)

Case of experiment	Distribution of evaluation					Median	Mode
	1	2	3	4	5		
EPE	0	0	0	7	5	4	4
Nothing	0	0	2	8	2	4	4

Case of the experiment: (EPE: The case with using emphasized pseudo expression, Nothing: The case without emphasized pseudo expression)
Evaluation items: (1: Strongly Disagree, 2: Disagree, 3: Neither Agree Nor Disagree, 4: Agree, 5: Strongly Agree)

the absence of the remote participant. It is thought that the difference became extensive because the number of times the group moved was 8 times, but they said "I saw the face of the remote area participant". So we showed an effect that makes it easier to recognize the operation of remote participants.

Figure 6(b) shows the difference between using the emphasized pseudo expression and the average is -0.33 times (SD $= 0.47$), and the difference without emphasized pseudo expression is -1.0 times (SD $= 0.82$) on average. In both cases, participants in the shared space were aware that remote person operated the cards. In fact, this group found it easy to recognize the operation of remote participants, additionally from the viewpoint of the card moving in the emphasized pseudo expression, no difference was found between the presence and absence of expressions as numerical values.

Figure 6(c) shows the difference between using the emphasized pseudo expression and average is -1.33 times (SD $= 0.94$), and the difference without emphasized pseudo expression is -1.0 times (SD $= 0$) on average. It was thought that there was no difference in recognition because recognition was dependent on the presence or absence of expression and the emphasis was on the work regardless of the presence or absence of the emphasized pseudo expression.

Figure 6(d) shows the difference between using the emphasized pseudo expression and the average is -1.0 times (SD $= 0$), and the difference without emphasized pseudo expression is -1.33 times (SD $= 0.47$) on average. In both cases, participants in the shared space were aware that a remote person operated the cards. In this group, we showed an effect that makes it easier to recognize the operation of remote participants, but no difference was found between the presence and absence of expressions as numerical values. From these results, it can be seen that the emphasized pseudo expression can help making it simple to recognize the remote participant's operation, but there was no significant difference in recognition from the case of non-expression.

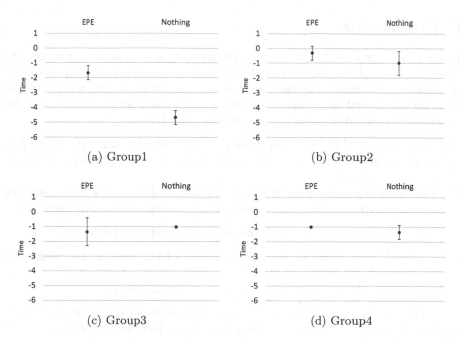

Fig. 6. Difference between the number of operations and the number of recognitions (Case of the experiment: (EPE: The case with emphasized pseudo expression, Nothing: The case without emphasized pseudo expression))

5.3   Discussion the System

In the description of the system, there were opinions such as "The face was displayed and the track of the card was easy to understand" and "There was an impact", but there were also opinions that required improvement such as "I felt that it would be nice to know the position when showing the location to the other party with the command language", "I cannot tell which one to move because the preliminary movement to move the card is not transmitted". With regard to the opinion, "I felt that it would be better to know the position when showing the place in the directive language", in the shared space, the card was pointed during the experiment; however, it was not clear which point was assigned to the remote side. From these results, it seems that using the face of the individual for the emphasized pseudo expression contributes to help the recognition of their presence and contribution. However, by not using the expression at the time of preliminary operation, there was confusion on who was moving because the expression for indicating which card was being moved has not been made, and the instruction in the conversation also mentioned the problem of what was being pointed to; these issues need to be corrected.

6   Conclusions

In this paper, we proposed an emphasized pseudo expression aiming to improve the recognition of the presence and contribution of remote participants. This expression is to display the movement (card movement) by the remote participant on the shared space side. The result of the comparison experiment with the use or not of this expression, showed the following:

(1) The emphasized pseudo expression can help the recognition of remote participants, but there was no significant difference in recognition from the case of non-expression.
(2) The count of the remote participants' operation does not have the condition of the cognition in the shared space if emphasized pseudo expression has.

Moreover, it became clear that the following points are problems.

(1) We need to add the preliminary movement of the card in the emphasized pseudo expression.
(2) We need to clarify which card is pointed to by the directive.

In the future, as a new form of emphasized pseudo expression, we plan to implement a display function to make the image intrude on the work screen using speech and experiment using it.

References

1. Higuchi, K., Kometani, R., Sato, Y.: An effect of grazing position visualization in the scenario of remote support system. In: WISS 2015, pp. 1–6 (2015)
2. Yamamoto, T., Otsuki, M., Kuzuoka, H.: An effect of body motion presentation at remote work orders on the expectation. IPSJ SIG Technical report, vol. 2016-HCI-167, no. 17, pp. 1–8 (2016)
3. Suzuki, Y., Fukushima, H.: Communication robot system with presenting existences and motions of the remote participants. OKI **75**(2), 22–25 (2008)
4. Doucette, A., Gutwin, C., Mandryk, R.: Effects of arm embodiment on implicit coordination, co-presence, and awareness in mixed-focus distributed tabletop tasks. In: Graphics Interface Conference 2015, Halifax, Nova Scotia, Canada, 3–5 June 2015, pp. 131–138 (2015)
5. Suzuki, S.V., Saito, R., Ogata, H.: Influence of presence from an embodied agent expressed with a silhouette. In: The 31st Annual Meeting of the Japanese Cognitive Science Society, pp. 504–510 (2014)
6. Ruiz, J.A., Xu, J., Shimamoto, S.: Experimental evaluation of body channel response and digital modulation schemes for intra-body communications, communications. In: 2006 IEEE International Conference on Communications, vol. 1, pp. 349–354 (2006)
7. Ruiz, J.A., Shimamoto, S.: Propagation characteristics of intra-body communications for body area networks. In: CCNC 2006: 3rd IEEE Consumer Communications and Networking Conference, vol. 1, pp. 509–513 (2006)
8. Varga, V., Vakulya, G., Sample, A., Gross, T.R.: enabling interactive infrastructure with body channel communication. J. Proc. ACM Interact. Mob. Wearable Ubiquitous Technol. Arch. **1**(4), 1–29 (2017). Article 169

9. Onishi, Y., Tanaka, K., Nakanishi, H.: Embodying a part of remote partner's video enhances social telepresene. Inf. Process. Soc. Jpn. J. **57**(1), 228–235 (2015)
10. Bentley, F.R., Tejaswi Peesapati, S.: SearchMessenger: exploring the use of search and card sharing in a messaging application. In: CSCW 2017, pp. 1946–1956 (2017)
11. Fedosov, A., Kitazaki, M., Odom, W., Langheinrich, M.: Sharing economy design cards. In: Proceedings of the 2019 CHI Conference on Human Factors in Computing Systems, Paper No. 145, pp. 1–14 (2019)
12. Hayashi, Y., Ogawa, Y., Nakano, Y.: Visualizing learners' attitudes based on non-verbal information in collaborative learning. Inf. Process. Soc. Jpn. J. **55**(1), 189–198 (2014)

Author Index